LUDWIG WITTGENSTEIN'S TRACTATUS ODYSSEY

The Great War and the writing of the Tractatus-Logico-Philosophicus

Ludwig Wittgenstein's *Tractatus* Odyssey
The Great War and the Writing of the *Tractatus-Logico-Philosophicus*
Edited by Radmila Schweitzer

Published by DoppelHouse Press in cooperation with
the Wittgenstein Initiative 2023

Book design: Tauras Stalnionis

Publisher's Cataloging-in-Publication data

Names: Schweitzer, Radmila, editor.
Title: Ludwig Wittgenstein's Tractatus Odyssey : the Great War and the writing of the Tractatus-Logico-Philosophicus / edited by Radmila Schweitzer.
Description: Includes bibliographical references. | Los Angeles, CA: DoppelHouse Press, in cooperation with the Wittgenstein Initiative, 2023.
Identifiers: LCCN: 2023940925 | ISBN: 978-1-954600-13-3 (paperback) | 978-1-954600-30-0 (ebook)
Subjects: LCSH Wittgenstein, Ludwig, 1889-1951. | Philosophers--Austria--Biography. | Analysis (Philosophy)--History. | Logical positivism--History. | Vienna (Austria)--Intellectual life--20th century. | Philosophy--History--20th century. | BISAC BIOGRAPHY & AUTOBIOGRAPHY / Philosophers | PHILOSOPHY / Logic | PHILOSOPHY / Movements / Analytic | PHILOSOPHY / Individual Philosophers | HISTORY / Europe / Austria & Hungary | LITERARY CRITICISM / Modern / 20th Century
Classification: LCC B3376.W564 L83 2023 | DDC 192--dc23

Dedicated to the scholars at Trinity College Cambridge, the Wittgenstein Archives in Bergen, and the Brenner Archive in Innsbruck, keepers of the light

Its whole meaning could be summed up somewhat as follows: What can be said at all can be said clearly; and whereof one cannot speak thereof one must be silent.

Tractatus Logico-Philosophicus, Preface
Ed. C. K. Ogden and F. P. Ramsey, Kegan Paul, Trench, Trubner & Co., 1922

Skjolden
1913
Cambridge
1911
Sokal
1915
Kraków
1914
Olomouc
1916
Vienna
1914 / 1919
Hochreit
1918
Oberalm
1918
Bukovina
1916 / 1917
Trattenbach
1920
Asiago
1918
Cassino
1919

TABLE OF CONTENTS

Who Is Afraid of Ludwig Wittgenstein? or, An Austrian Enigma

Radmila Schweitzer

This collection of essays started taking form in Vienna in 2018, 100 years after Wittgenstein finished the writing of the *Tractatus Logico-Philosophicus* in 1918. It took him until 1922 to find a publisher for his treatise, thus our present result celebrates 100 years since the *Tractatus's* entrance into the public sphere, where it was to wield an enormous influence, both in philosophical circles and on a broader audience. It remains one of the most famous books that only a few have actually read and even fewer fancy to understand.

But who was the author of this short treatise, claiming to have solved all philosophical problems ever? The complex and mysterious nature of the *Tractatus* has enveloped Ludwig Wittgenstein as a halo, causing him to be perceived as otherworldly, and all too often forgetting the human being underneath.

Our primary aim is to show the real man Wittgenstein, extraordinary and difficult as he was. It is important to apprehend the atmosphere in which he conceived and wrote the *Tractatus* and how it transformed him from a scion of a wealthy Viennese family into a self-proclaimed ascetic with nothing to his name. Amid the Great War, one of the greatest upheavals in modern history, Ludwig Wittgenstein went through a personal and intellectual transformation from which emerged the most influential philosopher of the 20th century and a modern cultural icon.

Throughout this journey, the *Tractatus* amassed its own singular, compelling language, which, as Marjorie Perloff writes, "we associate less with the philosophical than the poetic."

Today's knowledge about Wittgenstein's personality and philosophy is difficult to imagine without the work of the late Brian McGuinness, who has contributed more than anyone else to our understanding of Wittgenstein as a whole. McGuinness, who left us in 2019, was the main inspiration and authority I am indebted to when starting on this project. My gratitude goes in equal measure to the other great Wittgenstein biographer, Ray Monk, who contributed one of the odyssey stations.

The universities of Cambridge, Oxford, Bergen, and Innsbruck were unreservedly open to us from the very beginning, permitting us to publish, for the first time in print, facsimiles from Wittgenstein's Literary Estate (*Nachlass*) that illustrate Wittgenstein's personal narrative in the years leading up to the completion of the *Tractatus*, as well as his intellectual development. Special thanks are due to Nicolas Bell and earlier Jonathan Smith from the Wren Library, Trinity College, Cambridge and to Alois Pichler, director, and to Rune Falch of the Wittgenstein Archives at the University of Bergen, for a great deal of the documentary material that we have been able to reproduce. Our gratitude goes to Ulrike Tanzer and Ursula Schneider from the Brenner Archive Research Institute at the University of Innsbruck for allowing us to include unique facsimiles and photos from their collections.

For this book, we have been most fortunate to be able to assemble distinguished Wittgenstein experts from both sides of the Atlantic and, as luck would have it, some of them are from countries which are key to Wittgenstein's personal odyssey: Austria, Great Britain, Norway, and Poland. Some of them have provided us also with never-before-seen illustrations, notably Martin Pilch, Urszula Idziak, and Alfred Schmidt.

We are particularly grateful to the Austrian State Archive and its director, Dr. Helmut Wohnout, for allowing us to publish Wittgenstein-related military documents from the Great War.

The descendants of the Wittgenstein family have, as in all my work for the Wittgenstein Initiative, been wholeheartedly supportive and generous with family documents and photographs. Our gratitude goes to Françoise and Pierre Stonborough, Andreas and Annick Sjögren, and Florian Stockert, among many others.

If this book lessens the excessive timidity towards reading Wittgenstein, and encourages a new audience to become engaged with his unusual and powerful personality, and perhaps even to read the *Tractatus* (and the later Wittgenstein!), it will have been a success.

Last, and most important, my gratitude goes to Marjorie Perloff, an inspiration and a force of nature who didn't let me go until this book was ready to be published in English.

Vienna, June 2023
Radmila Schweitzer
Wittgenstein Initiative

What Is an Odyssey in Philosophy?

Allan Janik

Wittgenstein's way to his *Tractatus Logico-Philosophicus* can rightly be termed an Odyssey. Both in terms of his spatio-temporal meanderings and his intellectual development in the course of writing it, the *Tractatus* incorporated an exciting, improbable journey. The work, whose author had unpretentiously termed *Logisch-Philosophische Abhandlung* (*Logic-Philosophical Treatise*), entirely transformed philosophy.

The work first saw the light of day in a now-forgotten German journal in 1921, but it was only recognized as a milestone in Western thought with the publication of the dual language edition by Kegan Paul a year later. By that time, Wittgenstein was a very different person from the teenager who had first encountered philosophy in the work of the Viennese physicist-philosopher, Ludwig Boltzmann, around 1904. Up to the outbreak of World War I, Wittgenstein was one of the wealthiest people in Europe. And he clearly enjoyed all the privileges of wealth: exotic trips to Scandinavia, riding and tennis (then a sport for the elite), renting trains when none was scheduled when he desired to travel etc. By the time the *Tractatus* appeared, he had turned his back on all that. He gave his fortune to his siblings, as well as providing a princely sum to the support of Rainer Maria Rilke and other deserving artists, opting, instead, after World War I, for an ascetic way of living as a rural elementary school teacher in one of the poorest parts of Lower Austria. As a youth it was unclear to him which of his various interests he would follow professionally. From his early exposure to the popular lectures of Ludwig Boltzmann, he found both philosophy and high technology's latest challenge, aviation, equally tempting fields of endeavor. Later, through his acquaintance David Pinsent, a fellow student and pilot in Cambridge, he added the psychology of musical perception and the relationship between music and language to his list of gripping preoccupations. Thus, there was also the possibility of a career in psychology. But it was the alternative between philosophy and aviation, which tormented him. A mechanical engineer by virtue of his previous education in Berlin (to the end of his life he loved machines, according to G.H. von Wright), Wittgenstein had devoted considerable efforts to building something resembling a proto-jet engine for airplanes in Manchester in the years between 1909 and 1911. Aeronautical engineering offered him challenging

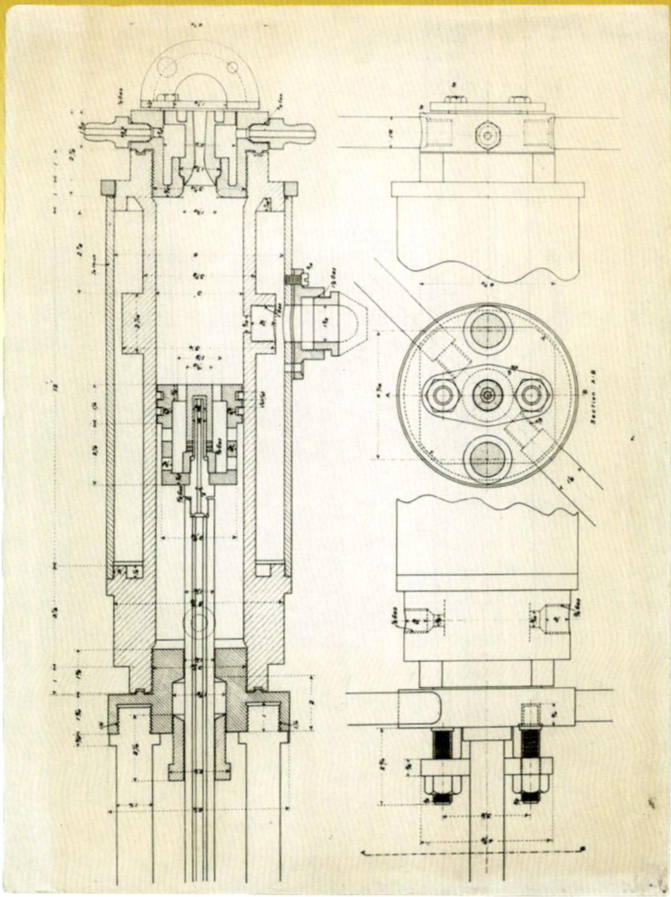

The plans of Wittgenstein's aero-engine Combustion Chamber Section

problems. But there was also philosophy, for which he had displayed prodigious gifts, as Bertrand Russell had been the first to observe. In his perplexity, he sought the latter's advice about his future course. Russell asked him to show what he could do in philosophy by writing a paper for him. The result was clearly brilliant and from 1912 on Wittgenstein devoted himself exclusively to philosophy. The way therein had not been smooth, but the matter was settled with typical Wittgensteinian resolve, such that we tend to forget that there had been alternatives.

His interest in philosophy had originally been awakened by Boltzmann's pioneering popular lectures on philosophy of science, which were covered in detail in the Viennese press (Boltzmann, like Gustav Mahler, was not only brilliant but also witty enough to make news regularly with his bon mots). Only when Boltzmann's death in 1906 prevented him from studying with him in Vienna, did Wittgenstein decide to study mechanical engineering in Berlin, which he did successfully for two years before going on to Manchester in order to work on problems related to propelling the flight of aircraft. The young man's philosophical interests in 1905, which were dominated by Schopenhauer's idealism, began to change radically in the years between 1906 and 1911, when exposure to the revolutionary works of Gottlob Frege converted him from idealism to a form of logical realism. Indeed, Frege became the very paragon of a philosopher for him and remained so throughout his entire life, despite the fact that he would later call some of Frege's central ideas into question.

Wittgenstein's early work in philosophy was the project of re-writing the first eleven chapters of Russell's *Principia Mathematica*. Following upon Frege's demonstration that logic was a kind of calculus, Russell's efforts were dedicated to show that all mathematics is based upon formal logic. He aimed at establishing the set of axioms and rules of inference in symbolic logic, from which the whole of mathematics could be derived. Wittgenstein should further sharpen the conceptual tools necessary for completing that task. In order to accomplish that, he turned to a central insight of Boltzmann's, namely, that successful attempts to grasp the way the world works scientifically are possible by virtue of the fact that we can picture reality to our self. If scientific propositions were accurate pictures of reality, we could get a firm hold of how they can represent reality clearly and distinctly. Logic provided the structure or syntax for combing the elements in the picture. The *Tractatus* would explain how this is possible and what further implications the "picture theory" entailed for our understanding of logic as the basis of all genuine knowledge. By the time Wittgenstein finished his task, he had moved a long way from where Russell left the project.

Far more than most people can imagine, Wittgenstein thrived on isolation. It was only when he was alone that he was capable of full concentration. That drove him to seek refuge in a remote fjord in Norway where he could work undisturbed. Ever drawing inspiration from Gottlob Frege, whose revolutionary *Concept Script* (*Begriffsschrift*) contains a strict presentation of logic as a calculus, and not a single word of German, he insisted that logic must take care of itself. Talking about the subject, even when that discourse was conceived as a "philosophy" of logic, had to be non-logical, and thus nonsense. Following a hint of Frege's, Wittgenstein devised a technique for representing logical relations exhaustive (as he then thought) on matrices. These "truth tables" were a mechanical technique or showing once and for all whether a proposition was a purely formal assertion of the sort "p is p," a formal contradiction, "p is not p," or a substantial statement of fact, "p is q." Since these were all the possibilities that the method allowed, he showed at the same time that there was no place in what he called "logical space" for metaphysical statements, i.e., substantial assertions about the world that are necessarily true. Moving outwards from the "inside" of logic to the world, he proceeded with the extraordinary singleness of mind typical of him to articulate the consequences of the notion that logic makes knowledge possible by providing the "syntax" for producing pictures of the world – and at the same time established the limits of what could possibly be pictured in the first place. He always looked back to Norway in 1913–1914 as perhaps the most productive period in his intellectual life. Then came World War I.

Wittgenstein enraged his family at the outset of the war by enlisting as a volunteer foot soldier, rather than buying a commission, as was customary among the wealthy and powerful. Among other things, the war would offer him the only opportunity he would ever have, after his work in Manchester, to exercise his skills in mechanical engineering in connection with the repair and construction of canons in the course of 1915. Little wonder that he would contribute a large sum to the Austrian government for the construction of a large mortar. But that was a bit later. His first assignment in 1914 as a searchlight operator on the Goplana, a river patrol boat on the Vistula in Galicia, brought with it mortal danger each night. In this situation he sought a common solution to the problem of coping with his intense fear of death and his problems concerning the foundations of logic. He was convinced that there had to be a single solution to these totally disparate conundrums. He could not rest intellectually until he produced a definitive, unassailable solution to all the problems, for which traditional philosophy had vainly sought to provide theories. The first step in the "mystical" direction that would emerge from his reflections came with his discovery of Tolstoy's *The Gospel in Brief* in a bookshop in Tarnów. What the unchurched young man discovered there would set his mind, and his body, to work for the rest of his days. The resolution to the seemingly insurmountable problem of reconciling his intellectual and existential problems, the redemptive word (*das erlösende Wort*), as he called it, began to dawn upon him in the course of the Brusilov Offensive, a series of battles extending over the whole of the summer of 1916. That response was a radical re-affirmation of Frege's distinction between that logic of what can be said clearly and the impossibility of speaking about how logic worked or how to live a meaningful life. It was a matter of accepting what had to be the case in logic and in life. It led to his dramatic reflections on God and the meaning of life at the end of the *Tractatus*, which appear to come out of nowhere when one reads the text but, nevertheless, make the work unforgettable.

This attitude to life was as realistic as it was amazing. During Brusilov's Offensive he insisted that he should continually have reconnaissance duty at the very front of the Front. This exposed him to enormous danger in a wholly chaotic situation. The attack began with deafening barrages of canon fire that produced thick clouds of fowl-smelling, toxic smoke, making observation all but impossible and normal breathing equally traumatic. But this was where he wanted to be. His incredible coolness in this hellish situation inspired the men around him to resist the temptation to panic, for which he was awarded some of the highest honors that the Imperial and Royal Army conferred. It also earned him a promotion to the rank of lieutenant. In that context he was posted to Olmütz (Olomouc) in Moravia for re-training as an officer.

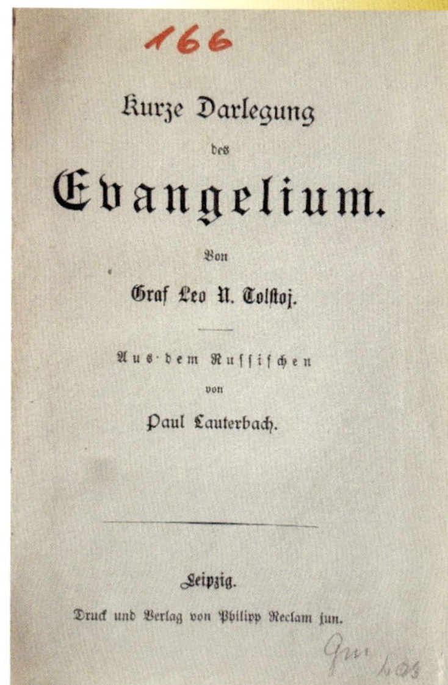
Kurze Darlegung des Evangelium.
Von Graf Leo N. Tolstoj.
Aus dem Russischen von Paul Lauterbach.
Leipzig.
Druck und Verlag von Philipp Reclam jun.

Title page of the German edition which Wittgenstein bought in a bookshop in Tarnów © Wittgenstein Initiative, photos: Alois Pichler

In Olomouc in the fall of 1916, he met the man who would become his most important interlocutor in the coming decade, the interior designer Paul Engelmann. Engelmann was part of a lively circle of intellectuals formed around his mother, Ernestine Engelmann, who came from a distinguished family of assimilated Jews. Paul Engelmann had studied architecture with Adolf Loos, who had suggested that Wittgenstein contact him when he got to Olomouc. Wittgenstein had been introduced to Loos by Ludwig von Ficker, the editor of Innsbruck's *Der Brenner* and the man he entrusted to dispose of the considerable sum from his inheritance that he wished to distribute to deserving artists. That was literally on the day before the war began in July 1914. Wittgenstein had come to appreciate Ficker's integrity on the basis of what Karl Kraus had written about him and the Brenner in *Die Fackel*. In Olomouc he and Engelmann would have ample opportunity daily to discuss Kraus, Loos and Otto Weininger, the philosopher whose startling book *Sex and Character* summed up the moral view behind their respective activities as social critics. Apart from having studied with Loos, Engelmann acted as a kind of secretary to Kraus during the war, collecting nonsensical/hypocritical newspaper articles for the latter's monumental anti-war docudrama, *The Last Days of Mankind*. Their work had its impact upon Wittgenstein in the course of Brusilov's Offensive as he came to realize 1) with Kraus, that ethical values, as much truth values (cf. his method of representing propositions) could only be shown and not said, 2) with Loos, that beauty was a deep matter of structural integrity, rather than dazzling facade and 3) with Weininger, that philosophy was a matter of humbly acknowledging the inherent limits of language, rather than sophisticated theorizing about ultimate reality. The three would help Wittgenstein to identify a further dimension, an ethical level, to the Fregean distinction between what we can assert in logic and what can only be shown by "waving" at it. In a sense, Wittgenstein's Vienna, the influence of Kraus, Loos and Weininger – emerged from his contacts with Engelmann in Olomouc, a place, whose self-image in those days was that of a suburb of Vienna and a microcosm. The Russellian project that Wittgenstein began in 1911 found its climax in the Viennese dimension of the work that its preface and concluding pages incorporate. Briefly, the telescoped style that Wittgenstein insisted upon employing fused two books: one inspired by Frege and Russell and another with a Weiningerian commentary appended to the first, undissolvably together in an incomprehensible way.

From the time of its original publication the *Tractatus* was an enigma to its first readers, all of whom eagerly sought to understand those 75 Sibylline pages. While Bertrand Russell and the group around Moritz Schlick in Vienna that would go down in history as the Vienna Circle were wildly enthusiastic about Wittgenstein's profound contribution to logic as well as his elegantly devastating critique of metaphysics, they could make neither head nor tail of its mystical conclusions. Russell admitted that he simply could NOT see the point of Wittgenstein's "mystical turn" at the end of the book, but seemed tacitly to admit that Wittgenstein must have had his reasons for writing what he did. Their first meeting after the war, which took place in Innsbruck in 1921, signaled the beginning of an irrevocable break. The Vienna Circle used Wittgenstein's slogan "what can be said, can be said clearly," blithely ignoring the rest of the sentence, "what cannot be said, must be passed over in silence," except for Otto Neurath who explicitly rejected the second half loudly and clearly. Wittgenstein was not amused to be found alongside Russell and Einstein (whose politics and public clowning annoyed him) as the most important representative of the Circle's "Scientific Conception of the World" in 1929.

The situation of Ludwig von Ficker, the Krausian in whom Wittgenstein had vested his last hopes to find an appropriate Austrian publisher, was not much different. His literary and religious concerns were somehow present in the *Tractatus* but he could not make head or tail of the largest part of the book. As one of the first rediscoverers of Søren Kierkegaard, he appreciated the relationship between existentialist ethics and biting social criticism, so he could well understand Wittgenstein's concerns about God and the meaning of life. The two had met in 1914 and became fast friends. They corresponded as regularly as their duties allowed in the first two years of the war. So, there were common interests and common experiences to build upon here. But they did not help Ficker one iota in trying to see the connection between the two sides of Wittgenstein's work. In the end his work remained enigmatic for fifty years and more after its publication.

Ludwig Wittgenstein was, indeed, an Austrian enigma. Absolutely nothing about him can be understood in conventional terms. His first thoughts after completing the *Treatise* that had preoccupied him for seven years were of committing suicide, presumably in a fit of depression at the recent news of David Pinsent's death in a plane accident. That, along with having lost the "graceful mercy of work" (*die Gnade der Arbeit*), had brought him to a state

Cassino – police barracks, from 1916, a prisoners of war camp. ©Collezione Mauro Lottici, with kind permission of Dr. Maria Ascher Corsetti

of total disorientation. This is hardly what you would expect of a philosopher who had just solved all the problems of philosophy for all time. But that was where it landed Wittgenstein. Yet, despite all that he had seen of the war, it was not yet over for him. At the end of September 1918, he would be posted back to Italy where he would find himself, ironically, fighting against the British in the vicinity of Asiago. As the Austrians sued for peace, Wittgenstein was taken prisoner and ultimately landed in the prisoner of war camp just below the Benedictine monastery at Cassino in January 1919. Here he would remain until the end of August, when he would return to the aborted project that he had begun a full year earlier: the search for a publisher for his *Treatise*.

In the light of all that, there is not much reason to be surprised that Wittgenstein would fail to find a publisher for the work. In the event, it was Russell, and especially his secretary, Dorothy Wrinch, who finally made it possible for the book to see the light of day. After five or six efforts of his own, Wittgenstein had thrown in the towel. It is noteworthy that his first choices were publishers, who were, in one way or another, connected with Karl Kraus. In fact, it was Russell's recommendation, rather than anything Wittgenstein had written, that got the book published.

Both Frege, who was skeptical from the start with respect to a book that was at once philosophical and literary, mixing the genres that he considered to be polar opposites, and Ludwig von Ficker, who was keen to repay his debt to Wittgenstein for supporting Georg Trakl and other Brenner authors, asked him to make changes in the typescripts they read. Frege would have been considerably happier if Wittgenstein recast the whole thing in essay form. Similarly, Ficker thought he should at least eliminate the numbering of the propositions. Both were equally anathema to Wittgenstein. The contents were painstakingly gleaned from his notebooks and, when we examine the surviving ones today, we can see at a glance that the printed text omitted many propositions that might have made this most difficult part of the book more comprehensible. But he would have nothing of it. Its final form was, indeed, something mystical in his eyes and absolutely nothing could be different from what it was. This was, after all, The Ultimate Solution to All the Problems of Philosophy. So, Wittgenstein's texts have provided an enormous challenge to putative editors right down until today. As for the author of the *Tractatus*, he had finished his job and could now turn to a very different form of "humanly useful work" (a favorite phrase of Wittgenstein's), namely, retraining as an elementary school teacher and living a Tolstoyan life. And so, the *Tractatus* odyssey came to its end.

Ludwig Wittgenstein's Youth

1889	26 April	Born in Vienna, in the family villa in Neuwaldegg
1903–1906		Staatsoberrealschule in Linz, Higher School Certificate
1906–1908		Engineer studies at the Technical University Berlin –Charlottenburg
1908–1911		Manchester, College of Technology: Research student in the laboratory of the engineering department, later also voluntary observer of the weather station
1911	21 June	Submission of a detailed draft for a flight propeller drive to the Patent Office
	Summer	First meeting with Gottlob Frege in Jena
	17 August	Patent for propeller drive is issued
	Autumn	Guest student in Cambridge
	18 October	First meeting with Bertrand Russell
1912	1 February	Cambridge Trinity College, as undergraduate meets David Pinsent
	7–27 September	Trip to Iceland, together with Pinsent
	12 October	Furnishing an apartment in Whewell's Court
	22 November	Lecture *What is Philosophy?* for The Cambridge Apostles
	December	Visit to Gottlob Frege in Jena
1913	20 December	Death of his father Karl Wittgenstein
	September	Trip to Norway, together with Pinsent (Christiania, Bergen, Øystese)
	October	Cambridge
	11 October	Norway – in Skjolden, staying with the Klingenberg Family
1914	April	Visit from G.E. Moore to Skjolden
	May	Return from Skjolden to Vienna
	14 July	Hochreit, letter to Ludwig von Ficker about a donation of 100,000 crowns to impecunious Austrian artists
	26 July	Vienna, first meeting with Adolf Loos
	7 August	Volunteers for service in the Austrian army

Ludwig

Ludwig Wittgenstein, approximately 1908

	9 August	Arrival in Kraków, assigned to one of the Vistula ships "for the operation of a spotlight"
	1 September	Starts reading Tolstoy's *Gospel in Brief*
	6 November	Learns of the death of Georg Trakl
	12 December	Transfer to the artillery workshop in Kraków
1915	February	Work as an engineer, supervision of the forge at the workshop
	July	Injury during a pipe explosion, stay in military hospital
	August	Transfer to Sokal, to artillery workshop train no. 1
1916	21 March	Transfer as a simple artilleryman to the front in the Bukovina
	June	Participation in battles during the Brusilov Offensive
	2 September	Vienna, meeting with Adolf Loos
	October	Officer training in Olomouc, meets Paul Engelmann
	November	Regular meetings with Engelmann's circle
	25 December	Vienna, meeting with Adolf Loos
1917	January	Return to the front in the Bukovina
	End of June	Home leave in Vienna
	July–December	In the field
	20 December	Vienna
1918	18 March	Transfer to the Italian front in Asiago
	8 May	Death of David Pinsent, killed in an airplane accident
	May–June	In the field
	August	Completion of the *Logisch-Philosophische Abhandlung* in Austria, during a home leave
	October	Again in the field
	3 November	Taken prisoner of war in Trento, Italy
1919	7 February	San Pellegrino/Bergamo
	9 February	Cassino
	21 August	Release from Cassino
	25 August	Vienna
	End of August	Meeting with Adolf Loos in Vienna
		Distributes his inherited wealth to his siblings, except Margaret
	16 September	Starts training for an elementary school teacher at the Training College in the Kundmanngasse
	13–20 December	Meeting with Bertrand Russell in The Hague

1920	7 July	Graduation certificate from the Teacher Training College
	19 July–23 August	Works as a gardener in the Klosterneuburg monastery near Vienna
	September	Elementary school teacher in Trattenbach, Lower Austria
	16 October	Moritz Nähr, Austrian photographer and friend of the family, visits him in Trattenbach
1921	August	Skjolden, Norway, with Arvid Sjögren
	September	Teacher in Trattenbach
	28 November	The *Logisch-Philosophische Abhandlung* is published in the "Annalen der Naturphilosophie" [Annals of Natural Philosophy]. In reality the issue appeared not before April 1922.
1922	22 June	Wittgenstein transfers the publishing rights to Kegan Paul in London
	10 August	Meeting with Bertrand Russell in Innsbruck
	September	Teacher in Haßbach, Lower Austria
	October	Move as teacher to Puchberg, Lower Austria
	November	*Tractatus Logico-Philosophicus* is published in an English-German version by Kegan Paul in London, with a preface by Bertrand Russell

1911: First Visit to Gottlob Frege in Jena

I wrote to Frege putting forward some objections to his theories, and waited anxiously for a reply. To my great pleasure, Frege wrote and asked me to come and see him.

When I arrived, I saw a row of boys' school caps and heard a noise of boys playing in the garden. Frege, I learned later, had had a sad married life – his children had died young, and then his wife; he had an adopted son, to whom I believe he was a kind and good father.

I was shown into Frege's study. Frege was a small, neat man with a pointed beard, who bounced around the room as he talked. He absolutely wiped the floor with me, and I felt very depressed; but at the end he said, "You must come again," so I cheered up.

I had several discussions with him after that. Frege would never talk about anything but logic and mathematics; if I started on some other subject, he would say something polite and then plunge back into logic and mathematics. He once showed me an obituary of a colleague, who, it was said, never used a word without knowing what it meant; he expressed astonishment that a man should be praised for this!

The last time I saw Frege, as we were waiting at the station for my train, I said to him "Don't you ever find any difficulty in your theory that numbers are objects?! He replied, "Sometimes I seem to see a difficulty – but then again I don't see it."

Ludwig Wittgenstein in a personal communication to Peter Geach
Courtesy Brian McGuinness, *Young Ludwig*, 1988

Gottlob Frege's house in Jena, 2018
©Wittgenstein Initiative, photos: Gregor Schmoll

1911–1913: Wittgenstein in Cambridge

Ray Monk

On 18 October 1911, Bertrand Russell was having tea in his rooms in Trinity College, Cambridge with his friend C. K. Ogden, when, as Russell put it in a letter to his lover Ottoline Morrell written later that day, "an unknown German appeared, speaking very little English but refusing to speak German. He turned out to be a man who had learned engineering at Charlottenburg, but during his course had acquired, by himself, a passion for the philosophy of mathematics & has now come to Cambridge on purpose to hear me." As Russell discovered in the following days, this "unknown German" was in fact an Austrian. Less than a year later, Russell would say he expected the next big advance in philosophy to be taken by him. His name, of course, was Ludwig Wittgenstein.

Though Russell does not mention this (presumably because Wittgenstein had omitted to mention it), Wittgenstein was then, and had been since 1908, a research student of engineering at the University of Manchester, specializing in aeronautics. His 'passion for the philosophy of mathematics' began in Manchester, where, soon after he arrived, he began attending J. E. Littlewood's lectures on mathematical analysis. With two other attendees of these lectures, Wittgenstein would meet once a week for discussion. These discussions led to the question of whether mathematics could be provided with logical foundations, which led in turn to Wittgenstein being advised by one of his fellow students to read Russell's book, *The Principles of Mathematics*, advice that would fundamentally change Wittgenstein's life.

Though he continued with his aeronautical researches, Wittgenstein became obsessed with the philosophy of mathematics, and, in particular, with trying to solve what is now called "Russell's Paradox," but which Russell in *The Principles of Mathematics* refers to as "The Contradiction." In *The Principles of Mathematics*, Russell had hoped to provide mathematics with a logical foundation. The system of logic he developed for this purpose centered on the notion of a class, which the German mathematician Gottlob Frege (who had, independently, developed a strikingly similar conception to Russell's of the logical foundations of mathematics) had defined as the extension of a concept. Thus, to the concept of a man, there corresponds the class of men, etc. An axiom of the system was that to every meaningful concept, there corresponds a class. Russell's Paradox threatened this axiom, and thereby the entire "logicist" project of building mathematics on a foundation of logic. The reasoning that led to 'The Contradiction' is as follows: the class of all classes has a peculiar property, namely that of being a member of itself. Most classes are not members of themselves. The class of tables, for example, is not itself a table. If we group all of these "normal" classes together, we form the class of all classes that do not belong to themselves. Call that class R. Now, if we ask, "is R a member of itself?" we seem to be trapped in a contradiction whichever answer we give. If we answer "yes," then we should infer "no," since it is the class of all classes that do *not* belong to themselves, But, if we answer "no," we should infer "yes," since, if it does not belong to itself, then it should be a member, since it is the class of *all* classes that do not belong to themselves.

The Principles of Mathematics by Bertrand Russell, 1903 Wikimedia Commons

Wittgenstein became *obsessed* with the problem of solving Russell's Paradox. As early as April 1909, during his first year at Manchester, he formulated his first attempt at a solution, which he sent to Russell's friend, Philip E. B. Jourdain. Jourdain's correspondence book records that on 20 April 1909, he wrote to Wittgenstein, after discussing his proposed solution with Russell himself. Neither, it seems, was persuaded by it. It was possibly this rejection of his 'solution' that persuaded Wittgenstein, for the time being, to stick to engineering.

He could not, however, stop thinking about philosophy. His sister Hermine says that at this time philosophy "took hold of him so completely against his will that he suffered terribly, feeling torn between conflicting vocations." In the summer vacation of 1911, Wittgenstein, "in a constant, indescribable, almost pathological state of agitation" (as Hermine described it), drew up a plan for a work of philosophy and travelled to Jena, where Frege worked, to discuss it with him. Wittgenstein later told friends that, on this occasion, Frege "wiped the floor" with him. He nevertheless was sufficiently encouraging to recommend to Wittgenstein that he go to Cambridge to study with Russell.

Russell at this time was having a passionate affair with Ottoline Morrell and wrote to her several times a day. In these letters we find a day-by-day account of Russell's relations with Wittgenstein. On that first day, Russell was pleased to see Wittgenstein at his lecture on mathematical logic (these lectures were very sparsely attended). The following day, he reported:

> *My German friend threatens to be an infliction, he came back with me after my lecture & argued till dinner-time – obstinate & perverse, but I think not stupid.*

A couple of weeks later: "My German engineer very argumentative & tiresome. He couldn't admit that it was certain that there was not a rhinoceros in the room." In later recollections, Russell embellished this and claimed that he had looked under all the tables and chairs in the room to convince Wittgenstein that there was no rhinoceros present, but his remark in a letter to Ottoline that Wittgenstein "was refusing to admit the existence of anything except asserted propositions" perhaps shines a light on what this dispute was *really* about. It suggests indeed that what Wittgenstein was expounding was an early version of the view he expresses in the very first two sentences of the *Tractatus*: "The world is everything that is the case" and "The world is the totality of facts not of things." The idea is that, if you list *all* the true propositions about the world, then you have a *complete* description of the world. To each of those propositions, there corresponds a fact, and the totality of those facts *is* the world. *All* of those propositions will be positive not negative. So, "Bertrand Russell's room has a desk in it" might be one of those propositions, but "Bertrand Russell's room does not have a rhinoceros in it" will not. Thus, this latter is *not* one of the facts of which the world is made (no matter how thorough you are in checking for rhinoceroses).

In November 1911, at the end of term, Wittgenstein came to Russell to say that he was facing the choice of whether to return to aeronautics or to switch to philosophy. Was he, he asked Russell, "utterly hopeless at philosophy?" Russell said he did not know, but thought not. He advised him to write something on philosophy during the Christmas vacation to help him judge. In the New Year, Wittgenstein showed Russell something he had written. It was, Russell told Ottoline, "very good, much better than my English pupils do," adding that he would certainly encourage him to switch to philosophy: "Perhaps he will do great things." Wittgenstein said later that Russell's encouragement had proved his salvation and ended nine years of loneliness and suffering. It emboldened him to finally give up engineering and to brush aside "a hint that he was *de trop* in this world."

Bertrand Russell in 1914
Wikimedia Commons

Frustratingly, neither the paper that Wittgenstein showed Russell in the New Year of 1912 nor *any* of the work he wrote in the succeeding six months have survived, so we do not know what exactly Wittgenstein worked on during that time. What we do know, however, is that Russell, one of the most respected philosophers of that time, was enormously impressed. "I love him & feel he will solve the problems I am too old to solve," he wrote to Ottoline in March.[1]

Though it is impossible to reconstruct from Russell's letters to Ottoline the details of Wittgenstein's philosophical work during his first year at Cambridge, they do contain some wonderful details that shed light on his personality. For example, in April 1912, Russell told Ottoline of a conversation he had had with Wittgenstein about Beethoven. Wittgenstein had told him about a friend of Beethoven's going to his house and hearing him "cursing, howling and singing." After an hour, Beethoven came to the door "looking as if he had been fighting the devil, and having eaten nothing for 36 hours because his cook and parlor-maid had been away from his rage." That, Wittgenstein told Russell, is the sort of man to be.

Russell's increasing admiration of Wittgenstein was bound to be noticed by the other members of the Cambridge elite, and for a while Wittgenstein was drawn into the circle of friends that constituted The Apostles, the most prestigious conversation society in Cambridge, dominated at the time by Lytton Strachey and John Maynard Keynes. From Strachey's letters we gain a rather different, less respectful, picture of Wittgenstein. Writing to Keynes, Strachey provided the following description of a meeting with Wittgenstein in the rooms of his brother James:

> *Herr Sinckel-Winckel hard at it on universals and particulars. The latter oh! So bright - but quelle souffrance! Oh God! God! 'If A loves B' - 'There may be a common property' - 'Not analysable in that way at all, but the complexes have certain qualities.' How shall I manage to slink off to bed?*

At around the same time as he was making an impression on The Apostles, i.e., the summer of 1912, Wittgenstein met the man who was to become his closest friend at Cambridge: David Pinsent. Pinsent was then in his second year as a mathematics undergraduate. The two met at a social evening in Russell's rooms. Pinsent's early impression was that Wittgenstein was "quite interesting and pleasant, though his sense of humour is heavy." Wittgenstein, however, seems to have taken to Pinsent straight away. Within a month of meeting him, he invited him on a horse-riding holiday in Iceland. "After my first surprise I asked what he estimated the cost would be," Pinsent recorded in his diary, "upon which he said - 'Oh, that doesn't matter: I have no money and you have no money - at least, if you have, it doesn't matter. But my father has a lot'."

After a little hesitation, Pinsent accepted the invitation. The arrangement they made was to meet in London on 5 September, stay a night there and then travel up to Edinburgh, where they would stay another night before sailing to Iceland from Leith. When Pinsent duly arrived in London, as planned, he saw how lavishly funded this holiday was going to be. Firstly, Wittgenstein (who was himself staying with Russell at his newly acquired flat in Bury Street, Westminster) had booked him into the Grand Hotel in Trafalgar Square, one of the most expensive hotels in London. Then, Wittgenstein handed him £145 in cash. At a time when the average annual income in the UK was less than £70, this is an astonishing amount of money, equivalent to more than £15,000 today. This was to be Pinsent's spending money for their month-long holiday. Wittgenstein had the same amount of cash, and also a letter of credit for a further £200. As Pinsent noted in his diary: "There is to be no sparing of expense on this trip!"

Lytton Strachey
Wikimedia Commons

John Maynard Keynes
Wikimedia Commons

Perhaps the most important thing that bound Pinsent and Wittgenstein together was a shared love of music. At Cambridge they had discovered they had similar musical tastes: they both loved Haydn, Mozart, Beethoven, Brahms and, especially, Schubert; and both disliked modern composers (anyone later than Brahms). In the summer term of 1912, they went to several concerts together. On the boat over to Iceland, they were delighted to discover a piano. They had taken with them an edition of Schubert's songs. Pinsent was evidently a fairly proficient pianist and Wittgenstein, as was noted with astonishment several times throughout his life, was

David Hume Pinsent
© Stonborough Family

an extraordinarily accomplished whistler. So, the two began to perform Schubert songs together, with Pinsent playing the piano while Wittgenstein whistled the vocal part. Within a year, they had a repertoire of over forty songs and were performing together almost every day.

When they reached Iceland, they spent two weeks trekking on horses in the extraordinary countryside outside Reykjavik. In the evenings, Pinsent read and Wittgenstein worked on logic, sometimes explaining his work to Pinsent. At the end of the trip, Pinsent exclaimed that it had been 'the most glorious holiday I have ever spent!'

When he returned to Cambridge, Wittgenstein moved into G. E. Moore's old rooms at the top of K staircase in Whewell's Court, Trinity College. He liked being at the top of the tower and kept the same set of rooms for the rest of his time at Cambridge, even when he returned later in life, when as a Fellow and then a Professor he would have been entitled to larger and grander rooms. From the very beginning of the academic year 1912–13, Wittgenstein was in an agitated frame of mind. Within days he had his first major disagreement with Russell, prompted by an article Russell had published in the *Hibbert Journal* on 'The Essence of Religion', which, Russell told Ottoline, "he evidently *detests*." Although he continued to lecture on the foundations of mathematics,

Russell had, for the time being, given up working on logic. He started a paper called "What is Logic?" but abandoned it, telling Ottoline that he felt "very inclined to leave it to Wittgenstein."

It was a mantle that rested heavily on Wittgenstein's shoulders. He seemed to Russell to be on the verge of a nervous breakdown, so anxious was he that he might not finish his work. He would spend hours in Russell's rooms, sometimes discussing logic, sometimes pacing up and down in agitated silence. Once, Russell asked: "Are you thinking about logic or your sins?" "Both," Wittgenstein replied, and continued his pacing.

The K staircase tower at Whewell's Court, Cambridge
© Stonborough Family

On 29 November, Wittgenstein gave a paper called "What is Philosophy?" to the Moral Science Club, whose minutes record:

The paper lasted only about 4 minutes, thus cutting the previous record established by Mr Tye by nearly two minutes. Philosophy was defined as all those primitive propositions which are assumed as true without proof by the various sciences. This defn. was much discussed, but there was no general disposition to adopt it.

In the New Year of 1913, Wittgenstein extended his time at his family home in Vienna, because his father, who had been ill with cancer for two years, was dying. The end came on 21 January. It was, Wittgenstein told Russell, "the most beautiful death that I can imagine; without the slightest pains and falling asleep like a child."

Soon after he arrived back in Cambridge, Wittgenstein was asked to review *The Science of Logic* by Peter Coffey, an Irish Catholic priest and professor of philosophy, for the *Cambridge Review*. It was the first thing he published and remains the only book review he ever wrote. The review is unrelentingly scathing. As the champion of Russellian logic, Wittgenstein subjects the traditional Aristotelian logic presented by Coffey to a series of withering criticisms. "The author," Wittgenstein declares, "has not taken the slightest notice of the great work of the modern mathematical logicians - work which has brought about an advance in Logic comparable only to that which made Astronomy out of Astrology, and Chemistry out of Alchemy."

Throughout the Lent and Easter terms of 1913 - which turned out to be his last two terms at Cambridge until his return in 1929 - Wittgenstein's relationship with Russell grew increasingly strained. Russell had begun what he hoped would be a major work on the theory of knowledge. By the end of May he had written six chapters, and felt confident enough to show some of it, a section devoted to the theory of judgment, to Wittgenstein (whose criticism he had by this time come to fear). "He said it was all wrong," Russell wrote to Ottoline, "that he had tried my view and knew it couldn't work." As he was inclined to do, Russell acquiesced, not only in Wittgenstein's view that his theory of judgment was wrong, but also in his assessment that what was wrong was the *foundation* of the entire enterprise. In consequence, Russell abandoned his plans for a book on the theory of knowledge. Three years later, he described Wittgenstein's demolition of his theory of judgment as "an event of first-rate importance in my life," one that had "affected everything I have done since."

> *I saw he was right, and I saw that I could not hope ever again to do fundamental work in philosophy. My impulse was shattered, like a wave dashed to pieces against a breakwater.*

In the summer, Wittgenstein had promised to take Pinsent on another holiday, this time to Spain. When they met in London in August, however, Pinsent was told there was a change of plan. They were not going to Spain. Instead, Pinsent was given three alternatives: Andorra, the Azores, or Bergen, Norway. As it was clear that Bergen was Wittgenstein's preference, Pinsent chose that. When they arrived in Bergen, Wittgenstein asked the tourist office to find them a small hotel, somewhere on a fjord, set in pleasant country and away from tourists. Such a place was found on the Hardanger fjord, just south of Bergen. By now it was obvious to Pinsent what had prompted the trip to Spain to be abandoned: Wittgenstein did not want a holiday, he wanted somewhere to work in peace.

As soon as they were settled into their tiny hotel, they settled into a routine that suited Wittgenstein perfectly: they worked in the morning, went walking or sailing in the afternoon, worked in the late afternoon and played dominoes in the evening. There was, wrote Pinsent in his diary, "just enough to do to keep one from being bored." He found Wittgenstein a difficult companion, "in an awful neurotic state... as bad – (in that nervous sensibility) – as people like Beethoven were." He described Wittgenstein as being morbidly afraid he may die before managing to put in writing all his ideas. While in Norway, Wittgenstein wrote to Russell asking him to meet "*as soon as possible* and give me time enough to give you a survey of the whole field of what I have done up to now and if possible, to let me make notes for you *in your presence*." As their time in Norway came to an end, Wittgenstein said he had never enjoyed a holiday so much. Pinsent, on the other hand, swore never to go away with Wittgenstein again.

When he returned to Cambridge, Wittgenstein startled Russell by announcing a plan of living in Norway alone for the next two years while he finished his work on logic. It was a plan he had already discussed with Pinsent, telling him that he would do (in Pinsent's words) "infinitely more and better work" if he lived "a hermit's life" in Norway than if he stayed in Cambridge, where he would be constantly liable to interruptions and distractions. Unlike Pinsent, Russell tried to talk him out of it.

> *I said it would be dark, & he said he hated daylight. I said it would be lonely, & he said he prostituted his mind talking to intelligent people. I said he was mad & he said God preserve him from sanity. (God certainly will.)*

Before he left for Norway, it was important to both Wittgenstein and Russell that a written record of his thoughts on logic should be made. Wittgenstein was reluctant to write his ideas out himself, since he did not want to write them out in an imperfect form and he had not yet reached a perfect formulation of them. Instead, they asked a secretary to take shorthand notes while Wittgenstein talked and Russell asked questions. These notes were supplemented by a typescript that Wittgenstein dictated a few days later when he was in Birmingham to say his goodbyes to Pinsent. Together, the notes and the dictation constitute *Notes on Logic*, the first record of Wittgenstein's early philosophical ideas to have survived. Some remarks in these notes are recognizable as early versions of remarks that later appeared in *Tractatus Logico-Philosophicus*, most notably the following statements giving Wittgenstein's conception of philosophy:

> *In philosophy there are no deductions: it is purely descriptive.*
>
> *Philosophy gives no pictures of reality.*
>
> *Philosophy can neither confirm nor confute scientific investigation.*
>
> *Philosophy consists of logic and metaphysics: logic is its basis.*
>
> *Epistemology is the philosophy of psychology.*
>
> *Distrust of grammar is the first requisite for philosophizing.*

Wittgenstein left Birmingham on 8 October. "It was sad parting from him," Pinsent wrote in his diary, "but it is possible he may pay a short visit to England next summer... Our acquaintance has been chaotic but I have been very thankful for it: I am sure he had also." In fact, it was the last time the two saw each other.

Wittgenstein always regarded his year in Norway, 1913–14, as the most productive in his life, the time when his mind was at its most creative, when he had genuinely *original* ideas. As ever, though, his thinking about logic went hand in hand with thinking about himself. "Deep inside me," he wrote to Russell, "there's a perpetual seething, like the bottom of a geyser, and I keep hoping that things will come to an eruption once and for all, so that I can turn into a different person. "Perhaps you regard this thinking about myself as a waste of time," he added, "but how can I be a logician before I'm a human being! Far the most important thing is to settle accounts with myself!"

As Russell was soon to find out, part of that "settling accounts with himself," of becoming a different person, was purging from Wittgenstein's life what he called the "sordid compromise" of their relationship. In the New Year of 1914, in what was clearly intended to be his last ever letter to Russell, Wittgenstein said he had "come to the conclusion that we really don't suit one another." "*I shall be grateful to you and devoted to you* WITH ALL MY HEART *for the whole of my life, but I shall not write to you again and you will not see me again either.*" On 3 March, however, he *did* write again, because he felt that Russell's reply was "*so* full of kindness and friendship that I don't have the *right* to leave it unanswered." He tried to explain what the problem was between them. Its foundations, he said, lay in the fact that their *ideals* were so fundamentally different: "And that's why we haven't been able and we shan't *ever* be able to talk about anything involving our value-judgements without either becoming hypocritical or falling out." Instead of making a complete break, he suggested that they "write to each other about our work, our health, and the like, but let's avoid in our communications any kind of value-judgement." It was a plan to which he adhered for the remainder of his correspondence with Russell.

In November 1913, Wittgenstein had written to G. E. Moore urging him to come to Norway to discuss philosophy. There was no one in Cambridge, Wittgenstein argued, with whom this was possible; even Russell was "no more pliable for *this* purpose." Soon after the above exchange with Russell, Wittgenstein wrote again to Moore, this time with more insistence: "*You must come as soon as Term ends.*" Moore agreed to come and arrived in Bergen on 26 March 1914. He stayed with Wittgenstein for a fortnight, every evening being taken up with discussions ("*he* discusses," Moore complained in his diary).

On 1 April, Wittgenstein began to dictate to Moore a set of notes that was part of a work that he was writing with the working title of *Logik*. These notes have now been published with the "Notes on Logic'" as "Notes Dictated to G. E. Moore in Norway." Their importance lies in the fact that they contain Wittgenstein's first articulation of what he regarded as the central point of *Tractatus Logico-Philosophicus*, namely the distinction between *saying* and

George Edward Moore and John Maynard Keynes in 1914 Wikimedia Commons

showing. The propositions of logic, he maintained, do not *say* anything, but they "*show* the logical properties of logic." He regarded what he had dictated to Moore as a considerable advance on the "Notes on Logic," and he wrote to Russell urging him to read it: "Many things in it are new."

Wittgenstein asked Moore to enquire whether *Logik* might serve as a BA thesis. On his return to Cambridge, Moore did as he had been asked, and discovered that it might not. The regulations governing such theses stipulated that it should contain a preface and notes indicating what sources had been used and which parts of the thesis were claimed to be original work. Moore duly passed on this information to Wittgenstein, and received in response a letter that, until Wittgenstein's return to Cambridge in 1929, put an end to their friendship. "Your letter annoyed me," Wittgenstein wrote. "If I am not worth your making an exception for me *even in some* STUPID *details* then I may as well go to HELL directly; and if I *am* worth it and you don't do it then – by God – *you* might go there."

The ferocity and injustice of this letter shocked Moore and even made him feel physically sick. He did not reply. Two months later, he received a more temperate letter in which Wittgenstein told him that "my wrath has cooled down and I'd rather be friends with you again than otherwise." In his diary, Moore wrote: "Think I won't answer it, because I really don't want to see him again."

Throughout his turbulent dealings with Russell and Moore, Wittgenstein kept up a correspondence with Pinsent, and, despite what Pinsent had vowed after their time together in Norway, the two arranged to go to Andorra together in the summer of 1914. On 29 July, the day after Austria declared war on Serbia, Pinsent wrote to Wittgenstein that "in view of this European War business we had better not go to Andorra – it might be difficult to get back." Within a few days, Wittgenstein's country and Pinsent's were on different sides of the First World War.

Even during the war, however, Wittgenstein and Pinsent managed to get letters to each other. Pinsent wrote in his diary that he thought it "magnificent" that Wittgenstein had volunteered for military service, "but extremely sad and tragic." He writes, "praying we may meet again someday. Poor fellow – I hope to God we shall." Pinsent wrote back to Wittgenstein, but he didn't know whether his letters arrived or not. They did and were a source of great delight to Wittgenstein. Pinsent was rejected for service in the British Army and spent the first year of the war studying law. He was rejected again in 1916. He became a mechanic, and, in a curious echo of Wittgenstein's past, started specializing in aeronautics. On 8 May 1918, Pinsent was killed in an aeroplane accident, while investigating the cause of an earlier accident. The news reached Wittgenstein via a letter from Pinsent's mother, Ellen. "I want to tell you how much he loved you," she wrote. "I saw him the day before he was killed and we talked of you. He spoke of you always with great affection." In reply, Wittgenstein wrote: "David was my first and my only friend... the hours I have spent with him have been the best of my life." He told her that he had now finished the philosophical work on which he had worked at Cambridge.

> *I had always hoped to be able to show it to him sometime, and it will always be connected with him in my mind. I will dedicate it to David's memory. For he always took great pleasure in it, and it is to him I owe far the most part of the happy moods which made it possible for me to work.*

Following the war, Wittgenstein corresponded with Russell and then met him to go through his book line by line, after which Russell was instrumental in getting it published. And when he returned to Cambridge in 1929, he renewed his friendship with Moore. It is his friendship with, and love for Pinsent, however, which are immortalized on the first page of the only philosophical book he ever published, work on which had so dominated his time at Cambridge in 1911–1913:

Dedicated to the memory of
my friend
David H. Pinsent

Ms-104 VI (Prototractatus), dedication to Pinsent's memory
www.wittgensteinsource.org/BFE/Ms-104,VI_f

1913–1914: The Quiet Seriousness of Norway

Knut Olav Åmås

"This is an ideal place to work in." Such was Ludwig Wittgenstein's opinion of Skjolden in Norway after having spent just two weeks there in 1913. The letter is to Bertrand Russell.

More than twenty years later he would write something similar to another Cambridge philosopher, George Edward Moore: *"I can't imagine that I could have worked anywhere as I do here. It's the quiet and, perhaps, the wonderful scenery; I mean, its quiet seriousness."*

Skjolden: a tiny west Norwegian fjord community. Wittgenstein spent more than two years of his life there. It was perhaps little more than a whim that took him to Norway for the first time, but it was more than that which persuaded him to return so frequently. Why did he choose, during some of the most important and creative periods of his life, to live among non-academics in a country which was peripheral to the innovative intellectual culture of Europe?

Wittgenstein's visits to Norway aroused both interest and consternation among his friends and colleagues in Cambridge. In 1915, Cambridge economist John Maynard Keynes wrote to Wittgenstein, who was at the time serving his country in World War I. Keynes claimed it must be much more enjoyable to be participating in the war than it had been to think about logic in Norway ...

But Wittgenstein was never really happy – in Cambridge. He characterized the university town as *"a mutual admiration society."* Almost every move to Norway can be seen as an escape from the university community, or from Vienna. On several occasions he seriously considered settling permanently in Skjolden, *"the only place I know where I can have real quiet."*

The striking contrast between Wittgenstein's attitudes to Cambridge and Skjolden raises several questions: How are we to understand his hostility to the academic environment? – Wittgenstein had a strong dislike of academic life in general, but of Cambridge in particular. And what convictions and attitudes of his might throw light on his decision to live and work in Norway, especially during the extraordinarily creative periods of 1913–14, when he

Skjolden at the end of the 19th century
© University of Bergen, photo: Knud Knudsen

was occupied with preparatory work for what would become the *Tractatus Logico-Philosophicus*?

It was definitely Wittgenstein's own conclusion that his Norwegian sojourns were productive: *"Incidentally, when I was in Norway during the year 1913–14, I had some thoughts of my own, or so at least it seems to me now. I mean I have the impression that at that time I brought to life new movements in thinking (but perhaps I am mistaken). Whereas now I seem just to apply old ones."*

Skjolden provided what were for him excellent conditions for his exacting intellectual work: a fair degree of isolation; if not entirely from people, then at least from *"bourgeois society."* It has long been a kind of standard version that Wittgenstein isolated himself totally while in Skjolden. That´s not quite true. What is significant is that he could pursue social contacts on his own premises. Throughout his life Wittgenstein had serious difficulties in relating to his social environment.

In Skjolden he seems to have clashed with people less than he did while living elsewhere. What he valued among the Norwegians he met seems to have been a certain simple seriousness.

We find a clue as to what made it possible for Wittgenstein to work in Norway, to return several times, and to why he sought isolation in the first place, in what he said to his friend, the law student David Hume Pinsent, towards the end of their shared Norwegian holiday during the summer of 1913. Pinsent wrote:

Ludwig was very cheerful this morning, but suddenly announced a scheme of the most alarming nature. To wit: that he should exile himself and live for some years right away from everybody he knows - say in Norway. That he should live entirely alone and by himself - a hermit's life - and do nothing but work in Logic. His reasons for this are very queer to me - but no doubt they are very real for him: firstly, he thinks he will do infinitely more and better work in such circumstances, than at Cambridge, where, he says, his constant liability to interruptions and distractions (such as concerts) is an awful hindrance. Secondly, he feels that he has no right to live in an antipathetic world (and of course to him very few people are sympathetic) - a world where he constantly finds himself feeling contempt for others, and irritating others by his nervous temperament - without some justification for that contempt etc., such as being a really great man and having done really great work.

A month's holiday in the late summer of 1913 took them first to Christiania (now Oslo), Bergen on the west coast, Norway's second largest town, and then to the small village of Oystese in Hardanger.

Ludwig Wittgenstein had not originally intended to go to Norway on this trip. It seems probable that it was in order to work that Wittgenstein thought of Norway as an alternative, and probably also to avoid too many tourists. Before Pinsent and he could leave he had several important meetings to attend to in England. He visited Moore in Cambridge, Russell in London and Whitehead in Marlborough. The two latter meetings concerned his further development of Russell's and Whitehead's work *Principia Mathematica.*

After a night at the Grand Hotel on Christiania's central boulevard, Karl Johan, the two young men continued by train to Bergen. Pinsent was particularly enthusiastic about the journey on Bergensbanen, the Bergen line:

We were the whole day in the train, and it was the most wonderful railway journey I have ever made. ... The views, especially at the Bergen end, are magnificent.

For the two foreigners the best final destination in Western Norway seemed to be Oystese in the Hardanger fjord, from Bergen a ten-hour journey by steamboat. The first impression was good, according to Pinsent's diary: *"a tiny village in a little bay of the Fjord with hills rising straight behind. It seems the ideal place we want."*

David Hume Pinsent
© Family Stonborough

Ludwig conveyed much the same in a letter to Russell on the day after their arrival: *"I am sitting here in a little place inside a beautiful fjord and thinking about the beastly theory of types."* He concluded this letter in a way that illustrates his ambivalence about the value of his work, and his uncertainty about the future of both that work and himself – doubts which would never leave him:

> *I very often now have the indescribable feeling as though my work was all sure to be lost entirely in some way or other. But I still hope that this won't come true. Whatever happens don't forget me!*

In Hardanger, Pinsent had occasion to record his companion's changing moods. It is evident that the progress of Wittgenstein's work, whether good or bad, influenced his health and humor. Pinsent complained one day that his companion was gloomy and unapproachable and that he was constantly working at logic. In contrast he had seemed in good spirits only a short while before:

> *He is morbidly afraid he may die before he has put the Theory of Types to rights, and before he has written out all his other work in such a way as shall be intelligible to the world and of some use to the science of*

Oystese in the Hardanger fjord, 1912

Logic. He has written a lot already – and Russell has promised to publish his work if he were to die – but he is sure that what he has already written is not sufficiently well put, so as absolutely to make plain his real methods of thought etc – which of course are of more value than his definite results. He is always saying he is certain he will die within four years – but today it was two months.

A few days later Wittgenstein wrote a long letter to Russell about the progress he was making:

Types are not yet solved but I have had all sorts of ideas which seem to me very fundamental. Now the feeling that I shall have to die before being able to publish them is growing stronger and stronger in me every day and my greatest wish would therefore be to communicate everything, I have done so far to you, as soon as possible. Don't think that I believe that my ideas are very important but I cannot help feeling that they might help people to avoid some errors. Or am I mistaken? If so, don't take any notice of this letter. I have of course no judgment at all as to whether my ideas are worth preserving after my death or not. And perhaps it is ridiculous of me even to consider this question at all. But if this is ridiculous, please try to excuse this foolishness of mine because it is not a superficial foolishness, but the deepest of which I am capable.

From Pinsent's diary we read that they did not perceive themselves as tourists. This seemed an especially touchy point for Wittgenstein. But nevertheless, Hardanger was among the very most frequented tourist areas in Norway immediately prior to World War I. Germany's Emperor William II had, for example, visited the Hardanger and other west coast fjords twenty-five summers in a row, from 1889 to 1914 – and his visits attracted new crowds from many parts of Europe.

A week before leaving Norway, while rowing to an island in the fjord, they discussed their holiday.

"Ludwig says he has never before enjoyed a holiday so much as this," Pinsent notes. He records that his companion was convinced that, as soon as he could get back to Norway and resume his work, he would be – happy. Pinsent believed the work would be as good as any he had done in Cambridge, and Wittgenstein himself reinforced the impression: *"(H)e swears he can never do his best except in exile."*

On 1 October, Wittgenstein was back in Britain. Early in that same month he visited Russell and dictated his Notes on Logic, the first step on the road to the *Tractatus*. Around 12 October, he returned to Norway, this time further north than he had been during his holiday, but still in western Norway.

From Bergen, where he arrived on 14 October, the steamer took him to Skjolden in the Sognefjord, a village that was to become a favored place of residence at several times throughout his life. On that occasion he remained there until the tourist season approached, in July 1914.

It was Jacob Valentin Kroepelien Jr. (1863–1926), the Austro-Hungarian consul in Bergen, who served as the immediate reason for Wittgenstein's first visit to Skjolden, deep in the county of Sogn. Through his business relations, Kroepelien was acquainted with Halvard Dragni, a factory owner in Skjolden. Dragni ran a general store and a fruit processing plant in the village, from where he sold fruit juices and conserves throughout Europe. The factory was called *"Halvard Dragni, Sogn Fruit Conserves Ltd.,"* and had also supplied products to Kroepelien for resale to shippers in Bergen.

Dragni received a request from consul Kroepelien in Bergen to find a place for a young Austrian to live. Dragni was told that

Wittgenstein wanted somewhere quiet. Harald Vatne, a local historian, records:

> *At that time the Dragni family lived in 'Storehuset' ('The Big House') in the center of Skjolden, beside the fruit processing plant. Their closest neighbor was Halvard's sister, who was married to Klingenberg, the village postmaster. It turned out the Klingenberg family was able to house the 'researcher' from Austria. These were exciting days for the family. How would it be to have a strange young researcher in the house, a rich man from abroad? Not the least excited was Kari, the daughter of the house, who had just turned six years old.*

On 17 October, Wittgenstein was on his way by boat to Skjolden. From onboard "Kommandoren" ("The Commandant"), he wrote to Russell, informing him of his address in Skjolden and about his work on the theory of types: *"Identity is the very Devil! Types have got a good deal clearer to me on the journey."* In a postscript he added, *"I am not as far north as I thought I would be as the Inn I intended to stay at is closed during the winter."* A week after the letter to Russell, Wittgenstein wrote to Keynes giving his new address and signing off with the conclusion, *"This is a splendid place. Yours ever L. Wittgenstein."*

Skjolden is a small village lying deep in the Lustra fjord, a side arm of the Sognefjord, which is itself one of the longest fjords in the world. The village is surrounded by mountains, beyond which lie the bleak heights of Jotunheimen, one of the most imposing mountain areas of northern Europe, and Henrik Ibsen´s inspiration for his play *Brand*. Two rivers run into the fjord, one from Lake Eidsvatnet, which lies directly below the site on which Wittgenstein had a house built.

At the beginning of the 20th century Halvard Dragni's factory was handling some 100,000 liters of berries per year and selling its products throughout Europe. Another export article from Skjolden was natural ice to England, which was used for cooling foodstuffs. The postmaster Klingenberg was also manager of the ice company. But agriculture remained the staple industry, just as it did for most communities in the area around the turn of the century.

On the whole there was, during the first half of the century, a pretty high level of activity in Skjolden. The village was in no way

Skjolden at the end of the 19th century

"the end of the world", as several Wittgenstein biographers have suggested. It was bustling with life, as lived by its own industrious inhabitants as well as its demanding visitors. During the summers there was a fair volume of traffic across the mountains to Gudbrandsdalen (a valley). In 1878, alone some 16,000 people and 2,500 horses followed this route.

It is a part of the Wittgenstein myth that, while in Norway, he socialized first and foremost with *"the poorest of farmers and fishermen"*. However, if we are to simplify at all, we should rather say, very roughly, that it was people of a somewhat higher social standing whose company he sought, for instance the factory proprietor, the postmaster, the hotel manager's family and the highly regarded farmer and youth hostel manager. This caused most people in Skjolden to treat him with some respect, even if many of them found his behavior for the most part mysterious.

Wittgenstein also met factory owner Halvard Dragni´s family: his wife Ingeborg, his son Bjarne, and Halvard's brother Arne. The Dragni family was related to that of the postmaster, Hans Klingenberg, the latter being married to Halvard's sister, Sofia.

As mentioned earlier, Klingenberg was also the director of the Skjolden firm "The Icehouse" ("Ishuset"), which had been active since the beginning of the century. The export of ice was in decline, and the company went bankrupt around 1916. One of Hans' and

Sofia's children was Kari. She succeeded her father as postmaster in Skjolden and held this position until 1955. Little Kari used to make Wittgenstein his afternoon tea while he was living with the Klingenbergs in 1913–14 and working on the plans to build a house by Lake Eidsvatnet.

The youngster Arne Bolstad was a small-holder and gardener. He was the son of the farmer Johannes J. Bolstad, who leased the cottage site to Wittgenstein. Arne was only 14–15 years old when Wittgenstein first came to Skjolden, the latter being at that time 24 years of age. Arne had an aptitude for music, and often took walks with Wittgenstein or spent time with him in the latter's house. Wittgenstein bestowed the house on Arne shortly after World War I, in 1919.

Most of the time he spoke English with the people in Skjolden, and this is partly the reason why not everyone was able to communicate with him. The information we have regarding which dialect he used when speaking Norwegian seems somewhat inconsistent. *"As I hardly meet a soul in this place,"* Wittgenstein wrote to Russell in 1913, *"the progress of my Norwegian is exceedingly slow; so much so that I haven't yet learned a single swear word."* But after a year in Skjolden, he mastered enough Norwegian to be able to exchange letters with his friends in their own language.

During the stay in Skjolden in 1913–14, Wittgenstein rented two rooms in the Klingenberg house in the center of the village, next to the recently completed Skjolden Hotel. There he had both a study and a bedroom on the ground and first floors, with a balcony looking out towards the Lustra fjord. Not until the last half of his stay did Wittgenstein begin to entertain the idea of building a house of his own. In March 1914, Pinsent wrote that *"Wittgenstein was at the time occupied with these plans, and that the house was to be completed the following autumn."* The intention was that Wittgenstein would return to Skjolden after having spent the summer in England. But in the meantime, World War I broke out.

The house wasn't finished until long after Wittgenstein's departure, and it wasn't until the 1920s that he was able to make use of it himself. At any rate, his plans to build a house in Skjolden illustrate two things: firstly, that he aimed to return to Skjolden, and perhaps to settle there for an indefinite period; secondly, that he needed more complete peace and quiet than was to be found at the center of the village. With the hotel right next door, and the locals and tourists going to and from the post office, there was simply too much disturbance there. Finally, he found a site he considered suitable, 30 meters above Lake Eidsvatnet, in steep and rather inaccessible terrain. To get to the site it was necessary to row across the lake and then climb a steep path up to the ledge. In winter it was possible to cross the frozen lake on foot, provided the ice was thick enough. It was Halvard Dragni who coordinated the construction work in 1914. Whether or not it was based on architectural drawings we do not know for sure.

The cottage might equally have been called a house. Wittgenstein himself referred to it sometimes as a "house," sometimes as a "cottage." Its dimensions were those of a typical Norwegian cotter's dwelling, with a 7 × 8-meter floor plan. The fact that the gable faced towards the village was peculiar in the area, as was the fact that the porch was on that same side of the house, facing Lake Eidsvatnet. The view towards the lake, the village and parts of the Lustra fjord was excellent. Wittgenstein mentioned the scenery in many a letter he wrote from there. It is like a closed world, with mountains on three sides. The landscape is not so much spectacular as soothing and tranquil.

The paths used by local farmers ran past his house, which was more centrally placed than it might appear today. In addition to his contacts with the local community and the personal visits from abroad, there arrived a steady stream of letters, most notably from friends and colleagues in Austria and Great Britain. Another indicator of how well informed he was kept about intellectual events in Europe is the fact that he received Kraus' periodical *Die Fackel* while in Norway. He also received von Ficker's *Der Brenner.*

In the correspondence with Wittgenstein the Skjoldeners paint a picture of him as someone deeply sympathetic to both people and animals. Our oral sources, on the other hand, contribute an opposing shade to the portrait: that of a highly demanding and unusual figure.

The aspect of conflict was, in other words, not absent. The fact that he wished to dictate the terms of social contact did occasionally lead to friction. We know of several examples where this is the case.

The people in the village described him as *"austere and dominating, meticulous and determined."*

On one occasion a local worker was asked to tar Wittgenstein's cottage. The man arrived five minutes late for the appointment at which they were to discuss the work. Wittgenstein turned out to be very offended by this, and exclaimed that anyone capable of such a thing ought to have his head chopped off. He himself proved meticulous in keeping appointments.

For many of the villagers it was difficult to understand his strict demand for silence. There was at that time far more traffic back and forth past his house than there is today. One local, on passing the house on his way from the lake, was abused by Wittgenstein for having disturbed him and told that it would take two weeks for the philosopher to recover the thread of his thoughts.

For Wittgenstein, contact and communication with people around him was always demanding. He himself was acutely aware of this. During World War I he had written in his coded remarks: *"Oh, again: It is endlessly difficult not to fight against mań s evil. For human wickedness wounds you every time."* He felt surrounded by people who hated him in more than one place where he lived. In Skjolden he suffered less from his environment. He liked the people there and became fond of both the village and the surrounding nature. In fact, there are almost no negative comments about Skjolden to be found in his writings.

Whilst in Norway, Wittgenstein kept up a lively correspondence with colleagues in England. Among the most extensive exchanges were those with Russell and Moore. Both of these friendships were to undergo radical, one might say destructive, changes during the sojourn of 1913–14. For the most part the letters are concerned with academic questions, but they also discuss conditions in Skjolden and Cambridge. In the autumn of 1913, Wittgenstein wrote to Russell:

> *Identity is the very Devil and immensely important, very much more so than I thought. It hangs – like everything else – directly together with the most fundamental questions, especially with the questions concerning the occurrence of the SAME argument in different places of a function. I have all sorts of ideas for a solution of the problem but could not yet*

arrive at anything definite. ... – I have got two nice rooms here in the Postmaster's house and am looked after very well indeed.

In a letter to Russell from November or December, Wittgenstein discussed issues of logic and put forward several proposals. The letter displays something very characteristic of Wittgenstein's correspondence with his colleagues: the expression of professional and personal subjects in one and the same breath:

> *All sentences in logic are generalizations of tautologies, and all generalizations of tautologies are logical sentences. Other logical sentences do not exist. (I believe this to be definite.) For Christmas I UNFORTUNATELY will have to go to Vienna. My mother, you see, has such a strong desire to see me that she would have fallen seriously ill if I did not go. She has such bad memories about the same period last year, so I do not have the heart to stay away. However, I will return here very soon. I am in a rather mediocre mood, owing to the fact that I have no progress in my work, and due to the fact that the thought of going home is so terrible.*
>
> *The isolation here does me no end of good, and I do not think that I miss life among people. Everything is fermenting inside me! The major question now is: How must a sign system be constituted in order to make all tautologies appear IN ONE AND THE SAME WAY? This is the fundamental problem of logic! – I am convinced that I never will publish anything during my lifetime. But posthumously you must make sure to publish my diary, in which the entire story is to be found. Write me back soon and try and get something out of my confused explanations. Yours always, L.W. P.S. Your letters do me very good.*

Around Christmas that same year, Wittgenstein wrote to Russell from the Alleegasse in Vienna complaining that he couldn't work well there. So early in January he was back in Skjolden. The holiday in Vienna had reduced his capacity for concentration and he didn't feel able to work. In a letter to Russell he therefore reported that he had no news regarding his work on logic:

> *(T)hings have been very bad for me the last weeks. (A consequence of my 'holidays' in Vienna.) Each day alternated between terrible anxiety and depressions, and even when I did not feel this way, I was incapable of working. ...*

Only the last two days have I been able to hear the voice of reason through the noise of the ghosts and have again started to work. And perhaps I will now recover and be able to produce something decent. But I have never known what it means to feel only one step away from insanity. – Let's hope for the best!

In the winter of 1914, Wittgenstein wrote to Russell saying that he had come to the conclusion that the two of them didn't get on well together because they were simply too different. *"I DO NOT INTEND THIS TO BE A REPROACH!"* he wrote. *"But it is a fact."* He considered there to be *"vast differences"* between them in terms of nature and disposition. For instance, they had fundamentally opposing views on the value of a scientific work. They wouldn't be able to achieve genuine friendship, he claimed, and then concluded the letter by wishing Russell well and asking him to remember him with affection.

We do not know exactly what lay behind this dispute. Wittgenstein's biographer Brian McGuinness suggests it may have been a difference in their attitudes towards publication. All we know about it is what we find in the letter just quoted, and in another of March 1914. Between these two Wittgenstein had received a letter from Russell, the goodwill and friendliness of which made it impossible for him not to reply, as he said. In doing so he stressed that their dispute was due to anything but demonstrable causes, that it rather lay deep within Wittgenstein himself.

You might be right in saying that we ourselves perhaps are not so very different: but our ideals are so entirely. And therefore we were and will never be able to speak with each other about subjects that concern our values, without feigning or quarrelling. ... For we have both weak aspects, especially I, and my life is PACKED with the most disgusting and petty thoughts and acts (this is no exaggeration).

He then suggested that they communicate solely about their philosophical work and about how they are, but leave out anything that has to do with personal values. He expressed a profound respect for Russell and emphasized that it was in order to protect just this that they had to be on their guard against hypocrisy.

Towards the middle of 1914, he wrote again from Skjolden, thanking Russell for letters and telling him that his work had been

Skjolden, autumn 1914 at the earliest. View from the lake towards the site where Wittgenstein had his house built.

going well during the previous four to five months. At the time of writing, he was however once again unable to write or to explain what it was he was occupied with. He asked Russell to contact Moore, to whom he had given an account of the matter during the latter's recent visit to Norway.

As with Russell, so it was with Moore, that Wittgenstein's 1913–14 visit to Norway marked a decisive change in their relationship. During that period, Moore visited him in Skjolden for two weeks. The discussions they had while he was there were strangely one-sided. Wittgenstein talked and Moore listened. *"He discusses,"* as Moore noted in his diary... Wittgenstein also dictated his thoughts on logic to him. As a method of work, dictating to friends and colleagues was something he used on several occasions, both in Norway and in Cambridge.

The product of the dictations to Moore, begun on 1 April, amounted to more than two packed notebooks. The substance was a development of the Notes on Logic, which Wittgenstein had dictated in Cambridge in collaboration with Russell in October of the previous year. Several new logical terms were employed in the notes taken by Moore, such as that of tautology and the distinction between what a proposition shows as opposed to what it says.

Moore had to be persuaded to come to Skjolden at all. In a letter to him in January, Wittgenstein asked when the Easter vacation would begin. He added that he was learning to ski and found it very amusing. And he wrote: *"Have you ever thought about the nature of a tautology? That's what I am now bothered with."*

A couple of weeks later he wrote again to discuss logic but took the opportunity to repeat his wish to see Moore in Norway as soon as possible. *"You must come as soon as Term ends and I shall meet you in Bergen. I am looking forward to your coming more than I can say! I am bothered to death with Logik and other things. But I hope I shan't die before you come for in that case we couldn't discuss much."*

Moore booked in at the newly completed Skjolden Hotel overlooking the Lustra fjord. He and Wittgenstein spent the days separately until two o'clock in the afternoon, after which they came together at the postmaster's house. Moore stayed for 14 days.

Wittgenstein's correspondence with Skjolden after he had left in July 1914, allows us to add a few new details to our picture of the philosopher, since we observe him here in a rural setting which couldn't have been more different from Vienna and Cambridge. When he was away the locals wrote to him in simple, everyday language, and Wittgenstein evidently enjoyed replying in a like manner. The oldest letter preserved is from 1914, the most recent from 1946. Most of the letters are from Skjoldeners to Wittgenstein. The correspondence, collected and edited by Georg Henrik von Wright and Knut Olav Åmås, also includes five letters from Wittgenstein to Anna Rebni. All in all, 51 letters and postcards are included in von Wright's and Åmås' edition of the correspondence between Ludwig Wittgenstein and friends in Skjolden.

There are frequent references to the war and its consequences in the letters. And in the coded remarks from that period, Wittgenstein, for his part, often records the post he received from Norway. Thus, for example in October 1914, we find the name of Mrs. Klingenberg cropping up among those of the logician Gottlob Frege, the poet Georg Trakl and the editor Ludwig von Ficker.

Arne Bolstad, *"an easygoing man with a quiet sense of humor"*, usually strikes a somewhat lighter note in his letters to Wittgenstein – friendly but ironic: *"I am working hard here at home now. You are comfortable as usual, I suppose, probably doing*

Wittgenstein's house in Skjolden, after the reconstruction in 2019.

Wittgenstein's house in Skjolden, after the reconstruction in 2019.

nothing." This was written by the 16-year-old Bolstad in 1915. At that point Wittgenstein was serving in Kraków, in the middle of The Great War...

People in Skjolden had expected him back as soon as the war was over. Clearly Dragni was anxious to know whether anything had befallen Wittgenstein. Elsewhere in the correspondence the people of Skjolden deplore the horrors that Wittgenstein must have seen and experienced during the course of the war. We do not know exactly what it was that made Wittgenstein decide never to return to Norway. Probably it had to do with the fundamental experiences that the war forced on him (and which he also sought), experiences that in many ways led him to live a different sort of life after 1919.

Ludwig Wittgenstein broke off his contacts with a good many friends and acquaintances after the war. In fact, he seems not to have written to Skjolden during 1916, 1917 or 1918, either. His letters suddenly stopped coming in December 1915, at least if we refer to the correspondence known today. The Skjoldeners complained about not getting any answer from Wittgenstein but continued writing to him. They didn't hear from him until October 1919.

Wittgenstein's house in Skjolden, after the reconstruction in 2019.

The Klingenbergs wrote to Wittgenstein at Christmas that year:

It was, therefore, with regret that we learned from Halvard that you will never come back here. I have always said and believed that you would come as soon as everything was all right. And I still want to believe that, one day, with the help of God, when quieter and more prosperous times return to your native country, then you will make a journey up here to meet acquaintances and friends. We have spoken about you so often. Indeed, not a day has gone by without us thinking of you. You, who were so noble and considerate that you didn't want your fishing rights in Lake Eidsvatnet, because you didn't want to kill any living thing except mosquitoes. You, who were so noble: Your character. And now you've had to experience so much evil, oh, how we've remembered you and wished that you were here during this long and difficult time.

14 July 1914: Letter from Wittgenstein to Ludwig von Ficker

Hochreit
Hohenberg
Lower Austria

14 July 1914

Dear Sir!

Forgive me for asking you for a big favor. I should like to transfer a sum of 100.000 crowns to you with the request that you distribute this sum, at your own discretion, among Austrian artists who are without means. I am turning to you in this matter since I assume that you are acquainted with many of our best talents and know which of them are most in need of support. Should you care to fulfill my request, please write to me at the above address, but in any event, please keep this matter secret for the time being.

Very truly yours,
Ludwig Wittgenstein, Jr.

Hochreit
Post Hohenberg
N. Ö.
14.7.14.

Sehr geehrter Herr!

Verzeihen Sie, daß ich Sie mit einer großen Bitte belästige. Ich möchte Ihnen eine Summe von 100,000. Kronen überweisen und Sie bitten, dieselbe an unbemittelte österreichische Künstler nach Ihrem Gutdünken zu verteilen. Ich wende mich in dieser Sache an Sie, da ich annehme, daß Sie viele unserer besten Talente kennen, und wissen, welche von ihnen der Unterstützung am bedürftigsten sind. Sollten Sie geneigt sein mir meine Bitte zu erfüllen, so bitte ich Sie, mir an die obige Adresse zu schreiben, in jedem Falle aber die Sache bis auf weiteres geheim halten zu wollen.

In vorzüglicher Hochachtung
Ihr sehr ergebener
Ludwig Wittgenstein jun

Cover of the notebook Wittgenstein used from October 1914 until June 1915
(Ms-102 FCr in Wittgenstein's Nachlass).
Original in the Wren Library, Trinity College, Cambridge,
www.wittgensteinsource.org/BFE/Ms-102, FCr_f

1914–1916: Wittgenstein in Polish Galicia

Urszula Idziak-Smoczyńska

THE WAR

*"[The War] saved my life;
I don't know what I'd have
done without it."*

Ludwig Wittgenstein, private communication with Felix Salzer[1]

In July 1951, more than two months after Ludwig Wittgenstein's death, Bertrand Russell reminisced, in an obituary published in the prestigious philosophical quarterly review "Mind," about his contact with Wittgenstein as "one of the most exciting intellectual adventures of my life." In this very brief recollection, he found room to mention the event that had been the reason for their estrangement since wartime. He wrote: "Once in a village in Galicia during the war [Wittgenstein] found a bookshop containing only one book, which was Tolstoy on the Gospels. He bought the book, and, according to him, it influenced him profoundly."[2]

This reminiscence has been repeated by Brian McGuinness in his biography of the young Wittgenstein and after him by numerous philosophers and biographers who recast the village as a town and gave varying versions of its name – "Tarnów." As the town that was the first to proclaim the independence of Poland in 1918 (witnessing the fulfillment of a mythical foretelling in which Poland would gain independence once the River Dunajec was filled with blood up to the mountain of Saint Martin), Tarnów now obtained a place in the history of philosophy. In fact, it was probably among the Polish literature and pious books displayed in Tarnów's bookstore of Konstanty Jeleń, under which one the oldest Hungarian wine cellars in Poland can still be visited today, that Wittgenstein might have found perhaps the only book in German – Tolstoy's *Gospel in Brief*. A few days after Wittgenstein's visit, the town was occupied for a couple of months. This was the fate of such Galician towns as Szczucin, Tarnobrzeg, and Baranów that Wittgenstein mentions on the left pages of his diary between intimate remarks, prayers and descriptions of his everyday experiences. The towns were passing from hand to hand, burned and destroyed by their

Słowacki's Theater in Kraków and Russians crossing the Vistula beneath Zawichost in 1914
Collage © Urszula Idziak-Smoczyńska

original occupants just before being lost, and finally plundered by the infamously brutal Cossacks. The war was waged to dominate the Vistula River, on which Wittgenstein's ship was floating: it was a war to capture the river harbors where Wittgenstein was waiting for further orders, a war for the bridges that his unit was meant to supply through its construction efforts. The war was about the partition of Poland. Therefore, we can only speak about Wittgenstein in Poland if we turn from Verdun and the Somme to the Eastern Front of World War I, that is the "war of the Carpathian mountains," which brought about the blood-spattered sacrifice and great suffering of the various multinational armies dispatched to the Galician and Lodomerian lands.

The three notebooks from the years 1914 to 1917 (MSS 101–103), which contain an intimate personal coded diary on the left pages and philosophical remarks on the right ones, should be reread in the context of combat events that took place during the war. The imagery used by Wittgenstein, who read and worked on the *Tractatus* in the first months of war at the Austro-Hungarian Empire's periphery, gives a false impression of trench warfare, still allowing for a customary or normal life. Life conditions in Kraków were different from Wittgenstein's patrol mission on the boat sent to the northern front line. Between the two fortresses – Kraków, where Wittgenstein appeared on 9 August 1914, and Przemyśl – a symbolic line was drawn to stop the Russian forces from making their way towards Budapest and Vienna. The boat moved beyond the border and passed towns that within weeks were captured and consequently lost by either the Russians or the Austrians. Battles were taking place in close proximity to the route of Wittgenstein's boat (the Battle of Kraśnik, the Battle of Sandomierz).

The Hungarian writer Ferenc Molnár, at the time a war correspondent living in Kraków, described an evening at the Słowacki Theatre where he attended the opera show entitled "Pan Twardowski":

> *I realized that I am in a theatre by the river Vistula. How important is the word 'Vistula'? Vistula means a Russian war. The Vistula is the river of war. To the Vistula flow all the other war rivers, to the Vistula they carry blood – the rivers Dunajec, Białka, Nida – so often mentioned Nida...towards the Vistula head the waters of San, Pilica, Bzura... how much blood flows into the Vistula! Not so long ago a whole Siberian army corps drowned in its waters. The Germans have thrown 20,000 people into it. 20,000 dead bodies are floating down this river while we are sitting in a theatre on its bank and clapping our hands.*[3]

Molnár likened the theatre to a box whose lid can be opened in a way that permits the scenography to blend with the painful path of the Eastern Front. When the box opens to the bottom it is meant to *"spread the savage shouts of triumph in the dark night to reach the Russians."* During this evening the nymphs of Slavic mythology narrate the tragic fate of a nation that has been deprived of its land for nearly 200 years. This loss, this tripartite rupture, lay at the foundation of "The War of Three Caesars" that emaciated most of the multinational armies along Polish villages and towns. While the image of the Vistula River filled with blood symbolizes the artery of this land without body, on this river, on a boat named after another nymph from Slavic mythology – the Goplana – Wittgenstein had been on duty since the beginning of the war. Goplana is the name of a water nymph, goddess of Lake Gopło in the Kuyavian region of northern Poland, who played a Mephistophelian role in Juliusz Słowacki's tragedy *Balladyna*. She is a nymph fallen in love with a man, like Echo or Galatea in love with Acis. The boat that used her name, SMS (The Boat of His/Her Majesty) Goplana, was a side wheel steamer, one of the few river boats constituting the *Weichsel-Flottille*, obscure and modest compared with the Danube flotilla, although its fate during the first few months of the war was equally dramatic because her main waterway constituted the rift between the enemies (in northern Russia and Prussia, and in southern Russia and Austria).

The flotilla was established on 30 July 1914 under the command of Mijo von Philipović – the First Lieutenant of Engineers. Its main core included ships belonging to the Galician River Regulation Administration that was ceded to the 1st Austro-Hungarian Army. On 5 August, the flotilla captured two Russian ships near Brzesk Nowy,

Harbor in Nadbrzezie with steamroller boats
© Courtesy of Jarosław Malinowski, editor of the journal Okręty Wojenne (Tarnówskie Gory, Poland)

the "Nadwiślanin" and the "Goplana" (built in 1895 in Drezno under the name "Nixe"). The captured ships had been armed and equipped with lamps manufactured by the Zieleniewski factory in Grzegorzki, and were sent on further north in order to escort equipment on barges closer to the frontline. According to historians, the Goplana was one of the best armed patrol ships of the Vistula flotilla. It had two cannons, L26 with a 37 caliber, and a Schwarzlose machine gun.

In addition to firearms, a searchlight had been installed whose stream of light consisted of a combination of hydrogen and carbon. Two years before the war broke out, the inventor of this new form of lighting, Gustaf Dalén, lost his sight during an explosion because the hydrogen was highly explosive. When Wittgenstein was injured during an accident in the Kraków artillery workshop in 1915 (most probably on 17 July according to a letter to Engelmann from 24 July), he may also have been a victim of this substance. Wittgenstein was assigned to operate the searchlight due to his technical education and skills. This duty gives a specific character to his war experience: while operating the source of light he stood in a very exposed position and worked at night "till around 3:30 a.m." (29 August 1914). Therefore, his schedule diverged from the rest of the crew. On 16 August he wrote: *"The trip itself down the Vistula is beautiful."* When his "brothers in arms" – whom he truly despised – woke up, he could go to sleep.

When he wrote the next day that *"we are now in Russia,"* it meant that the Goplana had passed beyond the border posts. During Poland's partition the border checkpoint between the Austro-Hungarian Empire and Russia was a simple deckhouse with characteristic black and yellow stripes, which was situated on a river ferry crossing the Vistula at the level of Baranow Sandomierski. But at this time the borderline was moved 40 kilometers up north beyond the rivers San and Sanna – it is difficult to establish which border Wittgenstein was referring to. Nevertheless, around this time, on 19 August, the Fourth Russian Army set off for Przemyśl. Undertaking defensive actions, the "Krummer Group"[4] moved along the east side of the Vistula from Kraków while on both sides of the San River the troops of General Viktor Dankl's 1st Army were concentrating their forces. On 23 August, the first skirmishes took place between the 13th Cavalry Division of the Russian army and the Austrian cavalry close to Annopol, then around Janów Lubelski-Frampol; in effect the Russians were forced to withdraw to the east, first to Ludmiłowka and afterwards to Kraśnik, a town they also rapidly surrendered. If Wittgenstein was still near the border line on the Vistula, as it is believed he was, it means he was at the center of the fights that were the background of what has been called *"the Battle of the Vistula River"* (29 September – 31 October 1914). Therefore, we read with some anxiety in his diary that over three days they were immobilized on a sandbar (22 August 1914) because a couple of days later, under the same conditions and perhaps on the same sandbar, two Austrian ships had been lost and destroyed by the Russian artillery (SMS Wawel and another ship[5]). At the same time, a hundred kilometers east of Wittgenstein's position on the Vistula, at the same latitude in Izbica, on the north of Zamość, Paul Wittgenstein was shot in the right arm, also during a patrol mission. During those last days of August, the young brothers Wittgenstein represented the two extreme points of the frontline that was meant to stop the Russian "steamroller."

THE DIARY

"If I had no paper I would write on sand."

Remark to a friend during WW1[6]

In 1929, Wittgenstein wrote:

> *Strange that for so many years now I have scarcely ever felt the least need to make notebook entries. The very first time in Berlin when I began to write down thoughts about myself on slips of paper it was a need. It was an important step for me. Later it came partly from the impulse to imitate (I had read Keller's diaries) and partly from the need to preserve something*

of myself. So, it was in large part vanity. But it was also a substitute for a person in whom I could confide. Later I added an imitation of (Samuel) Pepys's diary. Of course, it is hard to be fair here, as always, because natural motives and vanity were thoroughly intermixed in what I was trying to do. (MS 107, 74)[7]

This remark draws our attention to the importance of keeping a diary during the war. In his memories of the Great War, Ferenc Molnár remarked that sometimes one had the impression that everyone was keeping a diary.[8] If he were right, how much better our understanding of war would be, at least from the perspective of everyday life. Writing down one's recollections was nevertheless a luxury which required some spare time and tools. Wittgenstein noted that he was writing on a table made from a wooden box that cost 2.5 Kroner. Only three notebooks survived; there is a nine-month-long hiatus in the war diaries between MS 102 and MS 103. Following a remark from a letter to Russell sent after the war (in 1922), in which Wittgenstein suggested that Russell might use pages from his journals for kindling,[9] we are sufficiently convinced that he was not intending to publish them. This fact might be also considered in terms of vanity, as mentioned in the previous quotation. Wittgenstein was torn between confession and vanity, between the urge *"to preserve something of himself"* and to be vain about that something. The repetitive forms appearing in the coded diary are comparable to sketches in which two realms meet – the external world and the hand movements of a draftsman who examines his soul. This metaphor could be supported by the image of color samples that must have been made with color pencils in the notebook MS 102 between the entries of 18 December and 20 December 1914.

This leads me to think about the famous exchange between Wittgenstein and Paul Engelmann concerning the poem by Ludwig Uhland, "Count Eberhard's Hawthorn":[10] The count cuts a *"little fresh green spray"* from a hawthorn that he passed during his pilgrimage to Palestine; back home he *"placed it in the earth"* and from that sprig a tree grew under which he could *"sit in reverie"* and remind himself about *"Palestine's strand."* The metaphor of a branch that retains a germ of life and becomes a link between past and future resonates with the diary. In keeping a journal, the facts are not the most significant but life itself. Within this perspective it is important to analyze the role of Gottfried Keller,[11] whose stories and famous novel *Green Henry* (1855) were highly regarded by Wittgenstein. After enduring a disappointment in his plans to become a painter,

Heinrich Lee, the main protagonist of the novel, decides to write his memoirs. Upon finishing them, he brings the pages to a bookbinder who mistakenly wraps them in a luxurious green silk cover with golden fittings. In effect his journal becomes a valuable object, a piece of art that plays an important role in Heinrich Lee's future life. This story draws our attention to a remark from *Culture and Value* that once again evokes Paul Engelmann:

> *Engelmann told me that when he rummages round at home in a drawer full of his own manuscripts, they strike him as so glorious that he thinks it would be worth presenting to other people [...] But when he imagines a selection of them published he said the whole business loses its charm & value & becomes impossible.*[12]

Wittgenstein replied to him with a metaphor:

> *Let's imagine a theatre, the curtain goes up & we see someone alone in his room walking up and down, lighting a cigarette, seating himself etc. so that suddenly we are observing a human being from outside in a way that ordinarily we can never observe ourselves; [...] surely this would be at once uncanny and wonderful. [...] We should be seeing life itself. – But then we do see this everyday & it makes not the slightest impression on us! True enough, but we do not see it from that point of view. – Similarly when E. looks at his writings and finds them splendid [...] he is seeing his life as God's work of art, & as such it is certainly worth contemplating, as is every life & everything whatever. But only the artist can represent the individual thing so that it appears to us as a work of art; [...] The work of art compels us – as one might say – to see it in the right perspective but without art the object is a piece of nature like any other....*[13]

Reading the MSS 102–103 by Wittgenstein (alias Lee alias Keller), both the coded verso and philosophical recto of the pages, turns them into an artifact. Theatrical distance is also linked with an oral discourse which we have difficulty understanding because of our typographical sensitivity towards language. Wittgenstein preferred to speak rather than write; he enjoyed reading novels and fables aloud, and in the same way the diary took the place of a friend with whom he could speak and be heard by. Often writing was just a prelude to a face-to-face address, as in the 1930s when Wittgenstein

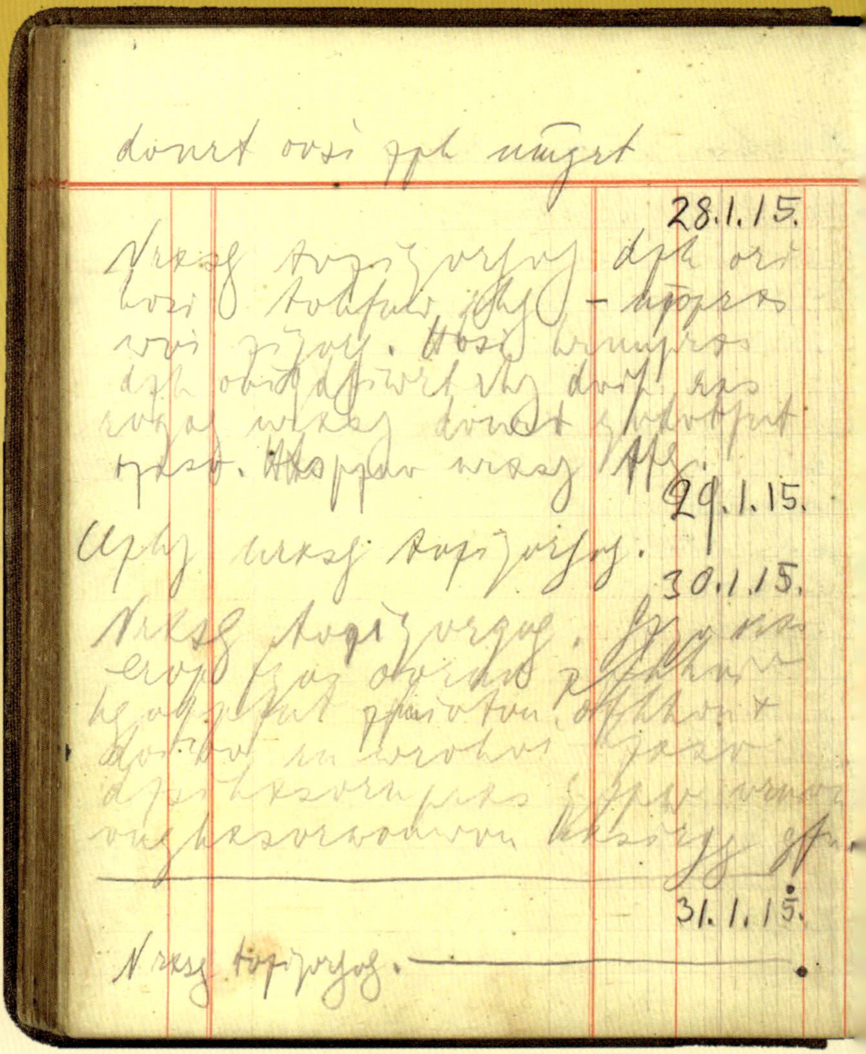
28.1.15.
29.1.15.
30.1.15.
31.1.15.

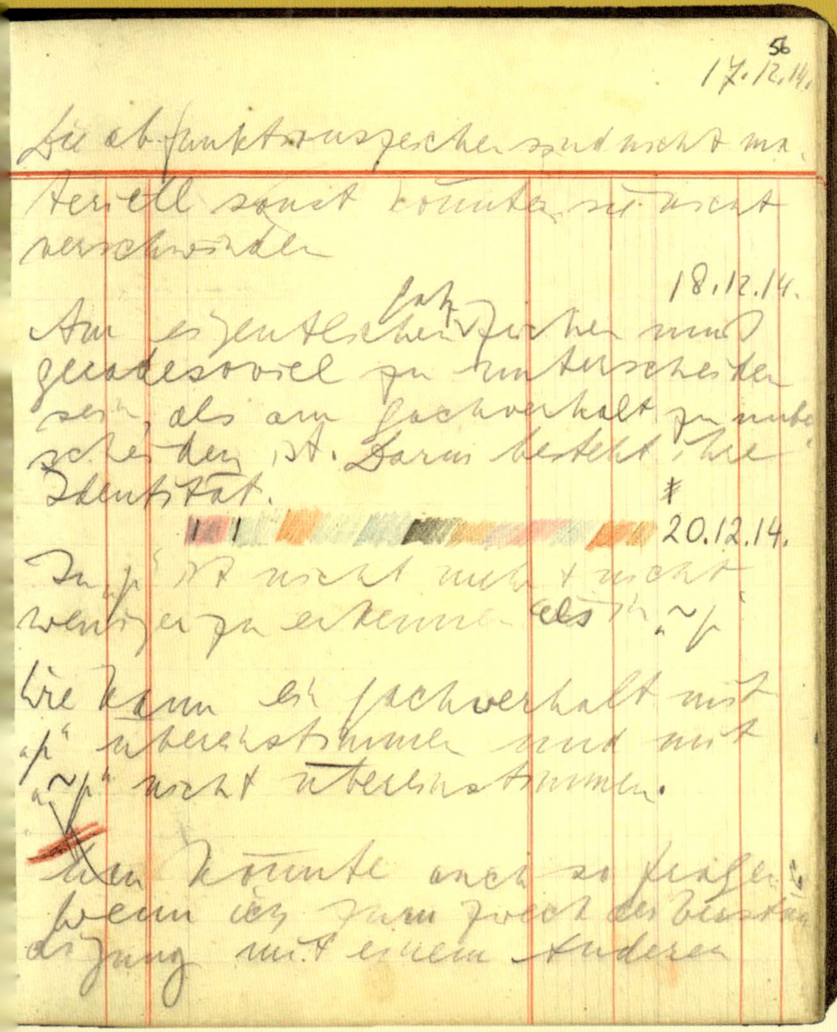
56
17.12.14.
Die ab-Funktionszeichen sind nicht materiell sonst könnten sie nicht verschwinden
18.12.14.
Am eigentlichen Zeichen muss geradesoviel zu unterscheiden sein, als am Sachverhalt zu unterscheiden ist. Darin besteht ihre Identität.
20.12.14.
In „p" ist nicht mehr und nicht weniger zu erkennen als in „~p".
Wie kann ein Sachverhalt mit „p" übereinstimmen und mit „~p" nicht übereinstimmen.
Man könnte auch so fragen: Wenn ich zum Zweck der Verständigung mit einem Anderen

felt an urge to confess and sent letters of confession from Norway to his friends and family members.[14]

In discussing the diaries 1914–1917, we usually refer to the philosophical reflections published for the first time in German and English in 1961 under the title *Notebooks 1914–1916*. These notes appear on the right (recto) pages of the notebooks. The "proper" diaries, however, consist also of writings on the left (verso) pages, the so-called "secret diaries" (*Geheime Tagebücher*), written in code. The contents of the coded pages remained unpublished until the 1990s, following G. E. M. Anscombe's decision.[15] The code used by Wittgenstein to keep his entries secret from his war comrades, in which a = z, b = y, i = r, (j = r), n = n etc., was the one used in his family and he had known it since childhood. It is only while reading the notebooks in their totality as a *"work of philosophical art"*, page after page, that we are able to grasp the tension between meaning and life.

On 5 October 1914, in the coded part, Wittgenstein recalled Russell in the context of a significant remark that at times of well-being one does not think about the weakness of the body, but when things get worse one immediately realizes it and hence turns to the spirit.[16] On the same day in the philosophical part of the notebooks he remarks that *"Logic is interested only in reality. And thus in sentences ONLY in so far as they are pictures of reality. But how CAN a single word be true or false?"*[17] The next day they received the order to sail to Russia, which meant that they were expected to recapture towns that had been lost about three weeks earlier.[18] On 7 October Wittgenstein must have been in Ostrowek in the place where the Wisłoka River flows into the Vistula; he wrote about being "ice-cold inside" and noted down one of the most existentially intensive fragments of the *Geheime Tagebucher*:

> *I can still not conceive myself to do my duty only because it is my duty while preserving all my humanity for the life of spirit. I can die in an hour, I can die in two hours, and I can die in a month or (only) in a few years. I can't know or help or do anything about it: that's how life is. So how do I have to be consistent in any of those moments (Augenblicke). Live in the beautiful and the good until life itself ceases.*
> (MS 101, 35–36v)

On 8 October they were already in Tarnobrzeg, an initially Austrian town some 15 kilometers from Sandomierz. Tarnobrzeg was ruined and devastated by the Russians, who had left but remained very close. Wittgenstein wrote down that he heard twelve hours of constant cannonade. These were battles with the Russians entrenched behind the banks of the River San; the cannonade took place in the vicinity of Zaleszany, some five kilometers from the borders of Tarnobrzeg.[19] On 9 October, on the recto philosophical page, Wittgenstein reflected on the *"relations between relations"* and observed that he must be somewhere fundamentally mistaken, writing: *"the question about the possibility of existence propositions does not come in the middle but at the very first beginning of logic".* On the same day, he wrote in the coded part: *"All day the heaviest cannon fire. Worked a great deal; there is at least one groundbreaking thought pending. —."* (MS 101, 37v) During those days, amid the tumult of war, Wittgenstein was examining the beginning of logic. If a statement is true only when it corresponds to an image of reality (see *Tractatus* 4.032., 4.03.), what about the truthfulness of a single word? Life corresponds to a single word. You can die in an hour or in a year, and live a meaningful life, or face a meaningless death. This is what troubled Wittgenstein logically and existentially, and explains why he was praying for both a meaningful life and meaningful death.

THE APOSTLE

"Tmgg org ori"
"Gott mit mir" [God be with me] in Wittgenstein's code[20]
MS 146 35v: 1933–34

"If you use a trick in logic,
who can you be tricking
but yourself?"[21]

At this juncture, we come to Tolstoy's book. Wittgenstein did not part with it throughout the entire war, to the point of being known by his comrades as "the man with the Gospels", which can also be taken to mean: the one who spreads the good message, the good word. When Wittgenstein found the *Commentary to the Gospel*[22] he must have been struck by the analytical division – surprising for a novelist – of twelve chapters into double points that aimed to mirror the verses of the Lord's Prayer.[23] Equally striking for us to read in the coded diaries is a repeated call to God in prayer, expressed particularly often with two expressions – *"God be with me"* [Gott mit mir] and *"Your will be done"* [Dein Wille geschehe].[24] Both of these correspond to the performative verse of the Lord's Prayer: *"Thy will be done on earth as it is in heaven."* This clause of the prayer constitutes a pivotal axis upon which the three first verses of "our Father", which glorify God (*"Hallowed by thy Name. Thy kingdom come. Thy will be done"*) change into an intimate appeal (*"and forgive us our trespasses [...] and lead us not into temptation But deliver us from evil"*). Wittgenstein expressed his fascination with the Lord's Prayer in a conversation with Maurice O'Connor Drury, adding that *"Christian religion does not consist in saying a lot of prayers [but] that in some way our lives are different."*[25] Instead of multiple words there should be one word, the Logos in the singular, coded and perhaps symbolized by the simplest sign, a straight line between two points, corresponding to life in its totality – meaningful or meaningless.[26]

Within this tripartite context of war experience, philosophical work and prayer, the "Secret" Diaries can be read as a variation on the parable of the rich young man who asks Jesus, *"What good deed must I do to have eternal life?"* (Matthew 19, 16).[27] Jesus' answer is deeply philosophical: *"Why do you ask me about what is good? There is only one who is good"* (Matthew 19, 17). Eternal life is therefore something different from this singular absolute good. Referring to this goal, Jesus advises the young man to *"keep the commandments."* But when it appears that the young man is righteous and has kept each of the commandments, Jesus gives an additional answer: *"If you would be perfect, go sell what you possess and give to the poor, and you will have treasure in heaven; and come, follow me."* (Matthew 19, 21) Jesus' answer corresponds to the singularity of the word "good" – "only one is good." Good is therefore not a relation, it is not an image of reality. "There is only one Good" is a tautology, and this goodness cannot be meaningfully expressed according to Wittgenstein's *Lecture on Ethics* (1929) because it corresponds to the absolute goodness that cannot be reduced to facts in respect of deeds. The next striking analogy between Wittgenstein and this parable corresponds to the desire to be perfect. According to Fania Pascal's memoir about Wittgenstein, this desire was explicitly and fervently expressed when Wittgenstein confessed his misdeeds to her, bursting out, *"Of course I want to be perfect,"* when she tried to soften (and possibly relativize?) his moral ambitions. There is only one good and it therefore cannot be meaningfully expressed, but the desire to be perfect – to be good

Contemporary Vistula and river boat at the gate of Kraków

in an absolute, unconditional way, is something that Wittgenstein *"personally cannot help respecting deeply and [...] would not for my life ridicule"* (*Lecture on Ethics*).

A final analogy is evidenced by the fact that after the war Wittgenstein eventually disposed of his fortune.[28] This analogical semblance gives the impression that we are dealing with a different but similar conclusion to this parable in Wittgenstein's life. Repeating nearly every day the words "God be with me," the philosopher followed the path of Leo Tolstoy and became just as he was, "another lieutenant whom war has turned into an apostle."[29]

Pictures, Models, and Measures

Susan G. Sterrett

On 29 September 1914, Wittgenstein recorded an incident in his Notebooks that he later mentioned to several friends as occasioning a major insight for his views in the *Tractatus* that propositions represent by being pictures. The entry reads:

> *In the proposition a world is as it were put together experimentally. (As when in the law-court in Paris a motor-car accident is represented by means of dolls, etc.)*
>
> *This must yield the nature of truth straight away (if I were not blind).*

Notebooks 1914–1916
ed. G.H. von Wright and
G.E.M. Anscombe
Oxford: Basil Blackwell, 1961

This incident, he said, was pivotal in coming to the view in the *Tractatus* that propositions represent by being pictures. In his later writings as well, investigations of what it is to understand a proposition remain tied to investigations of what it is to understand a picture.

The *Tractatus* was completed roughly one hundred years ago. That is recent enough that readers tend to feel comfortable taking the terminology of pictures, models, and yardsticks to have the connotations familiar to us today. This is likely attributable to lack of better options: Wittgenstein directed that all his books and papers were to be disposed of when he left Cambridge in 1913, so there is little to go on from that early period, in terms of his personal effects. Another shortcoming in historical sources commonly consulted is that history of science and technology has not been as integrated into philosophy as, say, history of logic and literature has. Though lack of his personal effects may be the reason for looking to Wittgenstein's milieu for the contextual cues in reading his works, in general there is something of value to be gained in looking at the context specific to an author at the time they wrote a text, anyway. The availability of materials following the

2.1 *We make to ourselves pictures of facts.*

2.11 *The picture presents the facts in logical space, the existence and non-existence of atomic facts.*

2.12 *The picture is a model of reality.*

2.13 *To the objects correspond in the picture the elements of the picture.*

2.131 *The elements of the picture stand, in the picture, for the objects.*

4.031 *In the proposition a state of affairs is, as it were, put together for the sake of experiment.*

Ludwig Wittgenstein: *Tractatus Logico-Philosophicus*, edited by C. K. Ogdenand F. P. Ramsey (Kegan Paul, Trench, Trubner & Co., 1922)

"Wittgenstein told me how the idea of language as a picture of reality occurred to him. He was in a trench on the East front, reading a magazine in which there was a schematic picture depicting the possible sequence of events in an automobile accident. The picture there served as a proposition; that is, as a description of a possible state of affairs. It had this function owing to a correspondence between the parts of the picture and things in reality. It now occurred to Wittgenstein that one might reverse the analogy and say that a proposition serves as a picture, by virtue of a similar correspondence between its parts and the world. The way in which the parts of the proposition are combined – the structure of the proposition – depicts a possible combination of elements in reality, a possible state of affairs."

Georg Henryk. von Wright
"Ludwig Wittgenstein, A Biographical Sketch"
The Philosophical Review 64: 4 (October 1955), 527–45

miles an hour, while the guaranteed speed was only 16 miles. The "Jupiter" is fitted with a single turbo-generator which supplies power for two separate motors, each of which drives one of the two propeller shafts. The placing of a dynamo and motor between the generator and the propeller shaft not only makes it possible to maintain the engine at its most efficient speed regardless of the speed of the propeller, but permits a more rapid and certain control of the ship's speed.

LAWYER STUDIES ACCIDENT WITH PLAT AND TOYS

A London lawyer, who specializes in personal-injury litigation, in studying a case to place the responsibility for the accident, and obtain a clear idea of the different phases of the affair, reconstructs the whole occurrence on a plat or plan of the locality, placing miniature vehicles representing the parties in such position that the question of right of way, traffic regulations, rules of the road, and such matters, are clearly shown. Thus equipped, he is able to place his case lucidly before the court.

NEW PARCEL-POST SCALE FOR POST OFFICES

The demand of postmasters throughout the country for a practical, simple

Scale Designed to Meet Parcel-Post Requirements

and accurate scale for use in weighing the many-shaped packages sent by parcel post, has resulted in the adoption of a new model, the invention of a Chicago man. The new scale is low, entirely constructed of steel, and the beam is below the level of the platform, so that projections from odd-shaped packages do not hamper the easy reading of the weight. The beam is set to ounces at one end and to pounds,

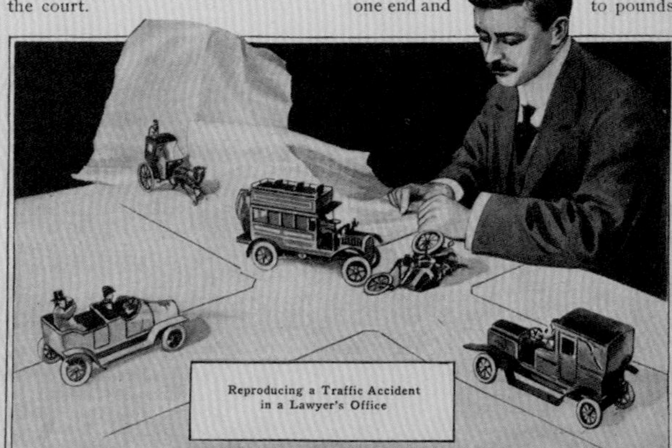

Reproducing a Traffic Accident in a Lawyer's Office

Courtesy L'Illustration

Communicated by Susan G. Sterrett.

massive digital archiving of magazines, newspapers, and journals that has occurred in the last two decades now makes it possible to bring things into discussion that were not as convenient to locate a decade or two ago.

Instead of relying solely on notions of model readily available to us, we can also look at the context in which Wittgenstein wrote this – the cultural context in which the German word *Modell* ought to be interpreted: how was the word used then? A look at the usage of the term "Modell" at the time Wittgenstein wrote this line in the *Tractatus* shows that in the late nineteenth and early twentieth century it was often used in conjunction with models of machinery, including steam boilers, engines, and automobiles, and that by 1914 it had become used frequently in association with model airplanes. It is anachronistic to look at the role experimental models have in scientific and technical practice today, however. Interest in miniature models of machinery was a cultural phenomenon. It cut across social classes, countries, disciplines, and professions.

For context here, we look not just at a particular point or period of space and time, but at how Wittgenstein navigated through the various opportunities the world presented to him.

The role of the event Wittgenstein placed so much emphasis on – of the miniatures being used in a courtroom to portray a traffic accident – is that intellectually the moment was more a matter of Wittgenstein's recognition that he had come across what he had been looking for, than it was a brand-new realization or a moment of transformation. Wittgenstein's ideas about propositions had already been developing, and seeing the use of miniatures to depict an accident used by a lawyer in a law court suddenly gave him a metaphor or a way of organizing those thoughts in an especially perspicuous way.

The context of the history of science and technology is especially relevant here, for it reveals that there was a time when miniatures were not just toys, but scientific objects. As for the depiction of the use of models of a traffic accident in a magazine, I have finally happened upon something close to it: a magazine account of the use of a miniature car and bus to depict a traffic accident, which was published in 1914. This is consistent with a report that Wittgenstein, much later, spoke of seeing "a newspaper notice" which said that in Paris at a legal proceeding about a traffic accident, the accident was presented with dolls and a little bus. The sketch of the lawyer using the miniatures is credited to a French publication published in Paris (*L'Illustration*). It is striking that the mention of dolls and a little bus match this illustration, too. We cannot be certain, in the sense historians demand, that it depicts the same accident, but it is at least fair to say that the illustration and accompanying text depict the sort of use of miniatures in a courtroom that was a newsworthy practice in 1914.

Adapted from *Pictures, Models, and Measures* by Susan G. Sterrett
(Department of Philosophy, Wichita State University)

The full article can be downloaded at
https://wittgenstein-initiative.com/pictures-models-and-measures/

1914–1918: The Genesis of the *Tractatus* in the First World War – Addenda to Previous Biographies

Martin Pilch

FIRST YEAR OF THE WAR – 1914–15

Transfer to Kraków – first trip with the Goplana

As early as 7 August 1914, ten days after Austria's declaration of war on Serbia, Ludwig Wittgenstein volunteered for military service. Two days after being "enlisted as a volunteer" in Vienna, he was already stationed with the 2nd Fortress Artillery Regiment in Kraków. His arrival at the war scene was so early that a real front against the Russian troops had not even been formed in Galicia. Nobody really knew what to do with this war volunteer from a wealthy family, who had previously been found militarily unfit and never received any military training. After a week he was therefore assigned to a ship of the Vistula flotilla, the Goplana, "for operating a searchlight."[1]

Wittgenstein's initially heroic attitude in anticipation of an "ordeal by fire of one's character" very quickly gave way to a disillusionment about "the stupidity, insolence and malice of these people" (16 August 1914), which nevertheless had to be endured "in humility" throughout the course of the war. We are informed in great detail about these early experiences of the war by the first of the three preserved war notebooks,[2] in which he not only entered his personal, melancholy remarks – soon switching to a special code to protect himself from being read by his comrades – but also recorded his philosophical reflections in the usual manner from the end of August on. In doing so, Wittgenstein directly followed up on the thoughts on logic and the philosophy of language that he had previously elaborated in Cambridge with Russell in 1912–13 and then refined further in the seclusion of Norway in 1913–14. At this point, Wittgenstein is still in the preliminary stages of the *Logisch-Philosophischen Abhandlung*, the writing of which did not begin until about a year later.

Before the beginning of November, Wittgenstein made two trips of several weeks each, traveling downstream on the Vistula River against the Russian positions. Although well equipped with weaponry (two cannons, one machine gun), the Goplana was not a warship intended for combat, but rather performed as a supply ship – a tow barge – to transport guns or other war supplies.

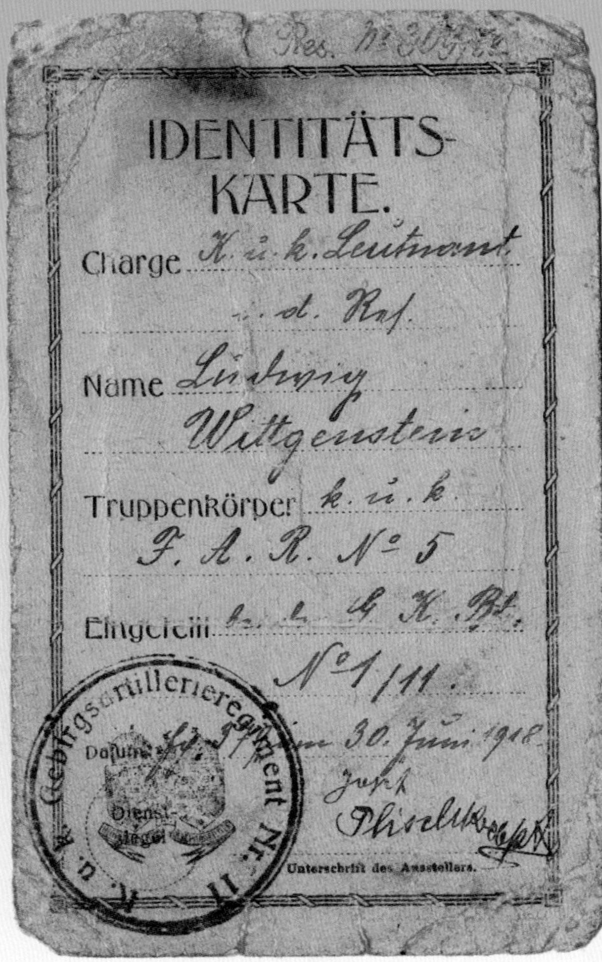

Wittgenstein’s military card, 1918

K. u. k. Gebirgsartillerieregiment
Datum Sg. 379, am 30. Juni 1918.
Unterschrift des Besitzers

SMS Goplana

The deployments remained flexible and were adapted to constantly changing needs on the front, so that Wittgenstein's personal impression that his life was in immediate danger, as often reflected in his diary, was mistaken.[3] Despite the close confinement on shipboard and Wittgenstein's aversion to his shipmates, the atmosphere on the ship was extremely favorable for philosophical work. While the ship was stranded on a sandbank for three days, Wittgenstein resumed his philosophical entries on 22 August 1914 with the confessional remark: "Logic must take care of itself." This remark opens a longer reflective section in the manner of an inner monologue about his connection to Russell's and Frege's philosophy. It also reveals the perspectives that would lead Wittgenstein away from and beyond Frege and Russell. Logic, according to his new view, no longer consisted of laws derived from the basic laws that Russell thought were immediately obvious. Instead, he posited that "language takes care of itself" (26 April 1915), and that "language itself prevents any logical mistake" (8 September 1914): "What makes logic a priori is the impossibility of illogical thought" (Ms 104: 53[1] = PT 5.30631),[4] which is to say that "in a sense we cannot be wrong in logic" (2 September 1914).

However, his change of scene did not immediately solve the old problems that hung over from Cambridge and Norway, with the most urgent among them being that of the properly understood relationship between sign and signified in language: "The obscurity

SMS Goplana with details of the cannon and the machine gun

obviously resides in the question: what does the logical identity of sign and thing signified really consist in? And this question is (once more) a main aspect of the whole philosophical problem." (3 September 1914)[5]. A major result of the Cambridge period was: "Propositions [which are symbols having reference to facts] are themselves facts: that this inkpot is on this table may express that I sit in this chair."[6] Facts, then, stand in for other facts; this is what constitutes meaningful propositions at their core. What remained to be clarified, however, was exactly how to think about the assignment of the constituents of both facts – the signifying and the signified – and the assignment between the relations that exist between the constituents. (23–25 September 1914). In the last days of September, Wittgenstein formulated the first reflections on the "picture theory of meaning," which would later become a central element of the *Tractatus*, to clarify these questions of attribution.

After five weeks on the Vistula, the Goplana reached Kraków again on 21 September 1914. The return had become necessary due to the unsuccessful progress of the Austrian troops' operations. The retreat to San and then further to Dunajec had to be ordered on 11 September 1914, thus drastically reducing the operational area on the Vistula. What Wittgenstein heard about it ("The news gets worse all the time." 12 September 1914) were mainly rumors about the advance of Russian troops, whereupon the crew reacted with panic ("At dawn this morning, we abandoned the ship with everything on it. The Russians are at our heels. I have experienced some terrible scenes. I have not slept for 30 hours." 13 September 1914). In fact, however, the Goplana managed to get safely up the Vistula to Kraków without contact with the enemy, taking on transport duties as a towboat ("On the way to Kraków with galleys.[7] The day passed quietly and was not unpleasant." 18 September 1914).

It is noteworthy that from this time on the concept of the image began to replace the concept of "correlation" [*Zuordnung*] in Wittgenstein's reflections and at the same time a new term for "the signified" [*das Bezeichnete*] was introduced: "state of affairs" [*Sachverhalt*]. It is very likely that both innovations go back to the newspaper article that Wittgenstein happened to read on his return to Kraków. This described a court case in Paris, in which an automobile accident was re-enacted with models and dolls.[8] He referred to this story in Ms 101 (29 September 1914) and later repeatedly emphasized the critical impact of this idea of having a *tableaux vivant* represent an actual event for the development of a picture theory.[9] What was new and promising about this approach

Tarnów 1912, on the right the bookshop (Księgarnia)
© Wittgenstein Initiative

was that it could solve the Russellian problem of negative facts, namely, that a proposition can also tell how something does not behave ("A picture can present relations that do not exist!!! How is that possible?" 30 September 1914).

The first trip on the Goplana also coincided with Wittgenstein's return to reading Tolstoy. From time to time the ship also sailed the Dunajec, a right-hand tributary of the Vistula, and on one of these occasions Wittgenstein must have stopped at the town of Tarnów, perhaps in the free hours while the ship was being loaded or unloaded.

In any case, as he later told Russell, in a bookstore he acquired the only German-language book available there, Tolstoy's *The Gospel in Brief* (presumably in the Reclam Verlag 1892 translation), a highly idiosyncratic gospel harmony of questionable theological orientation, but nevertheless with great influence on Wittgenstein's moral self-understanding during the war and beyond.

He began reading it on 1 September, and soon the book assumed a central role in his life when it came to enduring the adversities of war ("I carry 'The Gospel in Brief' by Tolstoy around with me, always, as if it were a talisman." 11 October 1914). The personal diary entries, which vividly describe his state of mind, are increasingly interspersed with short prayers ("God give me strength.

Amen. Amen." 12 September 1914) and invocations to God ("God be with me." 6 October 1914), which are also visibly colored by his reading of Tolstoy (again and again it is the "spirit", kept richly abstract in Tolstoy, that Wittgenstein invokes directly: e.g., "May the spirit grant me power!" 28 September 1914). This regular religious observation, which may surprise us in its intensity, led to Wittgenstein abbreviating many of these prayers, as a more efficient way of satisfying his need for complete records (especially concerning the progress of his philosophical work). Since his prayers did not vary much in their wording, he did this by inserting horizontal strokes between his punctuation (e.g.: "I am in a very good mood. – ! All day the heaviest cannon fire. Worked a great deal; there is at least one ground-breaking thought pending. —." (9 October 1914)[10]. Rather than documenting what he had prayed for, he evidently considered it more important simply to record that he had prayed.

Second trip with the Goplana

The second sailing of the Goplana (from 6 October 1914 to 5 November 1914) is documented in much greater detail than the first. Again and again, the diary mentions the places along the Vistula – Sandomierz, Tarnobrzeg, Szczucin – that the ship stopped at. During the two weeks in Kraków between the sailings, which Wittgenstein used productively to further develop the picture theory, there were movements at the front, and by 8 October, the German 9th Army and the Austrian 1st Army were again east of Sandomierz, where the San River meets the Vistula. On 6 October a plan was devised by the commanding Field Marshal Conrad, "to defeat the enemy stuck in the San-Vistula corner with the mass of the 1st Army"[11] and to make an advance on Lublin. The necessity of crossing the Vistula with the units at Zawichost meant that on the night of 7 October, the Goplana was ordered to leave Kraków and head down the Vistula again ("Just now the order came to take off for Russia. So, it's becoming serious again. God be with me. [...] Went to Russia through the night; hardly slept at all, on duty at the searchlight etc. We are soon to come under fire. May the spirit be with me." 6–7 October 1914). The prospect of "coming under fire" was not unfounded this time, for the Vistula flotilla was scheduled to assist in the crossing of the German troops across the river, in a spot where the Vistula also formed the front line. The nervousness on the ship was accordingly great and also affected Wittgenstein. For days there was a constant back and forth of advancing and retreating, as well as sudden deployment orders and their subsequent withdrawal. On 10 and 12 October 1914 Wittgenstein eavesdropped on the commander during briefings in his cabin, in which the name Zawichost was repeatedly mentioned as the place where the Goplana was to intervene directly in the fighting at the front. On 11 October 1914 he wrote: "Tonight we are supposed to move on to Zawichost to land troops & equipment; we must get there right before the Russians establish their positions. God be with me. – . 12 October 1914. We did not leave for Zawichost. Quiet night. [...]." The whole campaign failed so thoroughly that the only option was to retreat again and by mid-November Kraków itself was threatened by the Russians.

Given these conditions, it is almost incomprehensible that Wittgenstein managed, in the midst of all this excitement, to make sober analyses like the following:

> *But suppose that we did not bother at all about the question of analyzability? (We should then work with signs that do not stand for anything but merely help to express by means of their logical properties.) For even the unanalyzed proposition mirrors logical properties of its meaning. Suppose then we were to say: The fact that a proposition is further analyzable is shewn in our further analyzing it by means of definitions, and we work with it in every case exactly as if it were unanalyzable.*
> *(11 October 1914)*

Philosophically, the second trip was immensely productive: it was as if all the commotion of war did not inhibit Wittgenstein, but rather stimulated his thinking and productivity. A quarter of all the entries in Ms 101 and Ms 102 (from August 1914 to June 1915) were written in this one month on the Vistula. The picture theory was refined and the idea of the "logical place" was developed, a preliminary concept on the way to the conception of the "logical space." The 'state of affairs' [*Sachverhalt*] was determined as a 'possibility' and contrasted with the 'fact' [*Tatsache*].

The beginning was made on 20 October 1914 by the concept of "logical scaffolding": "The proposition constructs a world by means of its logical scaffolding [...]," whereby also "the completely general propositions are logical constructions from states of affairs." On 29 October, by analogy with ordinary space, "logical coordinates" and the "logical place" were introduced; three days later it reads: "The proposition must determine a logical place. The existence of this logical place is guaranteed by the existence of the component parts alone, by the existence of the significant proposition." (1 November 1914).[12]

The proposition in its composition of constituents – provided that it is legitimately formed to determine a possible logical place – also guarantees the possibility of the state of affairs isomorphically represented by the constituents.

Thus, on 4 and 5 November, Wittgenstein succeeded in summarizing the picture theory provisionally:

One name is representative of one thing, another of another thing, and they themselves are connected; in this way – like a tableau vivant – the whole images the situation. [...] Then in order for a proposition to present a situation it is only necessary for its component parts to represent those of the situation and for the former to stand in a connexion which is possible for the latter. The propositional sign guarantees the possibility of the fact which it presents (not, that this fact is actually the case) [...].

With the help of the logical place, it can also be determined what it means to negate a proposition.[13]

The return to Kraków, forced by the progress of the war, turned out to be difficult: on 28 October a paddle wheel broke and the Goplana had to be towed in the direction of Kraków. On the same day, Wittgenstein learned through letters, which reached him quite irregularly, that his brother Paul had been seriously wounded in the war and had lost his right arm. Two days later he also received field postcards from Gottlob Frege and the Austrian poet Georg Trakl. The connection with Frege had existed since the latter had advised him in 1911 to study with Russell in Cambridge, and that with Trakl had come about through Wittgenstein's generous donation of 100,000 crowns in the summer of 1914 to the magazine *Der Brenner* to support writers in need.

Trakl was currently in the garrison hospital in Kraków and asked Wittgenstein to visit him on 26 October. But this visit never came about; when Wittgenstein reached Kraków on 5 November, he noted in his diary: "It is too late tonight to visit Trakl"; the next day: "Into the city to the garrison hospital early this morning. Found out that Trakl had died there a few days ago!! This hit me very hard. How sad, how sad!!! I wrote to Ficker about it right away. Ran a few errands & then at about 6 o'clock came back aboard. Did no work. Poor Trakl! – .! Thy will be done. – "

In the weeks that followed, Wittgenstein worried about his immediate future. A prolonged siege of Kraków was expected, and it was primarily the prospect of being ordered to winter quarters with mass accommodations along with the rest of the crew that frightened him ("The siege of Kraków is now expected with all certainty. I must try to get away from this ship." 7 November 1914; "Now the word is that our crew will be departing from here since the ships are of no use in winter. What will become of me then??" 16 November 1914). When it was announced on 23 November that "Water-transport [is] discontinued," he made even greater efforts to obtain a transfer by approaching his superiors, pursuing every conceivable possibility, even that of being placed in a balloon corps (30 November 1914).

Georg Trakl in military uniform, 1912
Wikimedia Commons

Meanwhile, the philosophical "work" continued in the "lots of free time" (23 November), but in the struggle for the "one redeeming word" (21 November) he complained of a certain "standstill" (18 November), which increased into a fear of the drying up of his creative power: "Today I felt that the fertility of my mind may have dried up. The whole topic of my work seemed to move off into the distance. And indeed: my 3–4 months are over. Sadly, without any really major result.!" (26 November 1914). This disregard for his results of the past weeks is all the more remarkable, since it is precisely in

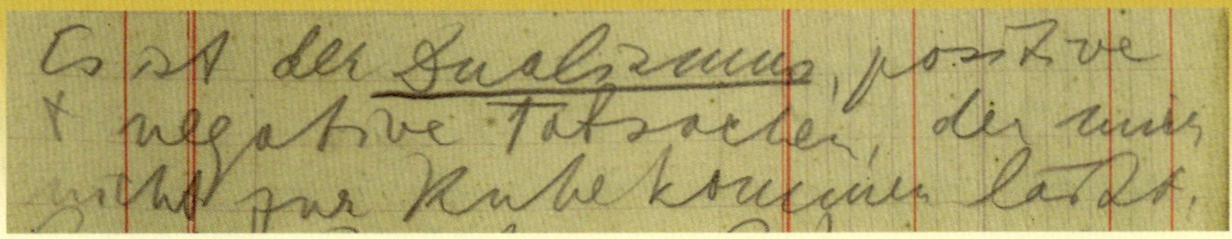

Ms 102 Excerpt from fol. 41r (www.wittgensteinsource.org/BFE/Ms-102,41r_f)

this short phase that key concepts of the future *Tractatus* take on their first contours, among them the picture theory of meaning, the conception of logical space, and the idea of the state of affairs as a possibility of how things stand. The reflections in these days circle again and again around 'negation' ("It is the mystery of negation: This is not how things are, and yet we can say how things are not" (15 November 1914); "the representation of negative facts by means of models" (14 November 1914) and the relation of positive and negative sign.

> *It is the dualism, positive and negative facts, that gives me no peace. For such a dualism can't exist. But how to get away from it? All this would get solved of itself if we understood the nature of the proposition.*[14]

On 23 November, in the midst of these reflections, Wittgenstein abruptly and quite independently – without any tangible analogous precedent in Hertz or Boltzmann – takes the step from "logical place" to abstract "logical space" (25 November 1915). The necessary completeness of this logical space, though not yet discussed at this time, will later solve the problem of negation in the *Tractatus*: "The totality of the obtaining states of affairs also determines which states of affairs do not obtain." (TLP 2.05 modified translation).

In the artillery workshop in Kraków

External circumstances changed abruptly for Wittgenstein when, on 3 December 1914, he met an *Oberleutnant* [First Lieutenant] at the commandant's office in Kraków, who was just taking over his new command there: Oskar Gürth. Two years older than Wittgenstein, this officer was apparently valued for his organizational talent and technical skills; earlier in the war he had briefly commanded a 9 cm cannon battery and worked as an 'automobile officer' with a 24 cm mortar battery. He was tasked with reorganizing Kraków's only industrial plant worth mentioning, the "Zieleniewski Factory," first into an "*Artillerie Autodetachement*" [workshop concerned with the care and repair of the various cars of the fortress-artillery in Kraków] and then into a full-fledged artillery workshop.[15] When, during a chance meeting, Gürth heard about Wittgenstein's engineer training, he promptly requested him from the fortress-command as a support for his task. Indeed, Gürth managed to secure Wittgenstein's longed for departure from the Goplana. For Wittgenstein, the release from the unloved ship's service initially meant monotonous clerical work, which, according to his personal entries, exhausted him to such an extent ("Office all day" 13 December 1914, and more often) that he hardly had time for philosophical work in the second half of December. The tasks were apparently not very demanding; on 10 December, for example, he was supposed to compile "a list of the chainsaws in a barracks." On this day, he also moved into a private room in Kraków and thus no longer had to spend the night in a barracks. On 24 December, Wittgenstein was very pleased to have been "promoted to military official – without stars."[16] This was probably only one of Gürth's unauthorized actions that would later cause Wittgenstein serious problems, because in the preserved files in the Vienna War Archives, in which every change of status in Wittgenstein's military career is meticulously recorded, there is no reference to an appointment to military officer of any rank. At the turn of the year, Gürth appointed Wittgenstein as his "adjutant" and took him on a ten-day official trip to Vienna, which meant an unexpected reunion with his family. On this occasion, Gürth "as delegate of the Kraków Fortress Command" also conducted direct negotiations with the 7th Department in the War Ministry about the further financing of the artillery workshop in Kraków.[17]

More recent research, carried out in 2021, on a wider selection of files from the Vienna War Archives that were not available to Brian McGuinness for use in his biography *Wittgenstein. A Life*,[18] show how provisional the conditions in the artillery workshop in Kraków actually were at the beginning of 1915. There was no order from a "higher authority" to set up such a workshop in the first place. Moreover, the rented "factory" and the hired workers caused unbudgeted costs. When in a list sent out by the War Ministry in Vienna (dated 26 January 1915) of all artillery workshops officially existing during the war, the workshop under Gürth's command was not listed,[19] the fortress command in Kraków hurriedly (on 13 February 1915) sought a subsequent extraordinary permit from the *Etappenoberkommando (EOK)* [Army Rear Area High Command].[20] The document is revealing of Wittgenstein's circumstances at the time. It not only describes the scope of activities and the capabilities of the workshop – repairs of heavy mortars, smaller field guns and machine guns up to field kitchens are mentioned – but it shows that the workshop was to remain mobile in case of a shift of the front and was "designated to follow the heavy assault artillery in the event of its action." This planned mobility of the workshop did not materialize, but the demand for it was apparently the nucleus of Gürth's broader intentions in March and April 1915 to develop plans for an entirely new mobile format for workshops, namely "artillery workshop trains," i.e., mobile modular railroad trains that could be flexibly deployed as full-fledged workshops near the front.

This newly developed idea was of great importance for Wittgenstein's wartime life, if only because Gürth, through perseverance, succeeded in obtaining permission from the highest level by the Minister of War himself,[21] for 'his' concept to be implemented. Two of these trains were in fact subsequently built under his direction in Kraków and Wittgenstein was assigned to one of these trains under Gürth's command from August 1915 to March 1916 as an artillery engineer.

However, Wittgenstein may have been more deeply involved in this development than previously assumed, because in a later report Gürth explicitly emphasizes to superiors that Wittgenstein "participated in the work on the trains [...]."[22]

This involvement may have taken two forms: on the one hand, it is likely that Gürth involved the technically far more experienced Wittgenstein[23] already in the planning phase in February or March – if the analysis of the workshop into individual functional modules and subsequent recombination into a linearly assembled overall functional unit was not Wittgenstein's own idea in the first place – or, on the other hand, he was involved as an engineer in the actual construction work on the two trains (from May to July 1915) in Kraków. The fact that we do not find out a single word about these plans or their implementation in the coded remarks of Ms 102 is probably due to the fact that the development of artillery workshop trains was treated as a military secret, also in the files. Wittgenstein, in contrast to his time on the Goplana, is conspicuously guarded when it comes to official matters or technical aspects of his assignment.

From February 1915 onward, Gürth was increasingly dependent on Wittgenstein's technical abilities[24] for his ambitious plans. He no longer used him only for auxiliary services in the *Autodetachement*, but, as he later reported to the ministry, assigned him "first as a supervisor, but then, because there was

Alleged forge of the artillery workshop in Kraków
https://filozoficznykrakow.files.wordpress.com/2014/12/celestat-warsztaty.jpg

a shortage of officers, as an operations engineer, in which position he performed splendidly."[25] Wittgenstein seems to have been much more skeptical when he wrote on 3 February: "Did no work. No ideas. I am now supposed to take over the supervision of our forge factory. How will that go?"

What he will have rightly anticipated is that, as a war volunteer and simple soldier without military rank, he could hardly give any instructions to the peer crew and higher-ranking non-commissioned officers (NCOs), so that, as Gürth puts it in his report, in the exercise of the supervisory function he "had difficulties in disciplinary terms vis-à-vis the professional NCOs."[26] Gürth eliminates the problem without further ado by having Wittgenstein wear the uniform of a *Landsturm*-engineer[27] – referring to certain ministerial decrees on the *Landsturm* – which gave him officer rank to the outside world. This recognition must have satisfied Wittgenstein's vanity at first, because the correspondence shows that the addresses on his mail changed very quickly from "To the war volunteer ..." to "To the *Landsturm*-engineer Ludwig Wittgenstein."[28] This is especially true in the numerous letters from his mother, but also from his former teacher in Berlin, Stanislaus Jolles, who reacted very ironically ("So you are a *Landsturm*-engineer, I did not suspect that, since I had pictured a man in his 40s. [...]" (20 February 1915). However, the title by no means eliminated Wittgenstein's problem, but rather made it worse when it became clear that the wearing of the uniform was only provisional and that no formal appointment had yet been made. On the contrary, the title may have led to increasing hostility, as an

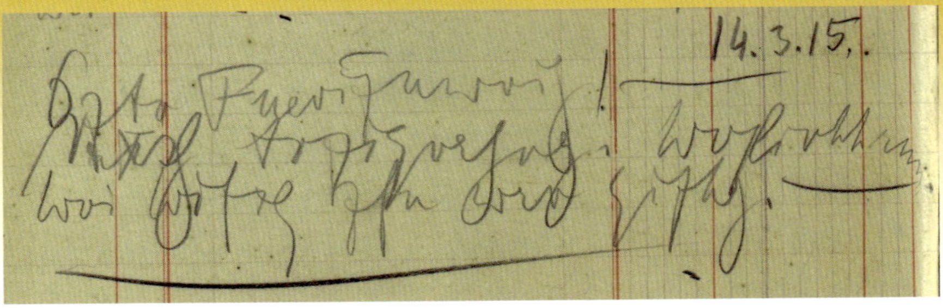

Example of a coded entry: the expression of increasing despair on 14 March 1915;
Ms 102 excerpt from fol. 67v (www.wittgensteinsource.org/BFE/Ms-102,67v_f)

entry of 11 February 1915 suggests: "Am now on very tense terms with one of the officers – Cadet Adam. It is possible that there may be a duel between us." Gürth should have realized that his solution was premature and unsound, and that it alone could have seriously compromised Wittgenstein, from the fact that Wittgenstein – as the later rejection of his application by his superiors makes clear – as a war volunteer belonged to the regular army (the *Landwehr*) and therefore could not hold a rank in the *Landsturm*, a militia made up of reservists of older age, which was strictly separate from the regular army in terms of organization.

In the notebook Ms 102 (30 October 1914 – 22 June 1915), at any rate, there is an increasing personal discomfort in the two following months about the "Unpleasantness with the crew. Trouble & agitation" (22 February), the "unworthy position" (5 March), the "undecided situation" (12 March), which increases the wish to switch to the infantry to the point of despair: "Situation unchanged!. —. Not worked, depression. Pressure on the chest. — . —" (14 March 1915).

Philosophically, his work did not progress well during these months. There are only scattered remarks with isolated flashes of thought, and not actually on the core issues of linguistic logic ("A tune is a kind of tautology, it is complete in itself; it satisfies itself." 4 March 1915; "The law of causality is not a law but the form of a law." 29 March 1915). Wittgenstein was, as a whole, quite disappointed in his efforts to elucidate the logic of the proposition, which he made a sort of a program for himself in Kraków ("My <u>whole</u> task consists in explaining the nature of the proposition. That is to say, in giving the nature of all facts, whose picture the proposition <u>is</u>. In giving the nature of all being." 22 January 1915). In mid-April 1915 he is at the height of this crisis and writes: "I <u>cannot</u> get from the nature of the proposition to the individual logical operations!!!" 12 April 1915; "That is, I cannot bring out how far the proposition is the picture of the situation! I am almost inclined to give up all my efforts. ——." 15 April 1915; the coded entry for the same date reads, "I can't think of anything new to say! (Gürth has been detached from here)[29] I can no longer think of anything new. And it probably shouldn't matter at all."

Following this outburst, something very strange happened. For instead of "giving up all efforts," a hopeful "I am working" soon followed, and on 1 May 1915 even a "The mercy of work," which means, in Wittgenstein's scheme of things, the highest level of philosophical creativity. It is not clear to what extent this sudden shift to new intellectual productivity, which will increase to longer and longer daily entries until the last remark on 22 June, has to do with Gürth's departure from Kraków.

What lay behind Gürth's sudden detachment can be reconstructed in relatively great detail from the surviving files of the Vienna War Archives. Gürth must have succeeded in convincing higher command levels of his "train project," i.e., the idea of a mobile artillery workshop in railway carriages, whether with Wittgenstein's cooperation or without it. On 12 April 1915, three days before Wittgenstein's diary notes his "detachment," a memo with the following brief content is recorded at the *k.u.k.*[Imperial and Royal] War Ministry at the *Stubenring* in Vienna: "The War Ministry intends to set up 2 artillery workshop trains, as discussed by Field Marshal Lieutenant Schleyer with Field Marshal Lieutenant Kanik, and to entrust *Oberleutnant* Gürth of the Kraków Fortress Command [...] with their implementation."[30] Two senior officers with the rank of generals, one, *Freiherr* Leopold Schleyer von Pontemalghera,[31] the highest responsible military official in the War Ministry for all technical matters in the war, the other, Franz Kanik,[32] head of the so-called *Etappenoberkommando (EOK)* [Army Rear Area High Command], i.e. responsible for the entire supply organization of the Austrian *k.u.k.* Army, thus agree to entrust a first lieutenant of the Kraków fortress with an idiosyncratic technical project according to his "own plans." Gürth apparently rushed from Kraków to Vienna immediately after receiving this news and was involved in the astonishingly fast preparation of "Decree 14,621" in the 7th Department of the War Ministry, with which the order for the development and installation of the trains was issued, personally signed by the Austrian Minister of War, Alexander von Krobatin, together with all the necessary enclosures with details on machines, tools, crew lists, etc.[33]

Meanwhile, a new commander was appointed in Kraków to replace Gürth,[34] and Wittgenstein was given overall supervision of the entire workshop, thus ensuring continuity through his technical expertise.[35] Wittgenstein, however, is obviously more involved in the new situation than he would like. "Working! Now frittering away my time in the factory!!! – – ," reads the entry of 27 April, and nothing changes in the basic problem of his precarious position.[36] On 3 May, the War Ministry's deployment order can be sent. Immediately afterwards, Gürth is sent on an official trip to Prague, Berlin and Leipzig to bring himself up to date with the latest technical developments in German army workshops.[37] After his return to Vienna in mid-May, he coordinates the installation work from the office of the Inspector of Technical Artillery at the Vienna Arsenal, to whom the supervision of the project has been assigned.[38]

However, the assembly of the trains themselves does not take place in Vienna, but in Kraków, in or near the "factory." From 10 to 13 May, the crews for the two trains arrived in Kraków; on 20 May, the first carriages for rebuilding; on 28 May, 66 boxes with tools – the machine deliveries, however, were delayed until July.[39] On 5 June the future commanders and officers for the trains are appointed: for Artillery Workshop Train No. 1, Gürth himself was designated as commander and Lieutenant Walter Wahle as his deputy.[40]

The third most important position in the two workshop trains according to the supplement, the artillery engineer in charge of operations (preferably a *Landsturm*-engineer), cannot be filled for the time being for lack of suitable engineers.[41] But this is precisely the position that Wittgenstein was, evidently, to hold in the Artillery Workshop Train No. 1 from the end of August on, and it is likely that Wittgenstein's entry of 8 June ("Will probably get away from here.") refers to the transfer to this newly created position. Gürth's appointment as commander of one of the two trains was approved just three days before that date, and it stands to reason that he will have immediately sought and notified Wittgenstein of the assignment as his principal engineer.

New advancements – the "mercy of work"

However, the visible resurgence of philosophical productivity in the Second War Notebook in mid-April 1915 could be due to a completely different source of inspiration. In his dissertation (completed in 2021) Shunichi Takagi argues, on the basis of detailed textual comparisons, that the philosophical remarks from April to June 1915 primarily

Oberleutnant Oskar Gürth (left picture and in the middle of the right picture). Pictures taken on 12 July 1916 in Kowel on the occasion of the inspection of an artillery workshop train by the German Colonel General Alexander von Linsingen (second from left).
© ANL, Sign. WK1/ALB94/27978 bzw. 27994

Russell's book *Our Knowledge of the External World as a Field for Scientific Method in Philosophy* (OKEW)
English edition 1914 (left) and American edition 1915 (right)
© Martin Pilch (Photo)

constitute an examination of Russell's book *Our Knowledge of the External World* (OKEW, Russell 1914), which contains his *Lowell Lectures* from that year.

So far, all that was known from the correspondence was that Wittgenstein requested urgently twice, to John Maynard Keynes and to David Pinsent, to send the book to him. However, there was no indication that he actually received it. Comparison of the text, with a number of striking correspondences, now suggests that this was the case after all. The 1914 book (OKEW) is closely related to Russell's essay *The Relation of Sense-Data to Physics*,[42] which we know with certainty that Wittgenstein received from Russell (around Christmas 1914).[43] Against the background of Russell's two texts, whose theses Wittgenstein clearly criticized and whose "scientific method" he relatively brusquely rejected ("Russell's method in his 'Sc.[ientific] Method in Phil.[osophy]' is simply a retrogression from the method of physics." 1 May 1915),[44] the considerations in Ms 102 appear in a different light.

Closer examined, it seems to me – this may be put here as a brief thesis – that a kind of triangular constellation of Russell's, Schopenhauer's and Wittgenstein's own positions becomes visible in the remarks from about mid-April to the beginning of June 1915. On the one hand, for example, Schopenhauer's conception of the *Satz vom Grund* [the principle of sufficient reason] as a causal law is rejected,[45] but on the other hand, in the course of far-reaching criticism, the construction of matter proposed by Russell is likewise rejected. With the help of Schopenhauer, Wittgenstein in turn succeeds in specifying his own position in the relationship between language and world. This step becomes comprehensible in the two remarks of 22 and 23 May 1915:

> *22 May 15*
>
> *The mathematical notation for infinite series like* '$1+\frac{x}{1!}+\frac{x^2}{2!}+\ldots$' *together with the dots is an example of that extended generality. A law is given and the terms that are written down serve as an illustration.*
>
> *In this way instead of (x)fx one might write 'fx.fy....'.*
> *Spatial and temporal complexes.*
>
> *23 May 15*
> *The limits of my language mean the limits of my world.*

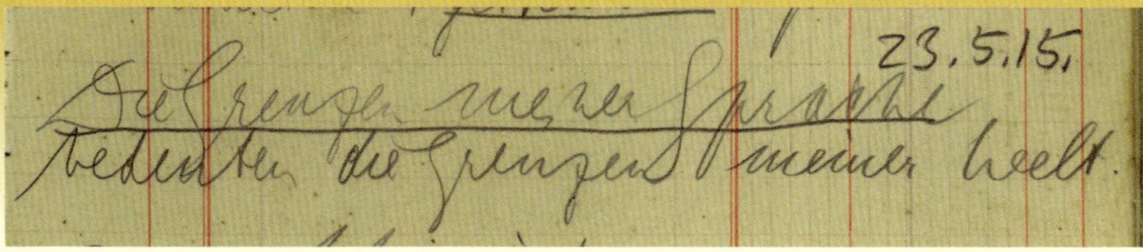

"23. 5. 15 Die Grenzen meiner Sprache bedeuten die Grenze meiner Welt"
["23 July 15 The limits of my language mean the limits of my world."]

Ms 102 Excerpt from fol. 101r (www.wittgensteinsource.org/BFE/Ms-102,101r_f)

> *There really is only one world soul, which I for preference call my soul and as which alone I conceive what I call the souls of others.*
>
> *The above remark gives the key for deciding the way in which solipsism is a truth.*
>
> *I have long been conscious that it would be possible for me to write a book: 'The world I found'.*

At first sight, the remarks of both days do not seem to be related to each other at all. The fact that Wittgenstein in the remark immediately before his famous formulation about "the limits of my language" comes to talk about infinite mathematical series, of all things, seems to indicate a completely different mental connection. But there is – if one includes the concrete background of Russell's considerations – a deeper immediate relation between both remarks.

Mathematical sequences and series play a central role in both of Russell's texts. In the logical construction of matter, which starts from "sense-data" or "sensibilia,"[46] a six-dimensional perspective-space is constructed from these, which is composed of a multiplicity of "private spaces" or "private worlds," each with its own perspectives on the world. The construction is described in OKEW[47] and carried out concretely in the sense-data essay.[48]

Roughly speaking, things are defined via series of such perspectival and mutually similar sense data. Rather than simply postulating things – physical objects – as existing, Russell attempts to construct them logically from sense data or from these abstracted physical *sensibilia*.[49] *Sensibilia* are themselves objects of physics and, according to Russell, become sense data in the strict sense as soon as they are perceived by someone.[50] The construction of the material physical objects from the sense data is done by a calculation of the limit (*limes*) of a mathematical series in the "perspective space [...] along a line of perspectives" of the "various private spaces"[51] – physical objects are thus logical constructions, namely limit values of series of sense data. The preference of construction over ontological assumption invokes Ockham's "principle of ontological parsimony."[52] This approach of replacing ontological assumptions by logical constructions whenever possible constitutes the core of the "scientific method in philosophy."

Russell's broad discussion of "private spaces" or "private worlds,"[53] also the closeness of this conception to solipsism, now meets elements in Wittgenstein's reflections that still stem from his early but continuing influence from Schopenhauer. That Wittgenstein was philosophically influenced by Schopenhauer is known from his self-testimonies.[54] Among the war diaries, remarks dealing specifically with Schopenhauer's conception of the subject can be found especially in Ms 103 (28 March 1916 – 1 January 1917). However, Schopenhauer also has a certain aesthetic-expressive role model effect on Wittgenstein. Most recently, in an online lecture of 12 June 2021 (*Possibility and Necessity in the Tractatus*),[55] Hans Sluga pointed out the striking literal correspondence between the opening sentences of Schopenhauer's *The World as Will and Representation* ("The world is my representation.") and those of the *Tractatus* ("The world is everything that is the case."). It seems to me that Wittgenstein, in his reception of Schopenhauer's introductory sentence, gets stuck, as it were, in the fourth word. From "The world is my representation" only the beginning "The world is mine" is taken over – with strong emphasis on the "my/mine," as we know it from the inherent solipsism of the *Tractatus*.[56] In contrast, the concept of a world constituted from 'representations' [*Vorstellungen*] is rejected. For Wittgenstein, the world is neither a logical-physical construction from sense data, as in Russell, nor one of subjective representations in the idiosyncratic Kantian succession of Schopenhauer. It is rather, in the sense of his picture or model theory, a *linguistic* construction in which linguistically significant facts stand as signs ("propositional signs") for other facts – "facts of the world". This *facts-for-facts* principle of language, which is quite fundamental to his thought, was developed by Wittgenstein in Cambridge as early as early 1913 and forms one of the starting points of his *Notes on Logic*.[57] Under the condition of language, the world is then the totality of these facts described by facts.

The term "limit" in the remark of 23 May about the 'limit of language', which at the same time means the 'limit of the world', would then be interpreted in its immediate context of origin not so much as an external limit or boundary, but in the sense of a limiting process (*limes*) of a mathematical sequence or series.[58] In the context of language, "limit" would then be understood concretely as a 'limit of a *law-guided* series of propositional operations'. Every proposition, i.e. every place in the (logical) space of all propositions, is such a limit of propositional operations and to every such point corresponds an equal limit (*limes*) of a series of facts in the world.[59]

The remarks of 22 and 23 May 1915 thus have in common a background of limit-processes of series. In the first remark Wittgenstein treats the special form of a *law-like* generality expressed in mathematical series (and their *limes*).[60] In the following remark, Wittgenstein reflects on his conceptual counterpart to Russell's discussion of "private spaces," based on an intensified solipsism with recognizable proximity to Schopenhauer. This is clearly evidenced by the sentences immediately following the remark about the limits of language, which are about "world soul" and the "soul of others."[61] This connection with his own experience of the world ("The world I found") explains why the remark does not simply say "The limits of language are the limits of the world." Wittgenstein's experience of the world as quite essentially 'mine' is philosophically much more original and fundamental than its later construction from language. But Wittgenstein has now, at the end of May, reached the point where he can express what has to take the place of Schopenhauer's 'representation'. The world, precisely as ever mine, is not 'representation' of some 'representing subject' but a factual totality – 'everything that is the case'. The world "divides into facts" (TLP 1.2) and not, as with Schopenhauer, divides into "object and subject" (*The World as Will and Representation* Book 1 § 1). The iconic phrase "everything that is the case" is coined around the same time and appears in the notebook (Ms 102) three days later, on 26 May:

> *But how am I to explain the general nature of the proposition now? We can indeed say: everything that is (or is not) the case can be pictured by means of a proposition. But here we have the expression 'to be the case'! It is just as problematic.*
>
> *Objects form the counterpart to the proposition.*

A little later, at the end of August or beginning of September 1915, the phrase "... everything that is the case" was combined with the three opening words of Schopenhauer's main work "The world is ..." and placed by Wittgenstein at the top of his first draft of his

Logisch-Philosophische Abhandlung[62] (the so-called *Prototractatus*, Ms 104). In the conception in May we clearly can find a preliminary stage of the six main propositions as formulated at the beginning of the *Prototractatus*.[63] In essence, it is about Wittgenstein's main task, set for himself in January 1915, the "explaining the [general] nature of the proposition," which consists precisely in the fact that (the totality of) propositions can represent the totality of facts, i.e. the totality of all that is or is not the case, through their general form.

In his mental upswing since mid-April 1915, Wittgenstein is far from having, as he writes, "to give up all [his] efforts" (15 April 1915). On the contrary, he succeeds in elaborating essential initial elements of his treatise within a relatively short time. Another focus in the philosophical work in May and June is the clarification of the syntactic role of 'names' referring to 'simple objects' inside and outside "of the context of the proposition" (14 June 1915) and the conception of a 'class-theory of propositions',[64] of which it is stated on 6 June 1915 that its relation to the 'picture theory of propositions' "will only become quite obvious later." The new methodological approach is also expressed in a letter to Russell of 22 May 1915, which states, "The problems are becoming more and more lapidary and general and the method has changed drastically."[65]

Despite the heavy demands of work at the artillery workshop and his continuing problems ("Renewed difficulties about my promotion. [...]. Often <u>very</u> depressed by the meanness of my associates, who exploit me in the <u>most shameful</u> way." 8 June 1915), the diary Ms 102 displays in its final sections extremely intensive intellectual work.[66] Its main focus is on the problem of the nature of the 'simple object' and that of 'logical inferences'. The way in which Wittgenstein, after reaching the last regular manuscript page, still draws pencil lines on the back endpaper in order to be able to continue writing, suggests that his writing flow, which was very intensive even by his standards, was by no means exhausted with the completion of Ms 102, but will have continued at least until 17 July, the day on which he was injured by a gun-explosion in the workshop.[67]

The explosion of a gun barrel in the workshop resulted in Wittgenstein's hospitalization for two weeks until the end of July. The injuries – in the correspondence we learn of a "nervous shock and a few light injuries" to the eardrum,[68] among other things – are

General view of the Artillery Workshop Train No. 2 "Allitsch" taken by the War Press Service on 12 July 1916 in Kowel on the occasion of the inspection by the German Colonel General Linsingen. © ANL, Sign. WK1/ALB94/27992

not so serious, however, that Wittgenstein would not have been able to write again after only about a week, including an extant letter to Ludwig von Ficker, in which he recommends Tolstoy's *The Gospel in Brief* to him with a remarkable statement: "This book has virtually kept me alive."

On 30 July, the two workshop trains were almost complete so that they could be examined by the Inspector of the Technical Artillery, Field Marshal Lieutenant Wilhelm Pucherna, who reported that "the equipment of these trains was found to be adequate for its purpose" and that "these trains [should] be at the disposal of the *k.u.k.* War Ministry on 10 August."[69] On 10 August, Gürth took over the command of Artillery Workshop Train No. 1, which was then stationed at Sokal, and for 11 August, an official trip of *Feldzeugmeister* [General of Artillery] Schleyer and Major General Kiss[70] to Moravia-Ostrava (the location of the Kraków Military Command) was scheduled "for the purpose of inspecting an artillery workshop train."[71]

At this time, Wittgenstein was already on a three-week leave in Vienna[72] after his stay in a military hospital. In that three-week period, Wittgenstein might have made the decision to summarize his previous results in a new attempt in the form of an *Abhandlung* [Treatise].

SECOND WAR YEAR – 1915–16

Transfer to Artillery Workshop Train No. 1 in Sokal and later to Stojanow – Progress in the War Ministry

Wittgenstein's circumstances changed once again after his leave from the front. After his return from three weeks of furlough at the end of August 1915 , he did not resume his post at the artillery workshop in Kraków, but was transferred further east to "Artillery Workshop Train No. 1 'Gürth',"[73] which was stationed at the time in Sokal[74] (now in the Ukraine) to support the Austrian 1st Army. As the newly appointed commander, Gürth apparently prevailed upon Wittgenstein to be assigned to the train as an engineer. With Gürth as commander and Walter Wahle as his deputy, Wittgenstein thus held the third most important (officer) post on the train, which consisted of a total of "16 four-axle carriages"[75] with a crew of eighty-nine men.[76]

Fortunately, an extensive series of photographs in the contemporary pictorial publication *Im Etappenraum der I. Armee* [*In the Rear Area of the First Army*, 1916] taken of the Artillery Workshop Train No. 1 allows us a direct insight into Wittgenstein's external living conditions at the time.

The train, which contained all the necessary elements of a full-fledged artillery workshop distributed in a modular fashion among individual railroad cars (metal foundry, forge, lathe shop, carpenter shop, saddlery, finishing facilities, office, quarters, etc.),[77] was stationed a reasonable distance behind the front at Sokal's shunting yard. According to Gürth's account, it had the task, apart from working on guns, of repairing "pretty much everything 'in between', starting with the pocket watch and ending with the railroad bridge [...]."[78]

On 25 August 1915, Wittgenstein is able to report his new field post address in a postcard to Frege and also writes in this message about "his treatise [*seine Abhandlung*]."[79] According to the description of Max Bieler, commander of a hospital train stationed in Sokal at the same time, Wittgenstein must have found ideal conditions for writing: quietness and little demand for repair work, "since things were at a comparative standstill on the front."[80]

It is not known what exactly triggered Wittgenstein's decision to start writing an all-summarizing *"Abhandlung"* [treatise] just now. In any case, there must have been further decisive progress beyond

General view of Artillery Workshop Train No. 1 "Gürth" at the end of August 1915 in Sokal. (from: *Im Etappenraum der I. Armee*)

the phase of June 1915 with respect to the detailed conception of *logical space*, the *logical status of facts* as the "obtaining and not obtaining of states of affairs" (PT 2.06 and 4.2) and the new distinction between "*Sachverhalt*" [state of affairs] and "*Sachlage*" [situation].[81] A certain role may also have been played by the injury experience in the Kraków workshop, which may have been a final impulse, as it were, a *memento mori*, in Wittgenstein's repeatedly attested notorious anxiety that his results might be lost as a result of his premature death.

The challenge of the *Abhandlung* was a great one in every respect. Several times before Wittgenstein had failed in a summary of his philosophical thoughts that would be readable and comprehensible for others. If one adds Frege's critical judgment of 1919,[82] this will also apply to the *Logisch-Philosophische Abhandlung* itself, which was just being started. What he had written to explain the thoughts developed in Norway in connection with his meeting with Russell in October 1913, did not manage to succeed. Also, a text with the title *Logik*[83] from March 1914, which is lost today, but of which there are several traces, did not lead to satisfying results. It must have become clear to Wittgenstein that, in addition to the extraordinarily difficult content of his work, he also had to deal with the equally difficult problem of the *form* of the presentation of his results. In the so-called *Prototractatus*,[84] the black-bound *Hauptbuch*

Interior views of the wagons "Lathe shop" and "Forge" of Artillery Workshop Train No. 1 "Gürth" in August 1915 in Sokal (from: *Im Etappenraum der I. Armee*)

Interior view of the wagon "Office" of the Artillery Workshop Train No. 1 "Gürth." The calendar page behind the registries on the far left reveals the week of 22–28 July 1915 as the time of the photographs. The two people in the background are most likely *Oberleutnant* Oskar Gürth (seated on the left) and *Leutnant* Walter Wahle (standing on the right). (from: *Im Etappenraum der I. Armee*)

[main ledger], there are clues at the beginning that can be interpreted as a struggle to find the right *form of presentation* that is equal in weight to the extraordinary and definitive content and is therefore just as astonishing.

The *Abhandlung* [*Tractatus*], as it appears today, is not a discursive philosophical text with arguments pro and con, but a sequence, not of 'aphorisms' as is sometimes claimed, but of concise remarks in an apodictic linguistic style and, as if to support its thetical weight, it is provided with propositional numbers in the style of Whitehead's and Russell's *Principia Mathematica*. However, an even closer examination shows that this famous propositional numbering was preceded by a textual conception that was as unusual as it was impracticable for a philosophical text.[85]

The 'primordial form' of the *Abhandlung* from about the beginning of September 1915 on can be reconstructed from the preserved mirror image of page 2a, which is lost today. The mirror image shows the (still numberless) immediate sequence of the main propositions 1–6 of the *Prototractatus* (in the wording of page 3 of Ms 104):[86]

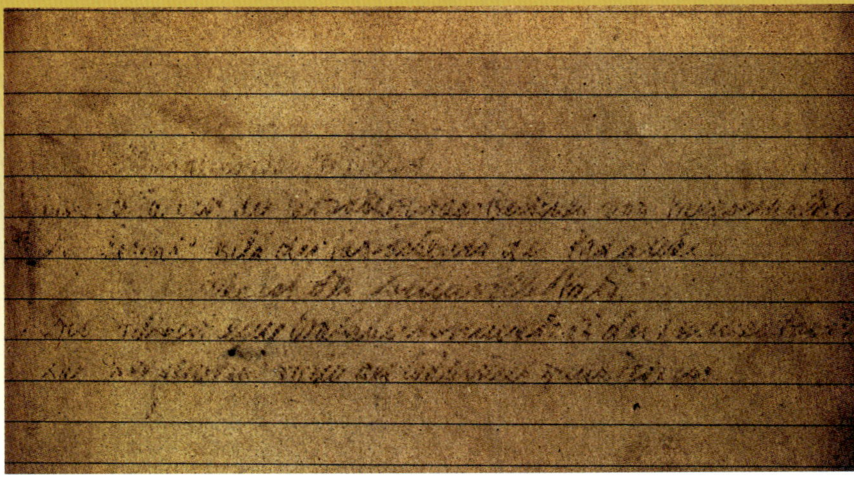

Detail from the faint mirror image of the excised page 2a in Ms 104, showing the main propositions 1–6 of the *Prototractatus* in their original as yet unnumbered form. (www.wittgensteinsource.org/BFE/Ms-104,2,reversed_f)

The world is everything that is the case.
What is the case, the facts, is the obtaining of states of affairs.
The logical picture of the facts is the thought.
The thought is the proposition with sense.
The proposition is a truth-function of elementary proposition.
The general form of truth-function is: $|N(\bar{p}_0), \bar{a}, N(\bar{a})|$

This is an account of the transition from the world as we know it to the proposition, which explicates its logical form. That summarizes the philosophy of the *Prototractatus* in its early form concisely.

In order to arrive at this solution, Wittgenstein – probably during his vacation in Vienna – may have specifically consulted certain philosophical works that were influential for him, as orientation and template. Among these works are most likely Schopenhauer's *The World as Will and Representation*, Frege's *Basic Laws of Arithmetic* or his essay "On Sense and Meaning" and Hertz's *The Principles of Mechanics*. But this is a speculation.

This six-line core form of the *Abhandlung*, which cannot be surpassed in brevity, was intended only as a starting point for further explanation, which was designed as a cascade of textual comments on descending levels. The first attempts at elaborating these textual levels led to great confusion, because no relationship was discernible between the remarks at one level and the comments explaining them at the next lower level. This problem was successfully overcome by Wittgenstein by introducing the famous propositional numbering.[87] The elaboration of the first commentary levels seems to have progressed rapidly after the introduction of the propositional numbers as an indispensable means of orientation, so that Wittgenstein can report to Russell on 22 October 1915 about the good progress of his work after reaching page 7 or 8 in Ms 104.[88] Quite unusually, he expresses satisfaction with his work ("I have recently done a great deal of work and, I think, quite successfully. I'm now in the process of summarizing it all and writing it down in the form of a treatise.").[89]

What is just emerging in these first weeks in the workshop train is a basic structure on the level of short remarks up to a depth of two decimals like "2.11 Pictures are models of facts." or "3.11 The propositional sign is a projection of the facts,"[90] which serve as a kind of framework for further elaboration. It is important to remember that, in its early sections, the *Abhandlung* is written neither in a room at a desk, nor – as is sometimes implied – in the trenches, but in a railway freight car among machines and guns to be repaired, cars and field kitchens, perhaps also in the train command's office compartment or at the rough wooden table in the crew carriage.

On the same 22 October 1915, the day of the letter to Russell, in some room of the huge War Ministry building on the Stubenring in Vienna – a building that had been in use for only two years, a file[91] was being prepared in the 7th Department, in order to forward an application contained therein to the "Inspector of Technical Artillery" for review. Its final negative outcome would have a decisive influence on Wittgenstein's further fate in the war. With this application from 3 September, Oskar Gürth made a new attempt to solve the main problem of Wittgenstein's inadequate position,[92] after having failed to have Wittgenstein appointed as a *Landsturm*-engineer by the superior authority. Correctly submitted through official channels, the request reaches the *k.u.k.* 1st Army Section Command (which declares itself "in favor of the request as being in the interest of the Supreme Command"), the *k.u.k.* 1st Op. Army Command and the *k.u.k.* Army High Command 13 October 1915 as received item No. 42,965 of the 7th Department of the *k.u.k.* War Ministry in Vienna and is thus in the decision-making and responsibility area of Gürth's former superiors *Feldzeugmeister* [General of Artillery] Schleyer (Section Chief) and Major General Kiss (Head of the 7th Department) from the time of the establishment of the artillery workshop trains.

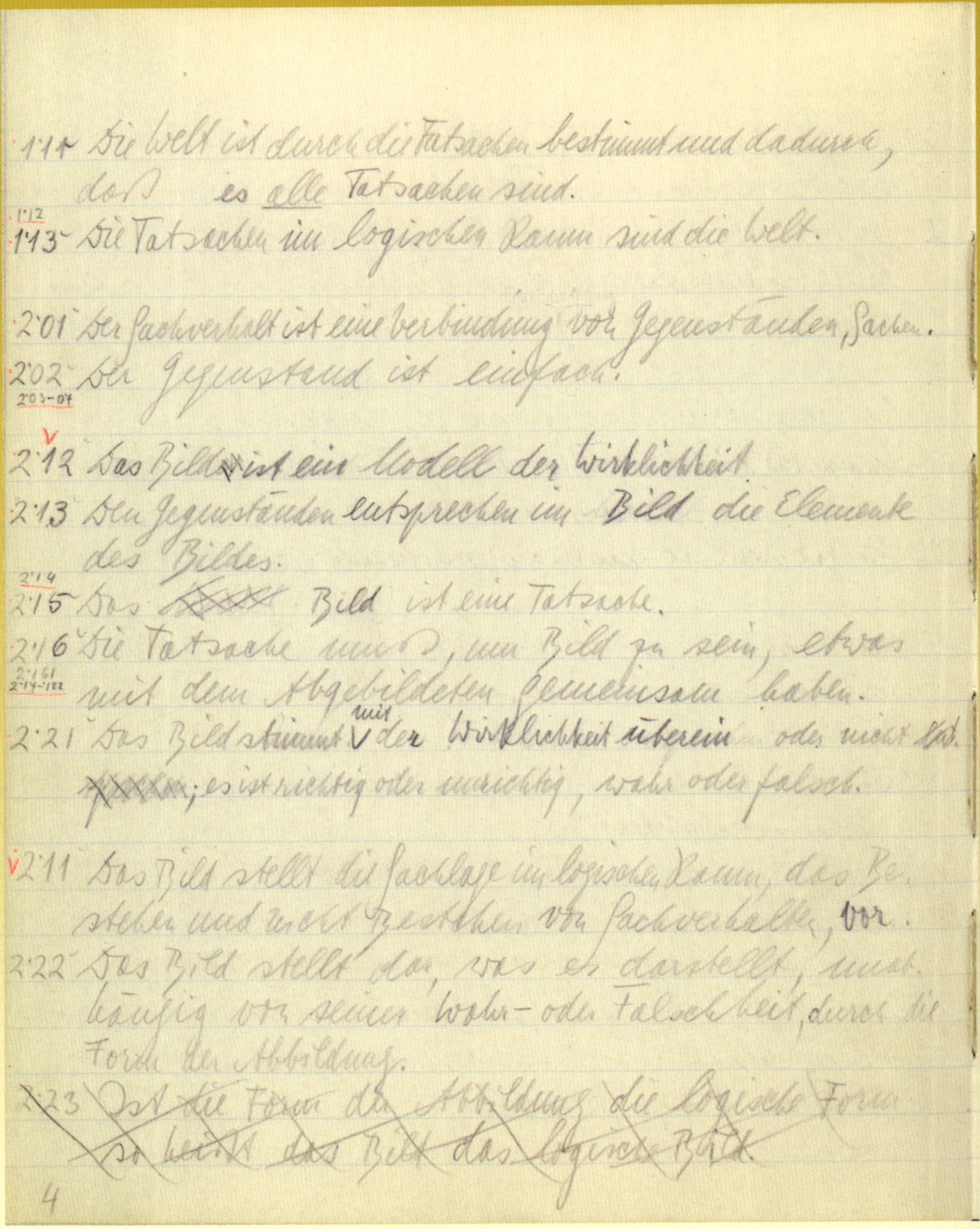
1·11 Die Welt ist durch die Tatsachen bestimmt und dadurch, daß es alle Tatsachen sind.

1·12
1·13 Die Tatsachen im logischen Raum sind die Welt.

2·01 Der Sachverhalt ist eine Verbindung von Gegenständen, Sachen.

2·02 Der Gegenstand ist einfach.

2·03–07

2·12 Das Bild ist ein Modell der Wirklichkeit.

2·13 Den Gegenständen entsprechen im Bild die Elemente des Bildes.

2·14
2·15 Das ~~[illegible]~~ Bild ist eine Tatsache.

2·16 Die Tatsache muß, um Bild zu sein, etwas mit dem Abgebildeten gemeinsam haben.
2·161
2·14–1[illegible]

2·21 Das Bild stimmt mit der Wirklichkeit überein oder nicht [illegible]; ~~[illegible]~~ es ist richtig oder unrichtig, wahr oder falsch.

2·11 Das Bild stellt die Sachlage im logischen Raum, das Bestehen und Nichtbestehen von Sachverhalten, vor.

2·22 Das Bild stellt dar, was es darstellt, unabhängig von seiner Wahr- oder Falschheit, durch die Form der Abbildung.

~~2·23 Ist die Form der Abbildung die logische Form so heißt das Bild das logische Bild.~~

4

Ludwig Wittgenstein Nachlass: Ms 104, pages 4–5
(www.wittgensteinsource.org/BFE/Ms-104,4_f; www.wittgensteinsource.org/BFE/Ms-104,5_f)

4

·3·01 Die Gesamtheit der wahren Gedanken sind ein Bild der Welt.
3·02

·3·11 Das Satzzeichen ist eine Projection des Gedankens.
·3·12 Die Projectionsmethode ist die Art und Weise der Anwendung des Satzzeichens.
·3·13 Die Anwendung des Satzzeichens ist das Denken seines Sinnes.

·3·21 Der Satz ist die Projection nach ihrer Methode.
·1·12 Denn die Gesamtheit der Tatsachen bestimmt was der Fall ist und auch was alles nicht der Fall ist.
·2·03 Im Sachverhalt hängen die Gegenstände ineinander wie die Glieder einer Kette.
2·031
·2·04 Die Gesamtheit der bestehenden Sachverhalte ist die Welt.
·2·05 Die Gesamtheit der bestehenden Sachverhalte bestimmt auch, welche Sachverhalte nicht bestehen.
·2·06 Das Bestehen und nicht Bestehen von Sachverhalten ist die Wirklichkeit.
·2·07 Die gesamte Wirklichkeit ist die Welt.
·2·031 Im Sachverhalt verhalten sich die Gegenstände in bestimmter Art und Weise zueinander.
·2·14 Das Bild besteht darin, daß sich seine Elemente in bestimmter Art und Weise zueinander verhalten.
·2·161 In Bild und Abgebildetem muß etwas identisch sein, damit das eine überhaupt ein Bild des anderen sein kann.

5

Interior view "crew quarters" of the Artillery Workshop Train No. 2 "Allitsch"
© ANL, Sign. WK1/ALB94/27989

It was requested that the "*Kriegsfreiwillige* [war volunteer] Ludwig Wittgenstein" be appointed, if not *Landsturm*-engineer, then as an "*Artilleriezeugsakzessist*"[93] for the duration of the war.

However, the responsible 7th Department obviously could not make a decision on its own. An extensive review procedure was necessary. The submission for the *Begutachtung* [expert opinion] of 22 October was addressed simultaneously to the 5th Department, the 2/W-Department in the War Ministry itself, and indeed to the Inspector of Technical Artillery, placed outside the hierarchy of the War Ministry. The 5th Dept. regretfully clarified, once again, that a promotion of Wittgenstein to a *Landsturm*-engineer was not possible for procedural reasons but at the same time "warmly endorses his earliest possible appointment as an '*Artilleriezeugsakzessist in der Reserve*'."[94] The opinion of the Inspector of Technical Artillery (from 1 November 1915), on the other hand, is unambiguously and uncompromisingly negative:

> *There is no reason to appoint the war volunteer Ludwig Wittgenstein as an Artilleriezeugsakzessist in der Reserve.; on the contrary, this would create a precedent for all those persons with university education who have volunteered. If for disciplinary reasons it is impossible to keep Wittgenstein in his present charge, he would have to be transferred.*[95]

What is hidden behind the harmless-sounding phrase "to be transferred" is nothing less than the deployment as an *einfacher Kannonier* [private gunner] directly to the Russian front, i.e., an announcement of that fate which – although repeatedly brought into play by Wittgenstein himself as a complaint for his "unworthy position" in the workshop – will actually and severely strike Wittgenstein in March 1916, after unsuccessful efforts by the 7th Department to avert it after all.

Leopold *Freiherr* Schleyer von Pontemalghera (AT-OeStA/KA BS I WKFronten Ö 1980)

Árpád Kiss de Nagy-Sitke (AT-OeStA/KA BS I WKFronten Ö 1985)
Both © Austrian War Archive

In his biography (p. 236), Brian McGuinness interprets Bieler's account to mean "that the personal difficulties Wittgenstein had felt in the workshop in Kraków no longer bulked large in his life." If this were so, then it would probably have been better to continue to handle things pragmatically in the seclusion of the provincial station at Sokal and later at Stojanow and to grant Wittgenstein, in effect, those privileges (authority to issue orders as operating engineer, to eat at the officers' table, to have a young Russian as his own servant) to which he was not legally entitled. Gürth must have been very sure of his case when he made the application, probably because of the reputation he had acquired during the "train work" and the good relations he had with the Ministry, especially with Schleyer and Kiss, to whose esteem he specifically referred in the application.[96] Nevertheless, he felt compelled to intervene on 8 November with Captain Haecht, who as the officer-in-charge in Kiss' department was responsible for the file management in the case and whom Gürth would have known from his time in the Ministry, "since no official settlement has yet come down in the matter of Ing. [engineer] Wittgenstein,"[97] as he wrote. He now considers a "negative settlement" at least possible and asks for hints for further possible intervention measures.[98]

At the end of November 1915, while the War Ministry was actually attempting, once again, to insure Wittgenstein's promotion, Gürth received (on 30 November) an information sheet on Engineer Wittgenstein that is preserved in the file. Wittgenstein concluded the first phase of his work on the *Prototractatus* on page 13 in Ms 104 and began a first revision in the following section (up to page 28).[99] Approximately at the beginning of January 1916, he thereby formulates remarks on the purpose of philosophy: "Philosophy aims at the logical clarification of thoughts." (PT 4.10014). "Philosophy is not a body of doctrine but an activity" (PT 4.10015). He thus also addresses the purpose of the *Abhandlung* itself – long before similar characterizations are expressed in the preface in the summer of 1918: "Philosophy should make clear and delimit sharply the thoughts [...]" (PT 4.100161). "It should limit the thinkable and thereby the unthinkable." (PT 4.10017). However, no connection is made at this time between the *unsayable* and the *passing over in silence* – the famous concluding remark 7 is not found in the manuscript until page 71 and thus belongs to a later stage of conception. It seems that in the early draft phase of his work the main proposition 6 about the general form of the truth-function was designed to conclude the *Abhandlung*, which at this time was still completely oriented towards the logic of language.

Alongside the work on Ms 104 (which is not mentioned by Bieler), there are, as Bieler reports, lengthy philosophical discussions, during which, according to an anecdote, even the ushering in of the new Year 1916 was missed.[100]

There are very important and very difficult sections worked out in January:[101] 'internal relations', 'propositional variable', 'formal properties' and 'formal concepts', as well as the important notion of a 'formal series' were developed. The 'formal series' [*Formenreihe*] however, is not yet called in this manner, but was only named so about two years later (PT 4.102251). One senses, when reading those remarks, written in the winter of 1915–16, that with the new formulations, for which there are hardly any precursors in the older manuscripts, at the same time the theory itself was expanding and advancing. In this phase, Ms 104 resembles a thought workshop. To this end, page 17 is a prime example of Wittgenstein's compositional method. We find remarks on four different main propositions (2, 3, 4, 5) side by side, seemingly independent and yet thematically intertwined. The line of thought is advanced simultaneously and in parallel at various places in the slowly growing *Abhandlung*.

Meanwhile, efforts in the War Ministry continued. On 26 January 1916, the head of the 7th Department in the War Ministry, Field Marshal Lieutenant Kiss, signed a document in which the matter of Wittgenstein's promotion was once again – and this must have been a quite unusual procedure – submitted to the Inspector of Technical Artillery (and the 1st Department) for review. The argumentation strategy was slightly changed to the effect that now, on the one hand, it is admitted that "*Oberleutnant* GÜRTH [...] has committed a mistake by awarding the *Landsturm*-engineer charge to war volunteer WITTGENSTEIN," but that, on the other hand, the cancellation of the appointment would punish Wittgenstein, "for which, however, any reason is lacking." To avoid cancellation, the appointment as "*Artilleriezeugsakzessist in der Reserve* to the technical artillery" is suggested again (fol. 7r). On 3 February, Pucherna, obviously unimpressed by these arguments, issued a new rejection, the tenor of which was completely unchanged (fol. 7v), and which the 1st Dept. endorsed "in full" on 12 February (fol. 9). It seems as if the balance of power in the Austrian War Ministry in the spring of 1916 left no possibility for the section chief Schleyer to overrule this negative vote. What can still be gleaned from the wartime file is the formulation of a final letter of rejection from the pen of Captain Haecht to the "Artillery Workshop Train 'Gürth'" (with a copy to the 1st Army Command and to the Army High Command), which was signed off by Kiss as head of the department on 22 February and by Schleyer as section chief the next day (fol. 1).

Before 2018, the "Inspector of Technical Artillery" who was responsible for this arbitrary rejection was not identified by name in Wittgenstein scholarship, and his name didn't appear in the Ministry of War file either. However, with the help of his rather idiosyncratic signature, three times – in the information in the preliminary note for Gürth's qualification description, and on a list of all field marshal lieutenants in the Austro-Hungarian army – he can now be identified as the very same Field Marshal Lieutenant Wilhelm Pucherna (1854–1936), who had already played an essential role in the set-up of the workshop trains in the spring of 1915. Pucherna, director of the *Artilleriezeugsfabrik* [artillery equipment factory] in Vienna since 1910, assumed the newly created position of Inspector of Technical

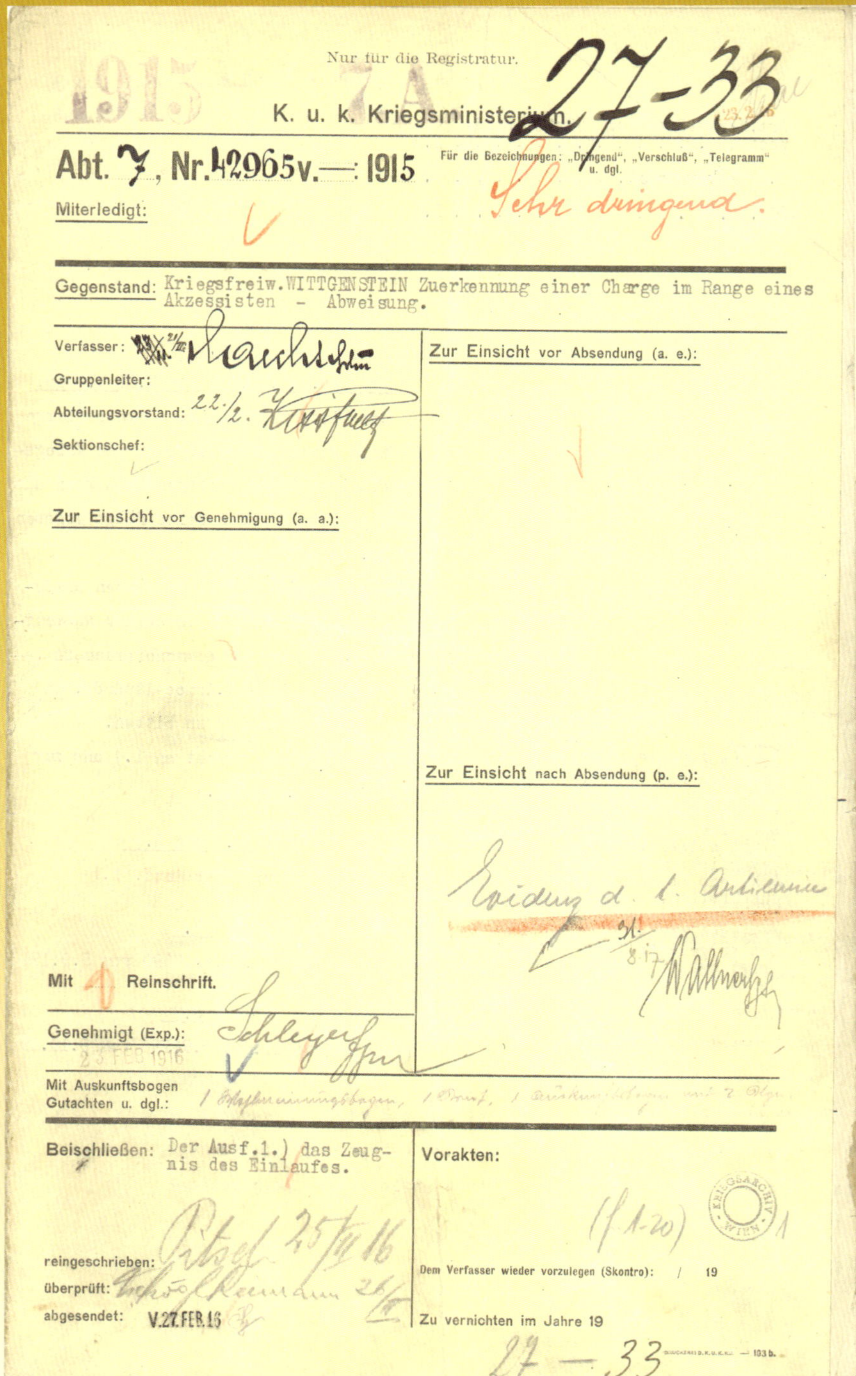

Nur für die Registratur.

1915 7A

K. u. k. Kriegsministerium. 27-33

Abt. 7, Nr. 42965 v. — : 1915

Für die Bezeichnungen: „Dringend", „Verschluß", „Telegramm" u. dgl.

Sehr dringend.

Miterledigt:

Gegenstand: Kriegsfreiw. WITTGENSTEIN Zuerkennung einer Charge im Range eines Akzessisten - Abweisung.

Verfasser:

Gruppenleiter:

Abteilungsvorstand: 22/2.

Sektionschef:

Zur Einsicht vor Genehmigung (a. a.):

Zur Einsicht vor Absendung (a. e.):

Zur Einsicht nach Absendung (p. e.):

Mit 1 Reinschrift.

Genehmigt (Exp.): 23. FEB. 1916

Mit Auskunftsbogen Gutachten u. dgl.:

Beischließen: Der Ausf. 1.) das Zeugnis des Einlaufes.

Vorakten:

(f 1-20)

Dem Verfasser wieder vorzulegen (Skontro): / 19

reingeschrieben: 25/II 16

überprüft:

abgesendet: V. 27. FEB. 16

Zu vernichten im Jahre 19

27 — 33

File KM 7. Abt. 27-33 (42.965/1915) of the *k.u.k.* War Ministry: filecover (fol. 1r on the left) and the draft of the ministerial letter of notification on the reverse side (fol. 1v on the right) with the formal rejection of Gürth's application

Art.Werkstättenzug „Gürth" Feldpost 12 . . . ." . . . . 1.)

1.Armeekommando . . . . 2.)

AOK.(Q.Abt.). . . . . 3.)

26/II

1.)

Auf Res.Exh.Nr.122 vom 3.Sept.1915.

Der Bitte um Verleihung einer Charge im Range eines Akzessisten an den Kriegsfreiwilligen Ludwig Wittgenstein kann aus prinzipiellen Gründen keine Folge gegeben werden.

Wenn es aus disziplinären Gründen unmöglich ist, Wittgenstein in seiner dermaligen Charge in seiner Kommandierung zu belassen so ist beim 1.Armee-EtpKmdo. um dessen Transferierung zu bitten.

Sollte Kriegsfreiwilliger Wittgenstein zur Transferierung beim AEK.beantragt, dessen Transferierung auch durchgeführt werden u. ein Ersatz für denselben unbedingt notwendig sein, so ist diesbezüglich um denselben durch das AOK.beim Kriegsministerium einzuschreiten, worauf ein ldstpflichtiger Maschinenbauingenieur zugewiesen werden wird.

Das vorgelegte Maturitätszeugnis folgt behufs Ausfolgung an den Genannten im Anschlusse mit.

Dieser Erlass ergeht an 1.) und zur Kenntnis an 2.) und 3.)

2.) und 3.)

Auf einer Abschrift der Ausf. 1.)

2.)

mit Bezug auf Res.Dl.Nr.7990 vom 5.9.1915

3.)

mit Bezug auf Dl.Op.Nr.91796 vom 9.10.1915

The "stoney guest" in Wittgenstein's biography: Field Marshal Lieutenant Wilhelm Pucherna
Wikimedia Commons

Artillery in 1912, was in charge of ammunition matters as section chief in the ministry in 1917–18, and briefly headed the liquidated War Ministry in 1919. He not only left behind a monumental tomb at the Vienna Central Cemetery, but ironically enough, he also – probably unintentionally – changed the history of philosophy. His intransigent attitude in the question of promotion was the cause of Wittgenstein's transfer and thus of his haunting experiences on the front in the Bukovina, which in turn led to the major transformation of the *Abhandlung*, which until then had concentrated entirely on logical problems.[102]

On the front in the Bukovina

In the nearly three weeks it took for the execution letter from the War Ministry to reach the artillery workshop train in Stojanow,[103] Wittgenstein was busy formulating the much-discussed remarks in *Tractatus* research about simple objects as the substance of the world: "Objects form the substance of the world. Therefore, they cannot be compound." (PT 2.021). The second remark on page 28 ("The configuration of the objects forms the state of affairs." (PT 2.0272) is the last remark before a distinctly visible break marked with a red horizontal line, indicating a longer interruption of the work on the manuscript. What follows on the next 35 pages differs clearly in methodology and on page 28 also in the typeface and even in the way the remarks are numbered (temporarily

Wittgenstein uses an additional comma after the second decimal place, e.g. "4.09,2" in Ms 104: 28[5]). There is good reason to believe that the obvious break in the manuscript is due to the events after 21 March 1916, when Wittgenstein learned of his imminent transfer to the front.[104] Max Bieler gives the following account:

> *In April (?) 1916 [actually, end of March, Ed.] Wittgenstein suddenly received orders to leave for the front. It was a heavy blow for us both. He took with him only what was absolutely necessary, leaving everything else behind and asking me to divide it among the troops. On this occasion he told me that he had had a house built beside a Norwegian fjord where he would sometimes take refuge in order to have peace for his work (I think also that Russell had visited him there). He now wanted to make me a present of this house. I refused it and took in its place a Waterman's Fountain Pen. Among a few other books he took with him The Brothers Karamazov [...]*[105]

Wittgenstein must also have been very anxious about his emerging work. On the front leaf of Ms 104 is the following undated instruction:

> *All the good propositions of my other manuscripts are to be fitted in among the propositions in this book. The numbers indicate the order of the propositions and their importance. Thus 5.04101 follows 5.041 and is followed by 5.0411, which is a more important proposition than 5.04101.*

This "instruction" can best be explained if one understands it as a guide for a potential editor for the completion of the work, should he himself no longer be able to do so, as a result of the course of the war. There was now a more than justified reason to make such a provision. Only someone who was very closely acquainted with Wittgenstein's thoughts could be considered as the addressee. The remark is therefore in all probability meant for Bertrand Russell in case Wittgenstein – which now becomes more probable than ever – would not live to see the end of the war.

The war records note that the "War Volunteer Cannoneer Ludwig Wittgenstein" was transferred by the 1st Army Command effective 21 March 1916 "from the *k.u.k.* Fortress Artillery Regiment No 2 to Field Cannon Regiment No 2." Shortly thereafter, on 16 April, in the course of a major reorganization of the Austrian artillery, his unit is renamed: from then on, he belongs to the

4th Battery of Field Howitzer Regiment No. 5, which is basically stationed in Sanok, but is currently preparing for front-line action near Czernowitz.[106]

The move to the war front is probably also the reason that Wittgenstein begins a new notebook (Ms 103), which gives a vivid picture of his changed living conditions, especially in his personal entries. In the notebook, the first page is missing and the entries begin with 28 March 1916, dramatically in the middle of the sentence with the words:

> *and must take my life. I suffered the tortures of hell! And yet the picture of life was so enticing to me that I wanted once more to live. I will take poison only when I really want to poison myself.*

The next day it says:

> *Forced to do much that is unfamiliar. I need great strength to endure it. Often I am close to despair. I have done no work for more than a week. I have no time! God! But it is, of course, only natural, for when I am dead, I will also have no time to work. Now the inspection. My soul shrivels up. God enlighten me! God enlighten me! God enlighten my soul.*
> (29 March 1916)

The "unfamiliar" he is forced to do refers to the completely different assignment compared to the highly qualified and privileged operating engineer in Kraków and in Sokal. He is now part of the crew of an artillery squad and, lacking experience, will initially have been called upon for physically strenuous auxiliary duties. The operating crew for a 10.5 cm howitzer forms a so-called *Halbzug* [half platoon] ("At the half platoon everyone hates me because no one understands me. And because I am no saint! God help me!" 23 April 1916). A battery comprises three platoons, i.e. six guns, and has 220 men and 180 horses. The 3rd and 4th batteries of Wittgenstein's regiment belonged to the 24th Field Artillery Brigade with the task of supporting Infantry Regiment 77 and with this and other infantry units in the larger formation of the 24th Infantry Division, which as part of the XI Corps (under General of Cavalry Korda) in turn belonged to the 7th Army under Colonel General Karl von Pflanzer-Baltin.

Example of a typical wooden construction of an observation post of the Austrian Army in the Bukovina during World War I © ANL

In April, the regiment took up its first position directly at the front: "I've been in firing position for the last few days. All day hard physical labor, which makes it impossible to think." (23 April 1916). The unaccustomed "hard physical labor" at this time must also refer to setting up and operating the howitzer. Wittgenstein soon tried to escape this situation and to get away from the hard physical work, and at the same time also to gain distance from the crew. The solution was to volunteer for artillery observation. He virtually begged to be placed with the observation troops, which combined a significantly higher personal risk with long periods of being alone. Both were welcome to Wittgenstein. According to the surviving photographs of the Austrian *Kriegspressedienst* [war press service], the observation posts in the Bukovina must be imagined as simple platforms, many meters high and accessible by ladders, on rickety wooden constructions that offered a wide view, often over the treetops, but no protection against enemy artillery and infantry fire.

After an interruption of more than three weeks, Wittgenstein was able to resume his philosophical reflections on 15 April. The first remark in Ms 103 reads: "Only that which we ourselves construct can we foresee!" (15 April 1916). He is now concerned with the special role of elementary propositions, which enter into truth-functions as their 'truth-arguments'. This conception already found its expression at the beginning of the *Prototractatus* (PT 5.011). The 'general form of the truth-function' as expressed by the formula in PT 6 allows to construct *all* propositions from the given set of elementary propositions with the help of a special 'truth-operation', the so-called 'N-operator' (introduced as "N($\bar{\alpha}$)" with Ms 104: 13[7] = PT 5.3001). Thus, Wittgenstein has found a way to re-construct ordinary propositions of language as 'truth-functions of elementary propositions' (PT 5). But this idea leaves open the question of a possible constructability of the elementary propositions themselves. What exactly is their logical status? Do they need their own form of construction by an analogous operation? Wittgenstein's reflections on this issue in April,

> *Every simple proposition can be brought into the form φx. (16 April 1916)*
>
> *We must be able to construct the simple functions [φx] because we must be able to give each sign a meaning. (15 April 1916)*

and also later in Ms 103 suggest that certain not insignificant details of the logic of the *Abhandlung* were still open at this point, although by reaching page 28 in Ms 104 the conceptual basis of the "*Core-Prototractatus*" was already completed. The ongoing process in Wittgenstein's theory in this dangerous phase of his life now takes place in the new notebook (Ms 103) while the other manuscripts, including Ms 104, are left in safety in Vienna.[107]

At the beginning of May, Wittgenstein succeeded in establishing himself permanently with the observation troops ("On the observation post, I'm like the prince in the haunted castle. Now all is quiet during the day, but at night there must be terrible things going on! Will I be able to stand it???? Tonight will tell. God help me!!" 5 May 1916). Remarks like "In constant danger of my life. The night went well by the grace of God." (6 May 1916) are now to be taken literally, in contrast to the impressions on the Vistula, and confirm the increased personal danger in his new activity, which became for him precisely a kind of school in adopting the right view of life.

The "third position" referred to in the notebook (16 May 1916), to which the battery was transferred in mid-May 1916 in anticipation of a major Russian attack, can be precisely located by the information in a later reward application concerning Wittgenstein. "Hill 417" at "*Kordenposten Sawokrynicznyi*" can be made out on detailed Austrian *k.u.k.* military maps of the time in the front section northeast of Czernowitz near Dobronoutz. Wittgenstein's observation post was located in the immediate vicinity of the *Kavalleriestützpunkt* [cavalry strongpoint] at "Hill 458," which was heavily contested and then lost in the initial phase of the Brusilov offensive. Thus, it was situated on the right edge of the section in the southern part of the Russian front that was most severely affected by the Russian attack on Okna.

Because we know the exact location at the beginning of the offensive, Wittgenstein's further movements can be reconstructed with very high accuracy from the fact that his unit was part of the 24th Infantry Division. This allows us to follow his trajectory even during the following June 1916, in which his diary is silent due to the ferocity of the war's events. Now, in the second half of May, there is tense anticipation ("Today or tomorrow there is to be a Russian attack. As God wills!" 27 May 1916). Also, the philosophical entries stop and after a last push prayer ("God be with me") on 29 May – the diary breaks off completely for over a month.

Wittgenstein's behavior during the three days of uninterrupted shelling from 4–6 June 1916 may have been, from his point of view, a personal appeal to God's judgment of his work and its value; it irritated his superiors extraordinarily and, strangely enough, had a calming effect on his comrades. Despite repeated requests by the battery commander to leave his high post in the heavy fire and seek cover, Wittgenstein continued to observe uninterruptedly, apparently also providing tactically valuable information.[108] The commander Heinrich Bertl was so impressed by Wittgenstein's courage that he not only applied for an award for bravery, but even four years later, after the war, he referred to this episode in a letter to Wittgenstein:

> *[...] Summer 1916, Brusilov offensive, Battery 4 of the Field Howitzer Regiment No 5, where you earned the small silver [medal] in the 'high' barge of an 'Einjährig Freiwilliger titular Vormeister'.*[109] *At that time I was your battery commander as Oberleutnant Bertl. I remember very well how I had to call you in from the 'fifteen-fold' [binoculars] at the observation post into cover from the murderous fire at the 'Koffer [a special form of infantry post] of the I.R. 77' near Dobronouc. Can you remember now? [...]*[110]

The confusion about the unusual courage, neglecting his own person, perplexed even the military administration, because not

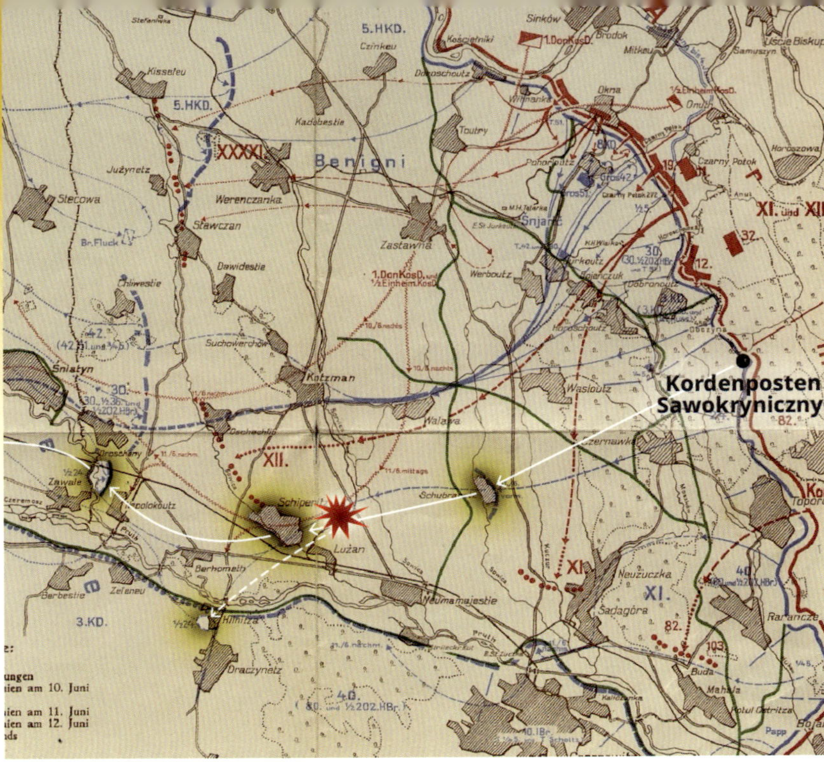

Map of the Eastern Front in June 1916. Blue lines represent movements of the Austrian army; red lines show movements of the Russian army; and white lines represent the trajectory of Wittgenstein's movements during the retreat of the Austrian army. Kordenposten Sawokrynicznyi was the exact position of Wittgenstein's observation post at the beginning of the offensive. © Martin Pilch

only *one* reward application was made, but two of them were written and – independently of each other – sent to the authorities for confirmation. Both documents, although with slightly different descriptions, unquestionably concern the same event on the observation post and both were successful and led to medals for bravery. First, he was found worthy of the *Silver* Medal for Bravery 2nd Class, but in the parallel application from the division command the award is downgraded to a *Bronze* Medal. In the end, he would be awarded both medals in Olomouc in the fall during his officer training.

In a way, this event and the experiences of those weeks changed everything for Wittgenstein, at least in the war. Not only did he receive the formal recognition he had long been seeking; he was selected to be trained as an officer, and he would return to his philosophical remarks in July as one inwardly transformed, taking up entirely new themes: God, the world, good and evil, the right life – a shift from the prior emphasis on logic.

But at first, he got caught in a series of overwhelming events. The collapse of the front near Okna (visible on the map) under the pressure of the Russian attack (red lines), led to chaotic retreats of the Austrian troops (blue lines). On the evening of 10 June, the entire XI Corps began to abandon its positions. Wittgenstein's 24th Infantry Division (white lines) retreated on the morning of 11 June roughly 15 kilometers to Schubranetz (the first "burn" mark in the line of retreat on the map) to take up a new position along a predefined north-south line with other Austrian units, as agreed. However, unbeknownst to Wittgenstein's division, the units to the north failed to take up their positions and moved further west than planned. The division was thus in the dangerous position of being cut off from its own troops. During the belated departure, an attack by Russian cavalry occurred (the jagged red spot on the map), splitting the division in two. One part escaped to the south across the Pruth River (diverging white arrow at the bottom of the map). Wittgenstein, though, seems to have continued westward, in the other part, with the artillery, to the provisionally established position at Śniatyn (visible on the left side of the map). He "himself later told a nephew of his long retreat from this offensive, in which he sat utterly exhausted on a horse in an endless column, with the one thought only of keeping his seat, since if he fell off, he would be trampled to death."[111]

By 12 June, only 3500 of the 16,000 men of the 24th Infantry Division were left. Since even the new positions could not be held under the pressure of the Russian onslaught, the retreat continued the following week. On 19 June, Czernowitz fell into the hands of the Russians. At this time the 24th Infantry Division was reassembled southeast of Kolomea between Roznów to the south and the Pruth River to the north. On 23 June, the division engaged in fighting near Kuty. In the next phase of the Russian offensive (the 'Battle of Kolomea'), from 28 June to 4 July, the 24th Infantry Division engaged in a rearguard action over another 50 km to the west to secure the important road to Delatyn. Since the division, in which Wittgenstein's artillery unit was located, had little fighting strength left, the army command decided to pull it out of the front and place it in reserve at Delatyn.

This is also the moment when the entries in the notebook resume. On 6 July Wittgenstein writes, "Colossal exertions this last month. Have thought a great deal about all sorts of things, but curiously enough cannot establish their connection to my mathematical line of thought." After the intense experience of the war, entirely new themes emerge in his philosophical remarks – in an entirely new tone (4 July 1916):

What do I know about God and the purpose of life?
I know that this world exists.
That I am placed in it like my eye in its visual field.
That something about it is problematic, which we call its meaning [Sinn].
That this meaning [Sinn] does not lie in it but outside it.
That life is the world.
That my will penetrates the world.
That my will is good or evil.
Therefore that good and evil are somehow connected with the meaning of the world.
The meaning [Sinn] of life, i.e. the meaning [Sinn] of the world, we can call God.

In the following days, these reflections on God, world, life, good, evil, etc., would continue, and quite a few of the remarks of the next weeks and months would later enter the *Abhandlung*, which now ceased to be merely a treatise on logic.[112]

The respite did not last long; in mid-July the remnants of the artillery were ordered to the ridges near Dora, an "important hilltop, a cornerstone of the front."[113] In the diary, it reads like this:

16 July 1916
Terrible weather. It's bad in the mountains, not sufficiently sheltered, icy cold, rain, and fog. An agonizing life. It's terribly hard not to lose oneself. For I am, after all, a weak human being. But the spirit helps me. The best thing would be if I were already sick, then at least I would have a little peace.

On 19 July, the army high command decided to transfer the 24th Infantry Division north to Army Group Hindenburg in exchange for a German division.[114] By all accounts, however, Wittgenstein's artillery unit was not affected by this decision and was instead detached from its previous division and assigned to support an infantry brigade deployed in the Carpathians. While the infantrymen were loaded onto trains at Nadworna on 23 July, Wittgenstein remained in his position on the heights of Dora and also became engaged in combat:

Yesterday, I was fired at. I fell apart! I was afraid of death! I now have such a strong wish to live! And it is hard to renounce

> *life once one is fond of it. That is precisely what "sin" is, an unreasonable life, a wrong view of life. From time to time I become an animal. Then I can think of nothing but eating, drinking, sleeping. Terrible! And then I also suffer like an animal, without the possibility of internal salvation. I am then at the mercy of my appetites and aversions. Then an authentic life cannot even be considered.*
>
> *(29 July 1916)*

THE THIRD YEAR OF WAR – 1916–17

In the Carpathians – A furlough in Vienna

In early August, the 4th Battery of Field Howitzer Regiment No. 5 moved by train from Nadworna, in a wide arc across Hungary, further south from its previous location into the Carpathian Mountains. This gave Wittgenstein the opportunity to send picture postcards home on the way, rather than just grey army postcards. The last leg of the journey to the new unit, to which the battery was attached, had to be made on foot: "After 3 days on the train, on the march to the firing line. Not in the best of health and sick to my soul due to the bigotry and meanness of my compatriots." (6 August 1916). Wittgenstein's third year in the war begins in the valleys of the Carpathian Mountains. He is now part of the 68th Infantry Brigade, which has been in action in the Carpathians for several weeks. Since 1 August, the Austrian troops had had to tolerate the humiliation of being placed under German command (Lieutenant General von Conta) because of their poor performance in the war. It is not quite clear to what extent Wittgenstein was involved in combat operations during this phase. In any case, he wrote nothing about it. It is also conceivable that in the difficult terrain the artillery might not always have been sufficiently mobile to follow the infantry. The extended philosophical entries in the notebook speak rather against too much involvement in the war. Between 11 and 13 August, for example, he drafted the passages on the "philosophical I" ("The I makes its appearance in philosophy through the world's being my world."), which would later be included in subsection 5.6 of the *Tractatus*. But he also succeeded in resuming lines of thought on the remaining logical problems, gaining important insights into the definition of 'operation' ("An operation is the transition from one term to the next one in a formal series. The operation and the formal series are equivalents." (17 August 1916; cf. TLP 5.232). But on 19 August, an end to the hardships and inconveniences finally emerged: "Shall be

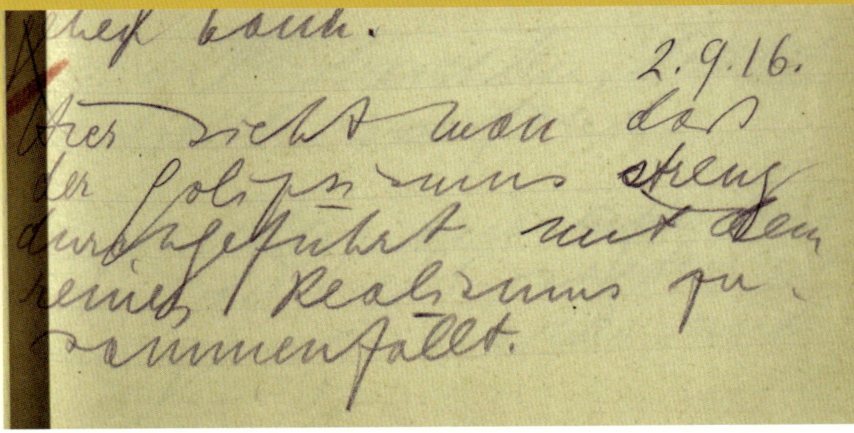

Ms 103 Excerpt from fol. 48r (www.wittgensteinsource.org/BFE/Ms.103,48r_f)

off to the cadre in the hinterland in the near future. I'm glad about it. Surrounded by viciousness. God will help."

This return to behind the lines was the prospective transfer to the reserve battery in Olomouc, for artillery observation officer training. Several war records agree that, until 2 September, Wittgenstein was "in the field," which presumably refers to the end of the front deployment that had lasted since March. If one interprets this wording to mean that he reached Vienna on this day – for a ten-day furlough before heading to Olomouc to begin his officer training – it would explain a striking coincidence which exists between the entries of 23 May 1915 and those for 2 September 1916 discussed above. The May entry in Ms 102 begins with the remark made famous in the *Tractatus*: "The limits of my language mean the limits of my world."

Wittgenstein then goes on to speak of world-soul, solipsism and that he could write a book with the title "*The world as I found it*." Exactly this peculiar formulation returns almost literally in the entry of 2 September 1916, which again deals with solipsism and the metaphysical subject being "the limit (not a part) of the world": "I want to report *how I found the world*." (my emphasis). My conjecture is that the initial word "Here" in the first sentence of 2 September 1916 ("Here we can see that solipsism coincides with pure realism, if it is strictly thought out.") does not refer to any preceding passage in Ms 103, but to this earlier entry of 23 May 1915, in the older notebook Ms 102. The later entry of 2 September 1916 thus comments directly on the May entry of 1915 in the light of recent existential experience.

In other words, on the very day he returned from the front, Wittgenstein could have retrieved his old notebook, which had remained in Vienna, in order to establish a connection between his thoughts from Spring 1915 and the newly gained ones. I also suspect that his haste had to do with the fact that he came to Vienna with a firm plan on how to proceed with the *Abhandlung*, in order to finish it as quickly as possible. To speed up the completion of the book, he might have resorted to the method that he had outlined in March on the flyleaf of Ms 104 (presumably for Russell), namely to insert all the "good propositions" of his other manuscripts at the appropriate place in the already worked-out text corpus of the *Core-Prototractatus*, with the only difference that he now planned to do this himself during the time he would presumably have in Olomouc. The change in the compositional technique from page 28 onwards certainly speaks for such an assumption.

But first a selection of the "good propositions" had to be made. If Andreas Geschkowski's reconstruction is right,[115] in Olomouc Wittgenstein corrected a special document, the so-called *Maschinschrift* [literally "typescript"] that had been dictated by him in September 1916 in Vienna, during his short leave. This item appears in the list of all manuscripts necessary for publication, which he dictated to his sister Hermine in January 1917.[116]

According to Geschkowski, in Vienna he used the opportunity to dictate to a typist, in order to produce a collection of excerpts along the lines of the dictation of the *Notes on Logic* in October 1913. The selection was taken from the Norwegian notebook of 1913–14, as well as from Mss 101 and 102, and in part from another, presumably lost notebook [NB IIa], which may have continued to Ms 102. It is explicitly noted on Hermine's list that the latter notebook was only partially included, and this could be because the ten days spent in Vienna were not sufficient to fully examine all the older notebooks, as Wittgenstein had intended. On 12 September, he took the *Maschinschrift* with him to Olomouc. A carbon copy, along with the original notebooks themselves, was left with the secretary of the Wittgenstein family, Adolf Trenkler, for safekeeping.[117] In Olomouc, the new compositional technique was first practiced on the *Notes on Logic* (or rather on the German original of these). In Ms 104, in this first step to go beyond the *Core-Prototractatus* (pp. 28–35), we can find (almost) exclusively remarks that go back to the *Notes on Logic*, and largely in the order of the former.[118] In September or October, already during the officer training, in a second step, the new *Maschinschrift*-collection was being processed and integrated remark by remark into Ms 104 (in the long section from pp. 35–64)[119] much in the same way as the insertion of *spolia* into masonry. In any case, a striking number of remarks in this section of Ms 104 can be traced verbatim to entries in Ms 101 and Ms 102. The remaining ones for which this is not possible, very often show a clear thematic proximity to Wittgenstein's Norwegian period as we know it from the *Notes Dictated to Moore*[120] of April 1914, or to considerations such as we may expect in NB IIa in the transition from Ms 102 to the beginning of Ms 104.[121]

Officer training in Olomouc and a preliminary completion of the Abhandlung

In Olomouc, Wittgenstein is known to have come into closer contact with the intellectual circle around Paul Engelmann,[122] and the descriptions of his encounters with this circle give the impression of a lively intellectual exchange that was in no way affected by oppressive military training duties. Various letters from comrades also give the impression that neither the duration nor the scope of the training met with any fixed expectations. Thus, Wittgenstein may have had sufficient time and resources to continue working, in addition to the classes and the hours spent with Engelmann. Indeed, the correspondence mainly reveals his concern about actually being awarded the medals for bravery that were envisaged. He also seems to have expected that the decorations would exempt him (at least in part) from the officer's examination at the end of the course.[123] This matter is somewhat unclear, because on the one hand Hermine consoled him about it at the beginning of December,[124] on the other hand the military files record his appointment as *Fähnrich der Reserve* on 1 December 1916. The appointment can actually only be connected with the successful completion of the training.

It is not clear whether Wittgenstein remained in Olomouc for the weeks of December until his documented Christmas sojourn in Vienna to work on Ms 104, or whether he returned to Vienna earlier. It is noteworthy that Ms 103 contains a longer gap between 2 December 1916 and 7 January 1917,[125] and that no military postcards have survived for this year after 6 December.

It is difficult to determine the exact writing progress in Ms 104 during the Olomouc period. Michael Potter is "inclined to think that he compiled everything up to at least the break point on page 64 by the end of November 1916."[126] However, a comparison of the contents of Ms 103 and Ms 104 shows that the remark 56[3] = PT 5.4 can only have been written after 23 November 1916,[127] which means that the

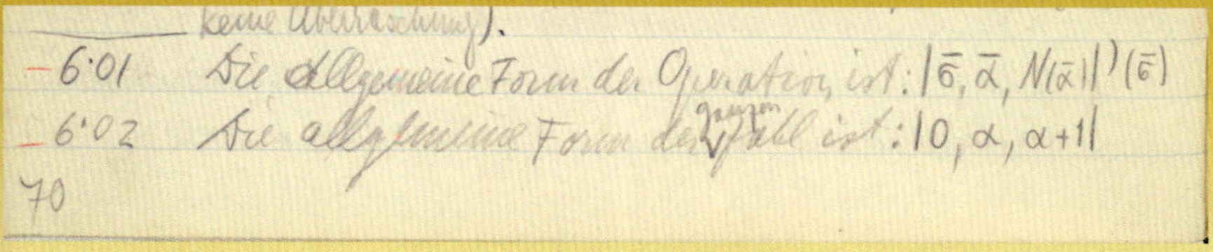
keine Überraschung).
6·01 Die allgemeine Form der Operation ist: $|\bar{\sigma}, \bar{\alpha}, N(\bar{\alpha})|'(\bar{\sigma})$
6·02 Die allgemeine Form der ganzen Zahl ist: $|0, \alpha, \alpha+1|$
70

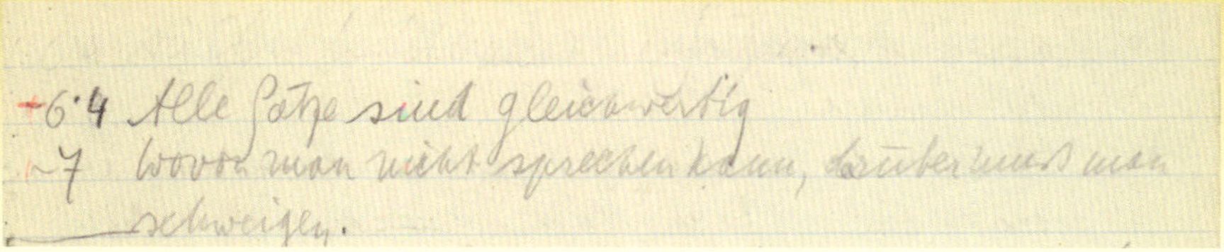
6·4 Alle Sätze sind gleichwertig
~7 Wovon man nicht sprechen kann, darüber muss man schweigen.

Ms 104 Excerpts from pages 70–71: remark 6.2 ("Ethics does not consist of propositions.") in the top line directly above the visible number 6.4 was subsequently erased by Wittgenstein (www.wittgensteinsource.org/BFE/Ms.104,70_f; www.wittgensteinsource.org/BFE/Ms.104,71_f)

breakpoint on page 64 was probably reached later, most likely around Christmas 1916. In any case, scholars are relatively unanimous with Brian McGuinness in assuming that in January 1917 a provisional final version of the *Abhandlung* was reached ("a provisional closing point"),[128] which McGuinness called *proto-Prototractatus*. It is disputed whether this version in January 1917 reached as far as page 70 or as far as page 71. The difference is made by five related remarks, set off by two horizontal lines, all marked on the left by a common margin sign "~". Among them is also the famous final remark 7.

6.01	*The general form of operation is:* $|\bar{\sigma}, \bar{\alpha}, N(\bar{\alpha})|'(\bar{\sigma})$.
6.02	*The general form of integer number is:* $|0, a, a+1|$.
6.2	*Ethics does not consist of propositions.*[129]
6.3	*All propositions are of equal value.*[130]
7	*About which one cannot speak, thereof one must be silent.*

These five remarks, however, still required intense reflections, in order to be able to formulate the general form of the operation (PT 6.01) or of the integer (PT 6.02), respectively, which still required time to be worked out. In particular, a comparison of the two variants of the final remark, one of which was certainly not written until June 1917, suggests that the five remarks are an addendum to Ms 104 from mid-1917.[131]

In any event, the *Abhandlung* in this 'provisionally final' version of January 1917 is still a purely logical treatise. This must be the work on which David Pinsent congratulated Wittgenstein in a letter of 31 December 1916. Wittgenstein had indeed been able to achieve the goal he had set himself in September of completing his work in Olomouc and Vienna.

To be sure, the *proto-Prototractatus* in the version of January 1917 no longer has, as in the original concept of 1915, proposition 6 on the general form of the truth function as a concluding proposition, but neither does it yet have remark 7. We are dealing here with a peculiar, interesting intermediate solution for the closing remarks, which can be reconstructed from the manuscript as follows:[132]

> *6.13 It is the characteristic mark of logical propositions that one can perceive in the symbol alone that they are true; and this fact contains in itself the whole philosophy of logic. And so also it is one of the most important facts that the truth or falsehood of non-logical propositions can* <u>*not*</u> *be recognized from the propositions alone.*
>
> *6.14 Logic is not a body of doctrine but a mirror-image of the world.*
>
> *6.141 Logic is transcendental.*

Consequently, in this version, the last word is given to logic, which is not part of the world, but its mirror-image that lies beyond the limits of the world.

Before he returned to the front again – this time no longer as a simple soldier, but as an officer[133] – Wittgenstein dictated to his sister Hermine a list of all those manuscripts and typescripts which, in the event of his death, Russell should receive in order to be able to publish the *Abhandlung*.[134]

Return to the front in the Bukovina

Wittgenstein left Vienna on 6 January 1917. However, he was only recorded as being "in the field" again from 19 January on. According to the correspondence, he spent the time in between again in Olomouc. About the months after his return to the Bukovina relatively little is known. The Field Howitzer Regiment No. 5 now belonged to the Honvéd Infantry Division 42, i.e. to the Hungarian Territorial Army (XIII Corps, 3rd Army).[135] What is known is that on 15 March 1917 Wittgenstein volunteered for a reconnaissance patrol at Dźwiniacz, and as a result earned the repetition-clasp to his Bronze Medal for Bravery (Files of the Vienna War Archives).

According to the correspondence, in his new situation, Wittgenstein felt able to "work."[136] What was he working on, one must ask, when the *Abhandlung* had just been finished? He might have regarded the missing formulations for the "general form of operation" as well as the "general form of integer" still as open gaps. Both are found on page 70, added at the very bottom with PT 6.01 and PT 6.02. In an often-quoted letter to Engelmann, there is also a thought ("If only you don't try to utter what is unutterable then nothing gets lost. But the unutterable will be – unutterably – contained in what has been uttered!"),[137] which, *mutatis mutandis*, also very well applies to the *Abhandlung*. As a logical treatise, it ultimately could not help but go beyond the purely logical. This transgression of the limits of the logical became clear as early as August 1916. ("Yes, my work has expanded from the foundations of logic to the nature of the world." 2 August 1916). But only now, gradually, was the overall character of the *Abhandlung* changing.

Bronze Medal for Bravery 1916, with repetition-clasp 1917
© Martin Pilch

One of the main reasons why the *proto-Prototractatus* version on p. 71 is likely to date from early July and not January 1917 is to be found in the way in which the final remark 7 has come down to us, namely, strictly speaking, a variant of the remark with the formulation "*Whereof* one cannot *talk*, thereof one must be silent." (my emphasis)[138] This version is not found in any manuscript, but it is found on a blank space in a letter from his sister Hermine of 7 June 1917 (in which she asks him for a better order in his disposal from January).[139]

The remarkable thing about this note is that it was written upside down on Hermine's letter, and so it is not an ironic comment on her somewhat pedantic reminders and complaints to her brother, but obviously the

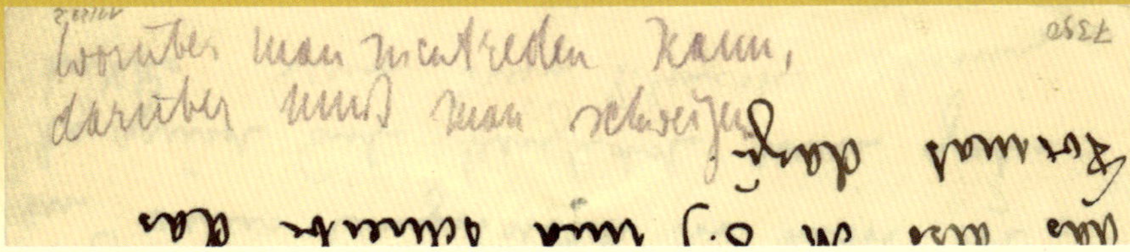

Excerpt from Hermine Wittgenstein's letter to Ludwig of 7 June 1917, with the presumably first version of the final remark of the *Tractatus* ("Whereof one cannot talk, thereof one must be silent.")

next best available piece of paper was used to record an important thought. For this reason, I think that it is likely that on this letter we have the actual original version of the final remark in front of us and not just another slightly different variant of a formulation written down half a year earlier. If this conjecture is true, the final remark PT 7 would have to be dated to June 1917, and the addition of the five remarks on pages 70–71 of Ms 104 to the beginning of July 1917 at the earliest. This is also supported by the fact that in the letter to Engelmann of April 1917, despite all mental proximity to the final remark, the moment of silence does not occur *expresis verbis*.

One can bring into play another assumption as an argument for a later genesis of the final remark.[140] It considers a key passage from Nietzsche. We know that Wittgenstein engaged with Nietzsche on several occasions: for example, in 1913 he spoke with Moore about *Zarathustra*,[141] in 1914 he read a volume of the Nietzsche Complete Edition in Kraków.[142] The preface of the second part of *Human, All Too Human* begins in a way that bears striking similarity to the final remark of the *Abhandlung*; Nietzsche's first sentence reads: "One should only speak where one must not stay silent." While there is no evidence of Wittgenstein's direct familiarity with this passage, it is conspicuous that a reference to it was made in Hermine's own philosophical journals, which are so closely aligned with those of her brother that Hermine's thoughts have even been edited under the title *Ludwig Sagt*.[143] In the same section, which dates from spring 1917, Hermine verbatim quotes from *Human, All Too Human*, so that it may be assumed that this Nietzsche work had also been the subject of a philosophical conversation between the siblings at that time (even if Nietzsche is not mentioned in Hermine's preserved letters to her brother).

The very last remark of the *Prototractatus* and later also of the *Tractatus* itself is embedded in a sequence of mantra-like phrases of sometimes slightly tautological character, that can be followed from 1915 onwards and even is detectable in middle Wittgenstein as documented in the following list.

Source	*Date*	*Remark*
Ms 102	27 May 1915	What cannot be expressed we do not express –.
Ms 103 (in code)	7 July 1916	What cannot be said, cannot be said!
Ms 104: 36[6] Ms 104: 36[6a]	ca. September 1916	Everything that can be thought at can be thought clearly. Everything that can be ~~said~~ uttered can be ~~said~~ uttered clearly.
Ms 103	15 October 1916	What you cannot think about, you also cannot talk about.
Letter to Engelmann	9 April 1917	If only you do not try to utter what is unutterable then nothing gets lost. But the unutterable will be – unutterably – contained in what has been uttered!
letter from Hermine W. 07 June 1917	June 1917	Whereof one cannot talk, thereof one must be silent.
Ms 104: 71[3]	June–July1917	About which one cannot speak, thereof one must be silent. [TLP 7]
Ms 104: 90[3]	ca. December 1917	What we cannot think, that we cannot think: we cannot therefore say what we cannot think.
Ms 104: 119 [TLP preface]	August 1918	The whole sense of the book might be summed up in the following words: What can be said at all can be said clearly; and about which one cannot speak, thereof one must be silent.
Letter to Ludwig von Ficker	20 October 1919	For I wanted to write, my work consists of two parts: the one presented here plus all that I have not written. And it is precisely this second part that is the important one. My book draws limits to the sphere of the ethical from the inside as it were, and I am convinced that this is the only rigorous way of drawing those limits. In short, I believe: All that many are blathering [*schwefeln*] about today, I have laid down [*festgelegt*] in my book by staying silent about it.

(*continued*)

Source	*Date*	*Remark*
Ms 107: 75	August 1929	What cannot be written, cannot be written.
Ms 108: 211	8 July 1930	What could not be foreseen, we just cannot talk about.
Ms 108: 248	26/ July 1930	What cannot be expressed cannot be talked about.

In July 1917, the final sequence of the *Abhandlung* assumes the following new form:

> *6.14* *Logic is not a body of doctrine but a mirror-image of the world.*
>
> *6.141* *Logic is transcendental.*
>
> *6.2* *Ethics does not consist of propositions.*
>
> *6.3* *All propositions are of equal value*[144].
>
> *7* *About which one cannot speak, thereof one must be silent.*

Even in this newly expanded version of July 1917, the *Abhandlung* is still predominantly a logical treatise, which only in the conclusion excludes ethics from the sphere of the sayable, i.e., of "propositions with sense." 6.2 is one of the five remarks (which was later erased in the further course of the revisions, but is still readable in the manuscript). More in-depth reflections, as we find them today in the *Tractatus* (e.g., "ethics and aesthetics are one" TLP 6.241, originally MS 103: 24 July 1916 on the Dora Hills), are still completely missing in this version. The systematic integration of the insights from Ms 103 will not occur until half a year later, in the winter of 1917–18.

On 22 June, Wittgenstein left the front for a short vacation. He invited Frege to Vienna for the following days, but Frege declined.[145] Probably on his way to Vienna Wittgenstein stopped for a short time in Olomouc, so that an episode reported by Engelmann would coincide with this period.[146] A photo showing Wittgenstein with the family at Neuwaldegg, wearing a uniform of a *Fähnrich*, can also be dated to this home leave. His brother Kurt can likewise be seen in uniform.[147]

The photograph shows a somewhat exhausted Wittgenstein, directly before or after the inclusion of remark PT 7 in Ms 104. At the same time, however, he must have been thinking about thoroughly revising the final sections of the *Abhandlung*. This could be

Kurt Wittgenstein, Paul Wittgenstein, Hermine Wittgenstein, Max Salzer, Leopoldine Wittgenstein, Helene Salzer and Ludwig Wittgenstein. Neuwaldegg, end of June/beginning of July 1917. © Research Institute Brenner-Archiv, "Wittgenstein Family – Collection Andreas Sjögren."

connected to the letter to Engelmann (CC 2011), which refers to their recent meeting in Olomouc and in which he also asks Engelmann to demand that Heinrich Groag return his manuscripts. According to this contextual reading, "manuscripts" would have to mean the 'loose-sheet collection',[148] which as an expandable working copy would be an indispensable tool for the new revision.

The compilations following the final remark 7 on pp. 71–78 give altogether the impression that Wittgenstein had again resorted to the *Maschinschrift* at the beginning of the section 6.3 on the Natural Sciences,[149] but not to the Mss 101–103 themselves. Accordingly, he would have kept to his cautious practice of taking to the front only as many manuscripts and working aids as necessary, in order to be able to publish the entire *Abhandlung* from the pieces safely stored in Vienna, if necessary.

Further work on the *Abhandlung* would have to wait for the time being. Immediately after returning to the Bukovina on 9 July 1917, his field howitzer regiment was engaged in heavy battles in an offensive in which all the terrain lost a year earlier, including Kolomea and Czernowitz, was recaptured by the Austrian troops. Wittgenstein's *Vormerkblatt für die Qualifikationsbeschreibung* [i.e. a template for the self-description of wartime missions by soldiers] for July 1917, filled out in his own hand, reads like a chronology of continuous battles:

until 9 July	positional warfare near Rosulna
9 July	battle of retreat to Łdziany
10–11 July	battle near Bania-Rosulna
12–22 July	battles near Kamin and Łdziany
from 23 July	offensive until the capture of Czernowitz
24 July	battle near Starunia
26 July	battle near Kolomea
29 July	battle near Kniaze
30–31 July	battle near Waschkoutz
01–02 August	battle near Hlinitza
03 August	conquest of Czernowitz

In the course of these battles Wittgenstein earns another decoration, the Silver Medal for Bravery 1st Class. His behavior is again quite similar to that at the beginning of the Brusilov offensive:

"*Fähnrich* Wittgenstein performed his duties as a reconnaissance officer in an exemplary manner during the fighting at Łdziany from 10 to 20 July last. Staying on his place in the heaviest artillery fire, it was only in this way possible for the battery to direct the fire on vulnerable points, which the battery commander could not see. In this way, considerable losses were inflicted on the enemy at decisive moments." (Files of the Vienna War Archives).

FOURTH YEAR OF THE WAR - 1917–18

Positional warfare near Czernowitz

From the beginning of August 1917, the eastern front in the Bukovina stopped moving.[150] Among the last advances in which Wittgenstein was involved was an attack on Bojany, east of Czernowitz on 27 August. In a way, it is embarrassing that this put him almost back in the same place he was 15 months earlier at the start of the Brusilov offensive. Bojany is only 15 kilometers south of the *Kordenposten* Sawokrynicznyi, where he earned the "small" Silver Medal for Bravery in June 1916.

In the absence of a preserved notebook to follow Ms 103, we know fairly little about his personal circumstances and mental development at this time. In a letter dated 22 August, Walter Wahle,

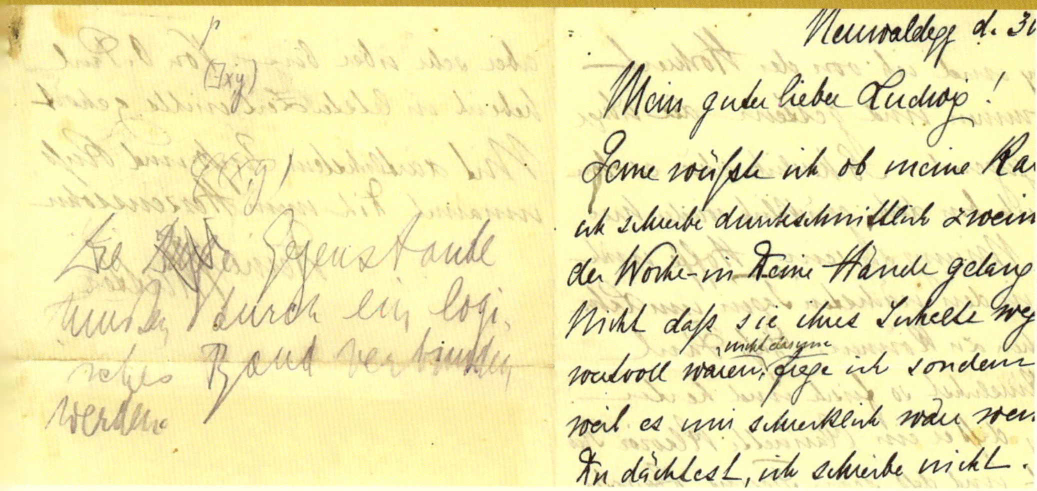

Remark on the "logical bond" jotted down by Wittgenstein on the letter from his mother dated 30 August 1917

the former deputy commander of Artillery Workshop Train No. 1, surprisingly contacted him. Wahle, who had been transferred to a research department of the Air Force in July 1916, after having been trained as a commander for artillery workshops,[151] tried to convince Wittgenstein to also seek a transfer to Wahle's unit, with the prospect of research work in aviation. Such a transfer did not take place, but Wittgenstein's documented participation in an aviation course in the winter of 1918 could be related to it (for background information, see Seekircher 2002).

On 27 August, in a letter to Engelmann, he wrote "My brain works very violently," which may be taken as an indication of intensive philosophical reflections and probably also of further work on the *Abhandlung*. One of the very few philosophical remarks from the "notebook-less" period has been preserved on the back of a letter from his mother (30 August 1917):"~~Things~~ Objects must be connected by a logical bond."

If we assume that Wittgenstein used his mother's letter to capture this thought rather promptly, then the 'violent work of the brain' might also have involved a reconsideration of the ontological remarks in section 2 of the *Abhandlung*. Several times in the final phase of the *Prototractatus*[152] we can find fresh additions to this section, also concerning the role of 'simple objects'. But none of these remarks ultimately interferes with the existing text as deeply as the remark about the "logical bond," which was probably not included in the final text for good reason. In the *Tractatus*, the simple objects connect themselves to *Sachverhalte* [states of affairs] by virtue of their own form alone. Concatenated with each other in this way they naturally build up configurations and therefore there is *no need* of any form of external connection, i.e. no additional 'logical bond' that would force them into *Sachverhalte* [states of affairs]. This accidentally preserved remark proves that Wittgenstein's unique ability of rethinking results already achieved again and again made him question the logical structure of *Sachverhalte* [states of affairs] once more in the summer of 1917.

After the fighting subsided, Wittgenstein was able to tackle the reworking of section 6 of the *Prototractatus* that had been planned for July. On pages 71–74 of Ms 104, he inserted a new subsection 6.2 on the Natural Sciences in a very orderly, i.e. thoroughly prepared, manner. This subsection, later at the beginning of 1918 renumbered to 6.3, consists of three textual layers.[153] The *first* of these textual layers was written between August and approximately October 1917 and remained largely unchanged until the completion of the *Abhandlung*. At the very center we find the idea from spring 1915, that there is no special form of necessity in the laws of nature comparable to 'logical necessity'. Rather, the law of causality is only a form of propositions and has no content ("The law of causality is not a law but the form of a law." PT 6.3; "Mechanics is an attempt to construct according to a single plan all <u>true</u> propositions which we need for the description of the world." PT 6.341).[154]

On p. 75, the final part of the *Abhandlung* is also reformulated again; the main remark of p. 71 on ethics ("Ethics does not consist of propositions.") is erased, but its thought is integrated into the new sequence of concluding remarks as 6.32; in October–November 1917, the very last remarks read like this:

6.3 *All propositions are of equal value.*

6.31 *The sense [Sinn] of the world must lie outside the world.*

6.32 *Hence also there can be no ethical propositions. Propositions cannot express anything higher.*

6.33 *There is indeed the inexpressible. This <u>shows</u> itself; it is the mystical.*

6.4 *For an answer which cannot be expressed the question too cannot be expressed.*

<u>The riddle</u> does not exist.

If a question can be put at all, then it can also be answered.

6.41 *Scepticism is not irrefutable, but palpably senseless, if it would doubt where a question cannot be asked.*

For doubt can only exist where there is a question; a question only where there is an answer, and this only where something can be said.

6.42 *We feel that even if all possible scientific questions be answered, the problems of life have still not been touched at all. Of course there is then no question left, and just this is the answer.*

7 *About which one cannot speak, thereof one must be silent.*

It is the purpose of philosophy as solution of all questions which forms the leading tone towards the resolution in remark 7, in this still not final version.

During this phase of writing also a new sequence on 'probability propositions' is developed on pp. 77–78 with PT 5.09 ff. In Geschkowski's opinion, the horizontal line after 78[10] = PT 1.21 marks the end of the evaluation of the *Maschinschrift* of September 1916.[155]

Armistice with Russia and completion of the Prototractatus

After the October Revolution (on 7 November 1917), the Russian Soviet government very quickly, on 28 November, proposed an armistice to the war opponents. Wittgenstein made a note of its effectiveness as of 29 November. As there was no longer any need for artillery observers and a letter from his mother of 2 November spoke of the prospect of a vacation, we may assume that Wittgenstein could return to Vienna in December.

In the following period between 29 November 1917 and 10 March 1918, the day of the departure for the Italian front in Asiago, pp. 79–103 in MS 104 were written down in an intensive final work phase, thereby completing the *Prototractatus*. The intensity of the writing is comparable to that in Olomouc, and some of the work is done again in parallel to a training course, this time for the Air Force. And once again, we are confronted with a major conceptual change; in this case, not in the methodology, since the integration of material from other notebooks remained predominant, but in the general theme of the *Abhandlung*, which underwent a transformation from a logical to a metaphysical treatise, in that he decided to incorporate the completely new thoughts set down in Ms 103 in 1916.

If we take a closer look at Ms 104, it is easy to see that Ms 103 is evaluated in a quite systematic way on pp. 81–86 of Ms 104, and remarks taken almost literally from the notebook are inserted at appropriate places in the *Abhandlung*. The text transfer proceeds entirely chronologically and not thematically.[156] Throughout Ms 103, the selected remarks show typical margin marks, slanted red dashes at the beginning of the remark, most of which are crossed out again with a delicate black dash. This suggests a method of pre-selection in Ms 103 (red line) and subsequent adoption in Ms 104 (black strike-out), or alternatively a dictation of an intermediate typescript comparable to the *Maschinschrift* of September 1916. From pp. 78–81 other material for which no precursors are known is apparently integrated in a very similar way. There is much to suggest that these parts were taken from the lost notebook NB IIa (from June 1915 to March 1916), which was after all only partially represented in the *Maschinschrift* in Olomouc.[157]

It seems, however, that this appropriation took place in reverse order, which means that the extraction process started with the final part of NB IIa that had not yet been used for the *Abhandlung*. An indication for this reversed procedure is that the theme of 'general constructability' that is visible in the first of the remarks in question,

> *That there is a general form is proved by the fact that there cannot be a proposition whose form could not have been foreseen (i.e. constructed).*
> (MS 104: 78[11] = PT 4.43012)

is appropriately continued by the first preserved philosophical remark in Ms 103:

> *Only that which we ourselves construct can we foresee!*
> (Ms 103: 15 April 1916)

Conversely, the last remarks of this sequence on p. 81 (immediately before the evaluation of Ms 103 begins) fit in thoughtfully with the topics in the transition from the end of Ms 102 (on 22 June 1915) to the beginning of Ms 104 (August–September 1915).

During this period, a new conception of elementary proposition and facts was at issue and the basic idea of the "immediate combination" or "concatenation" of objects in the facts must have been conceived for the first time. The remarks on p. 81 read:

> *It is obvious that in the analysis of propositions we must come to elementary propositions, which consist of names in immediate combination.*
> (81[1] = PT 5.4101)

It is a sign of an elementary proposition, that no elementary proposition can contradict it.
(81[2] = PT 5.4102)

If everything in the symbolism works as though a sign had meaning, then it has meaning.
(81[3] = PT 3.2522).

All these remarks, I think, originally belonged to a broader discussion within the lost NB IIa in order to clarify the relations between certain key-notions of the initial parts of the upcoming *Prototractatus*. Compared to the state of the late entries in Ms 102 Wittgenstein achieved a much higher degree of systematic order concerning concepts like 'object' [*Gegenstand*], 'state of affairs' [*Sachverhalt*], 'situation' [*Sachlage*] and 'fact' [*Tatsache*] and their counterparts, 'name' [*Name*], 'simple sign' [*einfaches Zeichen*], 'elementary proposition' [*Elementarsatz*] and 'proposition' [*Satz*] as truth-functions of elementary propositions.[158]

At the end of the long block of remarks from Ms 103, on p. 86, Wittgenstein proceeded to re-work once more the concluding sequence of the *Abhandlung*, almost reaching the final form known from the printed version of the *Tractatus*:

6.42 *We feel that even if all possible scientific questions be answered, the problems of life have still not been touched at all. Of course there is then no question left, and just this is the answer.*

6.43 *The right method of philosophy would be this: To say nothing except what can be said, i.e. the propositions of natural science, i.e. something that has nothing to do with philosophy: and then always, when someone else wished to say something metaphysical, to demonstrate to him that he had given no meaning to certain signs in his propositions.*

6.431 *This method would be unsatisfying to the other – he would not have the feeling that we were teaching him philosophy – but it would be the only strictly correct method.*

6.44 *My propositions are elucidatory in this way: he who understands me finally recognizes them as nonsensical, when he has climbed out through them, on them, over them. (He must so to speak throw away the ladder, after he has climbed up on it.)*

6.45 *He must overcome these propositions, then he will approach at the right level of what can be said.*

7 *About which one cannot speak, thereof one must be silent.*

In this version, four further remarks are inserted between 6.42 and 7, two taken from the end of Ms 103 (2 December 1916) and two completely new ones, among them the much-cited one about "throwing the ladder away."[159] The difference in comparison to the printed version, besides the deviant numbering, consists only in the fact that the penultimate remark at its end does not yet read: "[...] then he sees the world rightly." Instead of this, after overcoming the (nonsensical) remarks of the *Abhandlung* (i.e. after throwing away the ladder in 6.44) the reader "will approach at the right level of what can be said."

This idea, later replaced, shows that the ladder metaphor, at the time of its first formulation in Ms 104, is still closely connected with the problem of a correct type theory, which bothered Wittgenstein as early as in January 1913 in Cambridge.[160] Originally the metaphorical rungs of the ladder still stand for the ever-new logical types forming the 'hierarchy of propositions', which is generated step by step by the application of the logical operations.

The solution which Wittgenstein offers in 86[3] (= PT-remark without number) for this type and hierarchy problem is that "the lowest level and the operation can serve as the representatives of the whole hierarchy." However, this did not convince him in the end. With the later revisions of the penultimate remark "[...] then he will approach at the right level of what can be said." first to "[...] then he will approach the world at the right level" (still in Ms 104) and finally to "[...] then he sees the world rightly." (in Ts 202) the unsolved type problem is brought if not to disappear, then at least out of sight.

Regarding the origin of the famous concluding remarks, I would like to extend a bit the above conjecture by Nuno Venturinha, that PT 7 was inspired by the first sentence in Nietzsche's preface to the second volume of *Human, All Too Human.* Juxtaposing Nietzsche's words with the final remarks of Wittgenstein's *Abhandlung* (in reverse order), astonishing parallels emerge.

Human, All Too Human	PT	*Prototractatus*
Volume II – Beginning of Preface		**Concluding remarks in reversed order**
One should speak only where one must not stay silent;	7	About which one cannot speak, thereof one must be silent.
and then only of that which one has overcome [*überwunden hat*] – everything else is blather [*Geschwätz*], 'literature', lack of breeding.	6.55	He must overcome [*überwinden*] these propositions, then he will arrive at the right level [*Stufe*] of what can be said. ["All that many are blathering [*schwefeln*] about today, I have laid down [*festgelegt*] in my book by staying silent about it."[161]]
My writings speak only of my overcomings: 'I' am in them, together with everything that was inimical to me, *ego ipsissimus*, indeed, if a yet prouder expression be permitted, *ego ipsissimum*. One will divine that I already have a great deal – beneath me ...	6.54	My propositions are elucidatory in this way: Anyone who understands me finally recognizes them as nonsensical, when he has climbed out through them, on them, over them. (He must so to speak throw away the ladder, after he has climbed up on it.)
	6.53	The right method of philosophy [...]

So not only is Nietzsche's "silence" taken up in PT 7; both texts talk quite decisively about "overcoming," reject all "blather," and also share a special reference to the personal self ("My writings ..." – "My propositions ..."). After all we now know about Wittgenstein's existential wartime experiences and especially about the mortal danger on the artillery observation post, it is clear that ladders – i.e. those typical rough wooden ladders used to climb up to the high stand – many times meant for him the overcoming of his mortal fears, overcoming in the sense of the 'right life' as interpreted by Tolstoy's *Gospel in Brief*. Certainly, no one in the entire history of philosophy has ever had such intimate existential experiences with ladders as Wittgenstein did during the June Days of 1916. Thus, we might say, in the ladder metaphor, the logical demands of a correct implementation of types meet the ethical demands of a right living in the face of death. Both demands – the logical as well as the ethical – are of course transcendental.

Continuing from p. 87 to p. 100, there are still manifold additions to all the main sections of the *Abhandlung* (with the exception of the first, the commentary of which is concluded with 78[10] = PT 1.21). Among them is a remarkably orderly block of nine remarks on the "application of logic," (Ms 104: 97[1–9]) with which Wittgenstein probably intended to fill a gap he had perceived in connection with PT 5.4 and his rejection of the possibility of being able to show anything about the form of elementary propositions. On p. 98 the *third* textual layer on the propositions of natural science starts. It contains a clarification on the concept of causality following the mechanics of Heinrich Hertz.[162]

Surprisingly, on p. 101 of the manuscript, almost at the end of the *Prototractatus*, a new principal decimal is introduced (once again "6.2" which results in a cumbersome renumbering of remarks visible in many places in the manuscript), in order to give mathematics an appropriate place in the system of the *Prototractatus*: "Mathematics is a logical method." (PT 6.2). Mathematics is thus brought into immediate proximity to logic, but its propositions are nevertheless not supposed to be tautologies themselves, like the 'propositions of logic', but equations. The logical method behind is that of substitution of expressions in equations by other expressions ("For equations express the substitutability of two expressions, and we proceed from a number of equations to new equations, replacing expressions by others in accordance with the equations." PT 6.24). Later, during the major revision of the *Abhandlung* in the summer of 1918, in the transition from the *Prototractatus* to the *Tractatus* proper, Wittgenstein felt compelled to expand considerably the subsection 6.2 on mathematics, which had been introduced so late.[163]

With the first remark on p. 103 in Ms 104, the *Prototractatus* finally came to its conclusion at some point in the days before 10 March 1918. It is possible that the departure from philosophical positions, which Wittgenstein, by his own admission,[164] had adopted in his younger years, in the wake of Schopenhauer, also plays a role in the background of the whole arrangement of section 6. In any case, it is striking that the subsections 6.1–6.4 can be directly associated with the four different formulations of the *Satzesvom Grunde* [principle of reason] as developed by Schopenhauer in his early work *On the Fourfold Root of the Principle of Sufficient Reason.*

	Prototractatus	Schopenhauer
	propositions...	principle of sufficient reason ...
6.1	... of logic (tautologies)	... of recognition (logical truth)
6.2	... of mathematics (equations)	... of being (arithmetic & geometry)
6.3	... of natural sciences (forms of laws)	... of becoming (law of causality)
6.4	... of ethics (do not exist)	... of action (ethics)

Natural sciences: The departure from Schopenhauer concerns most explicitly the status of the "propositions of the natural sciences." Wittgenstein does not acknowledge any form of natural-law-like necessity that would be in any way comparable to logical necessity ("A necessity for one thing to happen because another has happened does not exist. There is only logical necessity." PT 6.37).

Ethics is likewise excluded from the logical realm ("Hence also there can be no ethical propositions. Propositions cannot express anything higher." PT 6.42; "It is clear that ethics cannot be expressed." PT 6.421).

Mathematics at least still touches the sphere of the logical in that the method in mathematics is explicitly called a "logical method" (PT 6.2; "Mathematics is a method of logic." PT 6.22). But the propositions of mathematics are mere pseudo-propositions. What they seem to express, in mathematics *is shown* with the help of equations, comparable to the way by tautologies something about the world *is shown* without saying anything ("The logic of the world which the propositions of logic show in tautologies, mathematics shows in equations." PT 6.21).

Altogether, subsections 6.1–6.4 offer a summary of Wittgenstein's break with his own former Schopenhauerian views, the original form of which, admittedly, we know little about.

On 1 February 1918, Wittgenstein was promoted to *Leutnant der Reserve*, and later that month he was allowed to participate in an aviation course at *Fliegerkompanie* [Aviation Company] No. 30 (near Czernowitz). At the beginning of March, he was back in Vienna, and Engelmann's account (in a letter to Friedrich von Hayek) states that Wittgenstein "dictated his manuscript to a typist in Vienna before leaving for the Italian front."[165] If one relates this information to March,[166] i.e., to the *initial* transfer to Asiago, and not, as McGuinness does, to September 1918, when Wittgenstein returned again to Asiago after the dictation of TS 204, then the completion of the *Prototractatus* must be dated to early March 1918. So, there must have existed a (not preserved) typescript of it (in the outer form probably very similar to the preserved Ts 204 of August 1918), which he would have taken with him to the Italian front for further revision.

On the Italian front in Asiago

From 10 March to 10 May, Wittgenstein, now attached to Gun Battery No. 1 of Mountain Artillery Regiment No. 11, noted in his own hand "*Stellungskrieg* [positional warfare] in Asiago" in the *Vormerkblatt für die Qualifikationsbeschreibung* as well as further: "10/05–25/05: commanded to the Art.[illery] Mat.[erial] Course of the 11th Army" and "25/05–05/07: June battle against Italy at Asiago". The latter refers mainly to his participation in the heavy offensive of 15 June, as a result of which he was recommended for the Gold Medal for Bravery for Officers for his typical behavior in combat, which is already known to us:[167]

> *In the battle near Asiago on 15–16 June this year, he went forward with the first waves of the assault battery as a reconnaissance officer. In the strong machine-gun and artillery fire he reconnoitered the battle conditions and 2 men of his patrol were wounded. In the heaviest drumfire he took care of the removal of the wounded, and returned to the assault battery, which was under the heaviest artillery fire. When the 1st officer and 3 men were buried by a 28-cm shell, he took over from them and, ignoring his own safety, led the rescue operations. When the order was given to withdraw the guns, within a short time he brought them back to the starting position through the furious barrage.*

However, Wittgenstein did not receive the Gold Medal for Bravery, due to the objection of a certain Colonel Danzer that the offensive had not been successful. Instead, he was awarded the Military Merit Medal on Ribbon with Swords on 22 September 1918.

In an (unpublished) report by Field Marshal Lieutenant Johann Fernengel, the commander of the 16th Infantry Division to which Wittgenstein's regiment belonged (which is why the former also signed off on the reward application concerning him on 10 July), one learns more about the background and the foreseeable failure of the offensive:

> *The preparations for the attack were unfavorably influenced by heavy downpours, too late arrival, laborious positioning of the heavy ordnance. [...] The troops intended for the attack had to carry the artillery ammunition into the battery positions every night in pouring rain due to the lack of other manpower. Under these circumstances, there was no question of recovery or of strengthening for the important task.*
>
> *[...] that we would not be able to finish the preparations by 15/06 early, requested him to ask the Army Command to postpone the order to attack for a few days. The answer was: "Impossible, it is requested from above for 15/06."*
>
> *[...] my troops entered the battle on 15/06 with full confidence. Fate willed otherwise: the artillery, which had the most important task for the first phase of the battle, gassing and smashing the enemy position, entered the battle with insufficient resources [...] of the 4 promised 30.5 mortars de facto only one was in firing position, the gas ammunition was much too little, [...] the light guns could accomplish nothing against the strongly fortified [...] position.*
>
> *Defectors from the neighboring D[ivis]ion to the east had disclosed the day and hour of our attack to the enemy. Thus it happened that the element of surprise was completely lost. [...]*[168]

During the second half of June, possibly also as a result of the battle, Wittgenstein was probably also in a hospital Bolzano, which is mentioned in a letter from Frege (12 September 1918). What Wittgenstein did not yet know in the spring on the Italian front was that David Pinsent had been killed in an airplane accident on 8 May 1918.

The long front leave – reworking of the Prototractatus Typescript to Ts 204

From 5 July, Wittgenstein was again on leave, this time a very long one, lasting until September 1918. It is not clear whether, as McGuinness supposes, he actually wanted to commit suicide out of grief over the death of David Pinsent and only a chance encounter with his uncle Paul at the Salzburg train station prevented him from doing so. The reply letter to Pinsent's mother, in which he informed her that he was dedicating his work to her son, sounds actually very composed. The letter from Ellen Pinsent is dated 6 July 1918, so if one takes into account the long postal routes, Wittgenstein could not have known about the death of his friend at the beginning of his furlough.[169] On the other hand, the uncle was thanked to an unexpected extent in the preface to the *Tractatus*. He was placed on the same level as Russell (however, this final word of thanks to both was later deleted, i.e. crossed out three times).

Paul Wittgenstein's Villa in Oberalm, near Hallein and Salzburg

By all accounts, Paul Wittgenstein's villa in Oberalm near Hallein (in the province of Salzburg) plays a significant role in the reworking of the *Prototractatus* into the actual *Tractatus* as we know it and as it was dictated – except for minor additions and corrections – in Vienna in August 1918 as Ts 204 (with carbon copy Ts 202). The villa (demolished in 2015) may thus be imagined as the place where the Herculean task of profoundly reshaping the *Abhandlung* was at least begun. However much time Wittgenstein had available in Asiago to correct the typescript of March, one may assume that there he did not get further than remark 3.1, because up to this point, the reconstruction of the changes, even if partially significant[170] and concerning the whole treatise, reads quite conventionally with insertions, deletions, shifts and corrections of individual words and parts of propositions.

However, as soon as Wittgenstein reached the remark 3.1. in his revision, he must have been radically dissatisfied with the basic structure and completely reworked the third section, later also the section 5 in a similar way, i.e. on the principal decimal level. This reworking is rightly regarded as extremely complex, Brian McGuinness even considers it hardly reconstructable. There has been much speculation in the literature about how it was even possible for Wittgenstein to manage this complexity. If one contrasts the

Prototractatus numbers with the new *Tractatus Logico-Philosophicus* numbers, if one follows how remarks and parts of remarks were shifted and changed, how they were combined under new numbers, how they were partly discarded and replaced by newly formulated remarks, then one is confronted with an almost unravelable structure of relations between numbers and contents.

After working out a detailed textual basis of both Ms 104 and the (still uncorrected) Ts 202, I proposed[171] to explain the revision process by the fact that Wittgenstein, similar to much later, for example, in the transition from Ts 208 to Ts 209, cut the typescript (or its carbon copy) into strips and rearranged the resulting textual parts. In the process, strips were sometimes discarded and replaced by new formulations. These were then additionally included in Ms 104 on pp. 103–118. This explains why there are still further remarks (revisions of earlier ones in the manuscript and supplementary new ones) in Ms 104, although the *Prototractatus* was concluded with p. 103. This additional section in Ms 104 (the so-called "*Korrektur*") between the actual *Prototractatus* and the preface to the *Tractatus* on pp. 119–121 also refers already to the process of renumbering, from which emerges the numbering system of the *Tractatus*. The order of the propositional numbers in the correction section at the same time gives information about the sequence of the revision with occasional jumping back and forward across section boundaries, which seems to be under the guiding principle of continuing to use as many remarks of the *Prototractatus* as possible. The presumed procedure explains why any new remarks were written down in Ms 104 at all, but it also explains why the "*Korrektur*"-section, at 16 pages, is much shorter than the *Prototractatus* itself. The bulk of the remarks just consisted of fragments of the March typescript. Probably the old and new material was pasted collage-like into a book to be dictated again. For the revision of the fifth section, Wittgenstein actually had to try twice, in order to find satisfactory new formulations. According to this idea of the revision process, however, the renumbering of the remarks must have been the last step and not, as Michael Potter suggests, the first.[172] This is also supported by the fact that the renumbering goes rather less deeply than that of the *Prototractatus*, and often several numbered remarks are combined under one new number. In many cases, this summary (in the reconstruction) follows exactly the structure of the hypothetical text snippets. A repeated dictation of the intermediate element reconstructed in this way (the "*Korrektur*") then leads exactly to the still uncorrected typewritten text of Ts 204 as it can be read today in the Austrian National Library.

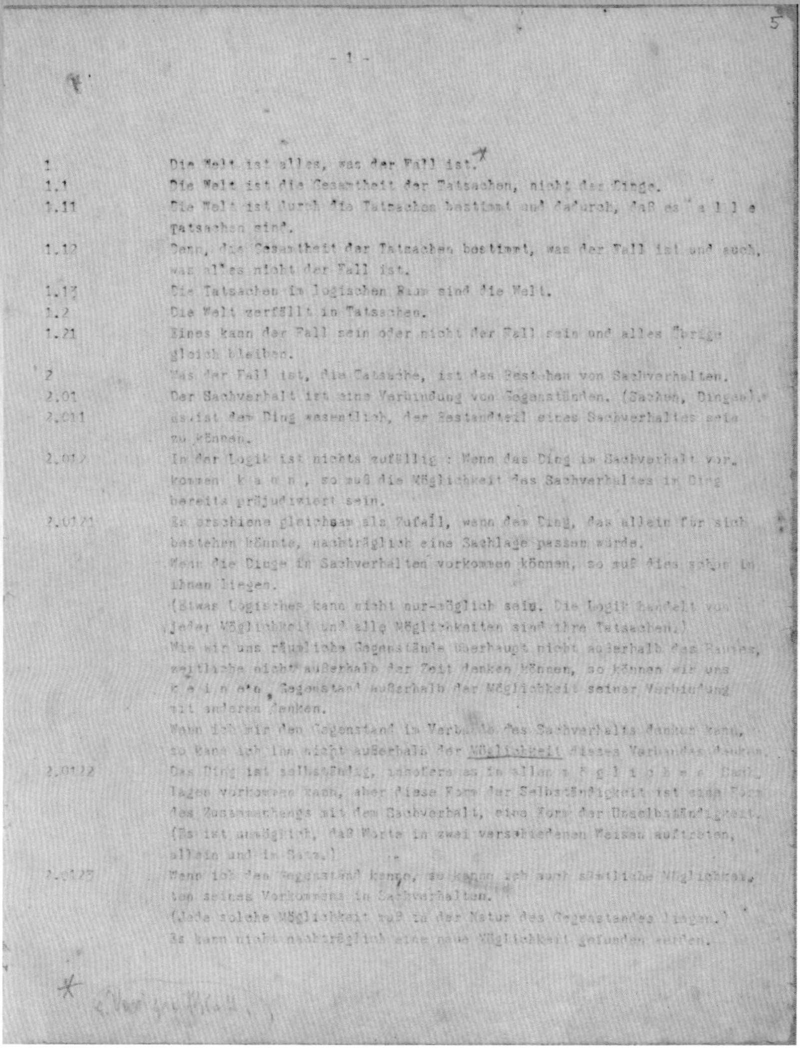

- 1 -

1 Die Welt ist alles, was der Fall ist.*

1.1 Die Welt ist die Gesamtheit der Tatsachen, nicht der Dinge.

1.11 Die Welt ist durch die Tatsachen bestimmt und dadurch, daß es a l l e Tatsachen sind.

1.12 Denn, die Gesamtheit der Tatsachen bestimmt, was der Fall ist und auch, was alles nicht der Fall ist.

1.13 Die Tatsachen im logischen Raum sind die Welt.

1.2 Die Welt zerfällt in Tatsachen.

1.21 Eines kann der Fall sein oder nicht der Fall sein und alles Übrige gleich bleiben.

2 Was der Fall ist, die Tatsache, ist das Bestehen von Sachverhalten.

2.01 Der Sachverhalt ist eine Verbindung von Gegenständen. (Sachen, Dingen).

2.011 Es ist dem Ding wesentlich, der Bestandteil eines Sachverhaltes sein zu können.

2.012 In der Logik ist nichts zufällig: Wenn das Ding im Sachverhalt vorkommen k a n n , so muß die Möglichkeit des Sachverhaltes im Ding bereits präjudiziert sein.

2.0121 Es erschiene gleichsam als Zufall, wenn dem Ding, das allein für sich bestehen könnte, nachträglich eine Sachlage passen würde.
Wenn die Dinge in Sachverhalten vorkommen können, so muß dies schon in ihnen liegen.
(Etwas Logisches kann nicht nur-möglich sein. Die Logik handelt von jeder Möglichkeit und alle Möglichkeiten sind ihre Tatsachen.)
Wie wir uns räumliche Gegenstände überhaupt nicht außerhalb des Raumes, zeitliche nicht außerhalb der Zeit denken können, so können wir uns k e i n e n Gegenstand außerhalb der Möglichkeit seiner Verbindung mit anderen denken.
Wenn ich mir den Gegenstand im Verbande des Sachverhalts denken kann, so kann ich ihn nicht außerhalb der Möglichkeit dieses Verbandes denken.

2.0122 Das Ding ist selbständig, insofern es in allen m ö g l i c h e n Sachlagen vorkommen kann, aber diese Form der Selbständigkeit ist eine Form des Zusammenhangs mit dem Sachverhalt, eine Form der Unselbständigkeit.
(Es ist unmöglich, daß Worte in zwei verschiedenen Weisen auftreten, allein und im Satz.)

2.0123 Wenn ich den Gegenstand kenne, so kenne ich auch sämtliche Möglichkeiten seines Vorkommens in Sachverhalten.
(Jede solche Möglichkeit muß in der Natur des Gegenstandes liegen.)
Es kann nicht nachträglich eine neue Möglichkeit gefunden werden.

First text page of Typescript Ts 202 (the so-called Engelmann Typescript) from August 1918 (www.wittgensteinsource.org/BFE/Ts-202,1r_f) © 2015 The Master and Fellows of Trinity College, Cambridge; The University of Bergen, Bergen

This dictation, which, according to a letter to Russell of 1919, took place in Vienna in August 1918,[173] completed, after three years of conceptual work, the *Logisch-Philosophische Abhandlung* which had been initiated on the train at Sokal. What followed were comparatively minor corrections during the war captivity in Cassino and in the course of the odyssey of various publication attempts, as described in Alfred Schmidt's article.[174]

A detailed timeline for March–September 1916 of Ludwig Wittgenstein's experience during the Brusilov Offensive in the Bukovina can be downloaded at https://wittgenstein-initiative.com.

Finding Our Way Home: The Philosophy of the *Tractatus*

Ian Ground

> 471. *It is so difficult to find the beginning. Or, better: it is difficult to begin at the beginning. And not to try to go further back.*
>
> — Ludwig Wittgenstein, *On Certainty*

One way to approach Wittgenstein's *Tractatus-Logico-Philosophicus*, especially for those new to it, is to understand it as an answer, or at least a response, to this fundamental question: How is the world thinkable?

We think and say true things about the world. And false things too. But how? What has to be the case if such thoughts and utterances are even possible? And what are the implications of how we answer this question?

Consisting of seven propositions, all but the last with multiple sub-propositions, the *Tractatus* is artfully structured, austerely beautiful, and technically demanding. It fuses the formal and the gnomic, the technical and the spiritual, the logical and the mystical. And, in the background, a further fusion: Wittgenstein's personal crisis and the crisis of his times. His lone struggles with his own identity – with self, sexuality and spirituality – and the global struggles – the mud, metal and murder – of the Great War.

These multiple fusions – and, as contributors to this volume do so much to illuminate, the work's complex genesis – invite divergent and disorientating interpretations. It may help new readers especially then to offer a broad-brush picture – a rational reconstruction – to give a sense of what the *Tractatus* centrally concerns and why it matters.

We can begin by seeing the book as a sublime distillation of a particular, historically dominant, conception of ourselves. That conception is this. First and foremost, we are conscious thinkers. Only after, are we active, embodied, speaking agents. Before we communicate with each other, we must first have something *to* communicate. Before we consider anything else – biology, psychology, the structure of the brain, or of social life or culture, or all the myriad possibilities of failures to communicate, the world must, first, be for us thinkable and speakable. In prioritizing the question of how it is that beings like us can think and speak at all, the *Tractatus* gives expression, austere and sublime, to a conception of ourselves that was already latent in our intellectual culture. It is a conception of ourselves as representing beings – minds – which can represent the world to ourselves, thinking and saying what is true or false. Minds are representational engines. This picture of the nature of mind, and hence of ourselves, continues, a century after the *Tractatus*, to be the default conception of the western tradition in cognitive science.

So, the question at the heart of the *Tractatus* is: how is meaningful thought and speech possible? Well, first of all, what, at the most general level, do we think and speak about? We think and speak about things and combinations of things – what Wittgenstein calls "states of affairs". The actual world consists of all the states of affairs – combinations of things – that obtain: the facts. But we can also represent to ourselves what does not obtain – the merely possible – so that, as well as thinking what is true, we can think what is not the case and so think falsely. What must be the case if we can have such true and false meaningful thoughts about the world? A century and a half before the *Tractatus*, Immanuel Kant asked: what must be the case – how must we and the world be – if *experience* is possible? Wittgenstein asks: how must things be if *meaning* is possible?

Wittgenstein's answer is that the world, language and thought must share a common form of elements and their possible arrangements. He calls this "logical form". Elements in our representations of the world, true or false, stand in the same relationship to each other as the elements constituting states of affairs stand to each other. Reality, language, and thought mirror each other. It follows that if we think or say anything meaningful, then what we think or say must be capable of being true or false. Only then will it picture or represent a possible state of affairs. Otherwise, what we say, or think, will not be meaningful.

Of course, this underlying form of reality, language, and thought is not, at least obviously, evident to us when we consider our actual complex, dynamic languages. But in what was to be a gift to the computing sciences that came after, the *Tractatus* shows how complex propositions that are the stuff of actual thought and speech, indeed the very idea of propositional complexity – can be generated from more elementary ones by carrying out the same operation repeatedly: a process of recursive negation. We take a simple proposition, negate it to make a new proposition, then add both to a new set, negate that, and so on. That is, all possible propositions, all possible thoughts, the form of everything that can be thought or said, by any meaning-capable being, can be generated from an elementary set, subject to this same operation, and inheriting the same logical form.

Much of the detail of the *Tractatus* lies in working out these ideas in comparison and contrast to contemporaries including Frege, Russell and others who had also worked in these and adjoining areas. The *Tractatus* did not appear *ex nihilo*.

What is wholly original about the *Tractatus* is how, in the way it gives expression to these ideas about logic and the possibility of meaning, it connects them, via Wittgenstein's own unique cultural inheritance and character, to even greater, though darker, themes. The *Tractatus,* Janus-like, confronts both what lay in the past and anticipates what was to come. Looking back through the *Tractatus* and its author, to the nineteenth century, we see the dark themes of the self, death, God, silence. Looking the other way, forward in time, we see the themes of modernism: self-subversion, a conception of limits and the liminal, the certain confidence of our civilization that science can tell us everything and the anxious conviction of our culture that along this road lies catastrophe. By way of beginning to grasp this connection between the meaning of meaning and the meaning of everything that – according to Wittgenstein – actually matters, we can draw out three implications of the *Tractatus* account.

One implication, only implicit, is this. Consider kinds of mind other than our own. If we think that Dolphins or Great Apes or, for that matter, aliens or A.I s *think*, then, if we follow the *Tractatus*, we must think that the same underlying structures that make meaningful thought and communication possible for us are in place for them too. Scientists studying cetaceans or waiting on signals from the stars can be assured that whatever its surface structure, the underlying structure of such alien communications and signals, if meaningful, will be fundamentally the same as ours. Such beings will, no doubt, think and talk about very different things from us. We may not, likely cannot, know the things they name. But if they do think and communicate meaningfully, then, biology and psychology aside, can we know how this, at least, is possible for them? The answer from the *Tractatus* is: *Yes, as it is for us*: in virtue of the shared form – the isomorphism – of world and thought. It is no accident then that researchers in machine intelligence were to show such interest in this implication of the *Tractatus*. *If* machines can think and speak, we may not understand them, but, according to the *Tractatus*, we can understand *how it is* that they *can* think and speak. And just that idea can be used, now, to build them. In unifying over diverse phenomena in this way – here very different forms of minded life - the *Tractatus* implies that we can do for meaning, something akin to what Newton did for gravity. The unifying, keystone idea of the *Tractatus* is then that meaning, and therefore mind, must be isomorphic with reality.

For the reader curious about how the more mature Wittgenstein of the *Philosophical Investigations* would come to regard his earlier work, we should notice this: the shared structure, which, in the *Tractatus*, makes meaning possible, is entirely independent of the species life of any meaning capable organism: the organism's bodily form, how it brings up its young or interacts with others: the contingencies that make up the weft and weave of its life. For the Wittgenstein of the *Tractatus*, the possibility of meaning is logically separate from how, for any particular creature, it comes about. The possibility of meaning is independent of form of life. This is a key point of contrast between the *Tractatus* and what was to come after in Wittgenstein's *Philosophical Investigations.* The keystone idea of the later work is that it makes no sense to say that living beings, and therefore meaning, are isomorphic with reality. Or to say that they are *not* isomorphic with reality. For the later Wittgenstein, the question of the relation of speaking mind to mute reality has gone wrong as soon as we ask it in those terms. Rather, we must understand living beings as acting and interacting *within* the world. Living and moving *through* it.

A second implication of the *Tractatus*, and more directly addressed, is for values. If I think or claim that my boat is on the lake, then, what makes that thought or claim meaningful is that it may be true or false. But when I think that, say, slavery is wrong, I think something that could not be otherwise than true (even if others should disagree). But then, according to the *Tractatus*, in such ethical thought, I am not representing the world as being one way rather than another. And so, I am not representing anything at all. So strictly speaking, ethical talk will lack meaning. The key to understanding the point of the *Tractatus* is to understand that still, according to Wittgenstein, we are ethical beings. The ethical is real. The demands of logic *and* ethics are inescapable. Teaching us how to live in the light of *that* thought – of the relation between the possibility of meaning and the meaning of everything that really matters is the true aim of the *Tractatus*. To understand why this apparent reverse turn in the argument is key to what the *Tractatus* really concerns, its originality and why it matters, we must consider a third implication: for the nature of philosophy itself.

The general constraint on what can be meaningfully said also applies to what philosophers have wanted to claim over the millennia. Philosophers purport to make claims not about what happens to be true, but what *must* be true. But what then is the status of philosophical theses, including those of the *Tractatus*? For the *Tractatus* itself purports to offer an account of what must be true if meaning is possible.

An analogy. We can use chess notation to describe an actual or possible position on a chess board. But we cannot use chess notation to say *how* chess notation *represents* such chess positions. That shows itself in the way the notation works. How we use the notation. Of course, we can use English (or any other natural language) to say or teach how chess notation works. Just as we can translate one language into another. But when we want to explain or translate not chess notation, or any particular natural language but language *itself* and thought *itself*, that recourse to another medium is not available. What is left? Only the showing.

With the relentless honesty and self-criticism that characterized both his character and his thinking, Wittgenstein applies just this thought to the philosophy of the *Tractatus* itself. It is evident that the relationship between thought and the world that the *Tractatus* purports to articulate is not one among all the facts there are and that we can think about. This relationship is a condition of there being any thinkable or speakable facts at all. Philosophy as envisaged by the *Tractatus*, and including the philosophy of the *Tractatus*, is, therefore, a futile attempt to say what cannot be meaningfully said but which can only show itself. How the world is thinkable will just show itself in our thought, our linguistic behavior, in what we do.

It follows that, philosophy, including the philosophy of the *Tractatus,* insofar as it is possible at all, cannot be a body of doctrines. It must be an activity. It must aim not, like science, at truth and knowledge, but only at clarity and, with the hope of achieving that clarity, a kind of freedom and peace. A freedom from the attempt to articulate what lies outside our representational capacities because it is a condition of the possession of such capacities. A peace which lies in only acknowledging, instead of trying to trap and tame, what is transcendent. The *Tractatus* is then trying to show us something that can't be said or thought and to show us this by saying something that *can* be said or be thought. This is why Wittgenstein claims that the propositions of the *Tractatus* are like rungs on a ladder. We use them to climb up to a position where we can see things as they are, where we can "see the world aright". But then we throw the ladder away. For Wittgenstein, that final discarding was at once a renunciation of the civilization from which he felt so alienated and a liberation from his struggles with the self.

The philosophy of the *Tractatus* then is a profound attempt to articulate a historically dominant conception of ourselves as first and foremost thinkers: representers of the world. It tries to represent ourselves, *to ourselves*, as representers, via the idea of isomorphism, and to do so with absolute consistency. But its conclusion, or better to say, its point, is that the consistent articulation of that representation must ultimately fail. We will be left with what shows itself in the thinking of thoughts, the speaking of words and the living of our lives. Nor can we succeed in articulating what really matters about *how* we should live our lives: the ethical. We can consistently represent to ourselves neither the possibility of meaning nor the possibility of the ethical. With that realization we see that nothing further, philosophically, can be said. To mark that limit there is only the eloquence of silence and what grace we can find in *showing*.

But why then should we care about the philosophy of the *Tractatus*? Would it have been better not to have set out on this journey at all, to have eschewed philosophical investigation of such questions from the beginning? To be content to think and say and mean the ordinary things we do, without asking how such things are possible? To lead a meaningful life as best each of us can manage without questioning why, in some absolute sense, that our lives should matter?

A second analogy. Consider the artistic genre of *trompe l'oeil*. The point of many such paintings is to "deceive the eye", giving the impression of real things in the world, laid out just as they would be in reality. Such painting is ingenious and technically demanding. This is perhaps something like the way the Wittgenstein of the *Tractatus* thinks of the philosophy of his times. Clever and exacting. But, for Wittgenstein, its depth is deceptive: illusory.

What then of the philosophy of the *Tractatus*? In the work of some *trompe l'oeil* artists - great ones, like, say, del Caso[1] - the objects so realistically depicted are only a means to an end. The real point is to teach us something about the nature of pictures, about perception and its limits, about the nature of appearance and the profundity of our relation to the *perceptual surface*. But to learn those lessons, we must, simultaneously, see the objects in the painting as real and know them as illusory.

And something analogous to this is perhaps the real point of the *Tractatus*. Its overt philosophical claims about world, logic and thought are like the depicted objects in a del Caso *trompe l'oeil* painting. We must "understand" those philosophical theses as we must "see" the depicted objects in the painting. We must see **what is painted** and engage with the philosophy of the *Tractatus*. But the point of doing so is not to learn more about the objects depicted or theses articulated, nor to reject them outright as illusory. It is to perceive and think through them. For in this way we learn to accept, or, if one has the character for it, to embrace: *how to live deeply on the surface of things*.

And this, perhaps, is also the point of connection between the *Tractatus* and what was to come after in Wittgenstein's *Philosophical Investigations*. We climb the ladder, throw it away, and then find ourselves, after all, back on the rough surface. And where are we now? We find ourselves back where our Odyssey started. Not further back. But at the beginning. In the midst of our lives.

Home again.

1919–1920: "To a Teachers' College to Become a Teacher"

Xenia Baumann & Students of the College Preparatory School Kundmanngasse in Vienna

And after that I shall embark on a career.
What career? You have time to guess till you come and visit me.

Ludwig Wittgenstein to Paul Engelmann, 2 September 1919[1]

Ludwig Wittgenstein's years as a primary school teacher in Lower Austria are a relatively well-researched part of his biography. In contrast, the year in which he trained as an elementary school teacher in Vienna has received much less attention.

Wittgenstein decided to become a teacher during his war captivity in Cassino. Through reading Tolstoy and Dostojevsky, the desire to lead a simple life and practice a meaningful profession took shape in his mind. Some of his fellow inmates in the POW camp were teachers, among them Ludwig Hänsel and Franz Parak, who immersed themselves, through books and conversations, in the idea of returning to teaching.

Convinced that he had solved all philosophical problems once and for all in the *Tractatus*, Wittgenstein decided to give up philosophy for good. At first, he thought of entering a monastery and becoming a monk, but Ludwig Hänsel advised him against this. It was Hänsel who encouraged Wittgenstein to become a teacher and who arranged a place for him at the teacher training college in the Sophienbrückengasse (later Kundmanngasse) in Vienna's third district.

On 21 August 1919, both men were released from captivity in Italy together with their comrades and started their way home to Austria. Wittgenstein arrived in Vienna at the beginning of September and initially spent about ten days at the Hochreit, the summer residence of the Wittgenstein family in Lower Austria.

At first, the family barely understood Ludwig's sudden ambition to become a teacher. His oldest sister Hermine wrote later:

Photograph for Wittgenstein's teaching license, 1919–20
© Wittgenstein Initiative

When I thought of him with his philosophically trained mind as an elementary schoolteacher it seemed to be like somebody wanting to use a precision instrument to open crates. Ludwig replied with an analogy that reduced me to silence. He said, 'You remind me of somebody who is looking out through a closed window and cannot explain to himself the strange movements of a passerby. He cannot tell what sort of storm is raging out there or that this person might only be managing with difficulty to stay on his feet.' Then I understood the state of mind he was in.

Hermine Wittgenstein: *My brother Ludwig*[2]

It was not only to his family that Wittgenstein felt he had to justify his decision to become a teacher, but to other people too. Moreover, immediately after his return from captivity, he had renounced his inherited fortune and divided it among his siblings Hermine, Helene and Paul. His experiences during the war, his period in captivity, and his subsequent decision to give up philosophy were a series of profound ruptures that would shape the next decade of Wittgenstein's life.

His letters from 1919 and 1920 do not give the impression that his new vocational choice had made him happier. In letters to Paul Engelmann, he repeatedly referred to suicidal thoughts and also commented on the horror of catching himself thinking about suicide, for example on 21 June 1920:

I know that to kill oneself is always a dirty thing to do. Surely one <u>cannot</u> will one's own destruction, and anybody who has visualized what is in practice involved in the act of suicide knows that suicide is always a <u>rushing of one's own defenses</u>. But nothing is worse than to be forced to take oneself by surprise.[3]

His two changes of address within the short space of nine months give the impression of a restless mind. He first gave up his dark sublet in the Untere Viaduktgasse, within walking distance of the teacher training college, to move in with friends – the Sjögren family – in the 13th district. However, when it transpired that the family's mother, the widow Mima Sjögren, was falling in love with Ludwig, he hastily moved out. Mrs. Sjögren's attempts to persuade him to return or to give an explanation for his departure are evidenced by the many letters she sent him in the spring of 1920. In addition, the search for a publisher for the *Tractatus* was a recurring subject in his correspondence throughout the school year. During

The school building in Sophienbrückengasse around 1900. The entrance to the teacher training college is visible in the lower right corner.
© Archive Dr. Christoph Römer, 1030 Vienna

the last months of the school year, Wittgenstein stayed with the Zimmermanns, a family who lived directly behind the teacher training college in the Rasumofskygasse.

The teacher training college as an institution

Maria Theresa's 1774 introduction of compulsory schooling for children in all the Habsburg hereditary lands necessitated the creation of teacher training institutions. Thus, from 1775 onwards, so-called *Normalschulen* (normal schools) were founded for this purpose, which were renamed *Lehrerbildungsanstalten* (teacher training colleges) following a further school reform in 1869. The one where Wittgenstein spent the school year 1919–20 had an even older history. Founded as the "School at St. Stephen's" in 1263, it became the first *Normalschule* in 1771. From 1775 it was housed for more than a century in the Monastery of St. Anne in downtown Vienna until the new school building in the Sophienbrückengasse was completed in October 1877. This was built on the site of the former Palais Rasumofsky as an almost mirror image of the side wing of the palace, but one floor higher. During Wittgenstein's time, Palais Rasumofsky housed the Imperial Geological Institute, and the garden of the palace was

The school building seen from the garden. The teacher training college was housed mainly in the rooms with the windows on the left side of the picture.
© Archive Dr. Christoph Römer, 1030 Vienna

available to the teacher training college as an experimental garden for the subjects of natural history and agriculture.[4]

The teacher training college shared the school building with the Landstraßer Gymnasium (college preparatory school), founded in 1869, which is still housed there today. This was built in the neoclassical style by the architect Frantisek Schmoranz Jr. The street was still called Sophienbrückengasse, even at the beginning of Wittgenstein's training, and was only renamed Kundmanngasse (after the sculptor Carl Kundmann) at the end of 1919. This was an outcome of the City of Vienna's plan to do away with street names that recalled the monarchy that had fallen in 1918, and Sophienbrückengasse was named after none other than the mother of Emperor Franz Joseph I.[5]

The year 1919 also marked a shift in education policy, when the education minister Otto Glöckel launched his pioneering school reform. This involved a democratization of schooling, a move away from "drill schools," the abolition of compulsory religious instruction, and free access to higher education for women. Wittgenstein's motivation for becoming a teacher was only partly aligned with Glöckel's agenda. His wish was to live a simple life with ordinary people in the countryside, to help them improve their lives. Although he was never a particularly devout individual, he intended to do this with the help of the Gospel, thereby revealing goals that differed from those of Glöckel.

He did not endorse all of Glöckel's approaches. Thus, his later fellow teacher in Puchberg, Rudolf Koder, wrote in his memoirs:

> *L. W. was never a supporter of Glöckel's school reform, he made fun of its excesses (e.g., cutting toilet paper in handicraft classes). He also never read the magazines 'Die Schulreform' (The School Reform) and 'Die Quelle' (The Source), which were very much propagated at that time. But although he was not a supporter of the school reform, in certain respects he taught in its spirit (e.g., self-activity of the pupils in the lessons, vividness of the teaching). He did this, however, not because it was demanded by the school reform, but because he thought it was the right thing to do. He would have worked in this way in school even without Glöckel. For example, he prepared the skeleton of a cat and reassembled the bones with a lot of care and perseverance, in order to be able to illustrate the physique of a predator to his pupils. Or: he had a carpenter make a potter's wheel according to his instructions, so that the children could try molding clay themselves.*[6]

The teacher training college continued to experience a very eventful history throughout the interwar period and after the Nazi annexation of Austria in 1938. The Nazification process of "Gleichschaltung" was reflected in the adaptation of the curricula to the goals and ideology of the regime. Staff and students with Jewish roots were expelled from the school. During the war, the school building was evacuated several times, and it was not until 1947 that regular school operations were resumed. In the 1960s, teacher training was fundamentally reformed and converted into a course of study taught at pedagogical academies. The last class of the teacher training college in the Kundmanngasse graduated in 1967.

The archive of the teacher training college, which is rich in documents but not without gaps, was handed over to the Archives of the Austrian Academy of Sciences a few years ago. It mainly contains class registers, examination records, a school chronicle and nine photographs of the premises from the 1902–3 school year.[7]

Ludwig Wittgenstein's daily life at the teacher training college

The teacher training college was an upper secondary school with four grades, but graduating it did not make students eligible for university studies. Wittgenstein had already completed such a course in Berlin and taken the Matura (graduation examination) beforehand, which set him apart from most of his classmates. He was listed in the class register as pupil no. 42 (out of 43 in total), and his address with the Sjögren family was noted as his place of residence. Although he was already 30 years old and a war veteran, the records list his mother Leopoldine Wittgenstein, living in Hochreit, Lower Austria, as his guardian. It is not known whether Wittgenstein was aware of this, or what he thought about it.[8]

As a 30-year-old man, Wittgenstein was by far the oldest in his class and felt awkward among his classmates. In a letter to Paul Engelmann of 25 September 1919, he wrote:

> *I'm attending a teacher training college in order to become a schoolmaster. So once again I sit in a schoolroom, and this sounds funnier than it is. In fact I find it terribly hard; I can no longer behave like a grammar-school boy, and – funny as it sounds – the humiliation is so great for me that I often think I can hardly bear it!*[9]

A little later, in a letter of 6 October 1919, he contacted Bertrand Russell with a similar message:

> *I have made up my mind to become a teacher and so must go back to school, at a so-called teacher training college. The benches are full of boys of 17 or 18 and I've reached 30. That leads to some very funny situations – and many very unpleasant ones too. I often feel miserable!*[10]

Wittgenstein also wished to keep a low profile and not be recognized as the son of a rich industrialist family. On 20 September 1919, he wrote to Ludwig Hänsel, who had arranged his place at the college:

> *My life is not without its difficulties. Today a teacher asked me if I was related to the rich Wittgensteins. I said 'yes'; whether closely related, there I lied and said 'no, distantly.' This is a point that may yet become fateful.*[11]

On the basis of his Matura certificate from the *Realschule* in Linz in 1906, Wittgenstein was deemed as proficient in many school subjects. This was indicated in the class register with an "M" next to the respective school subject. Similarly, this was the case with about ten others who were also career switchers in the teaching profession and had, for example, begun to study medicine. Only in pedagogy, teaching methodology, natural history, agriculture,

Wittgenstein's report pages from the class register of the fourth year of the teacher training college, school year 1919–20.
© Archive of the Austrian Academy of Sciences, St. Anna, No. 471a, p. 42

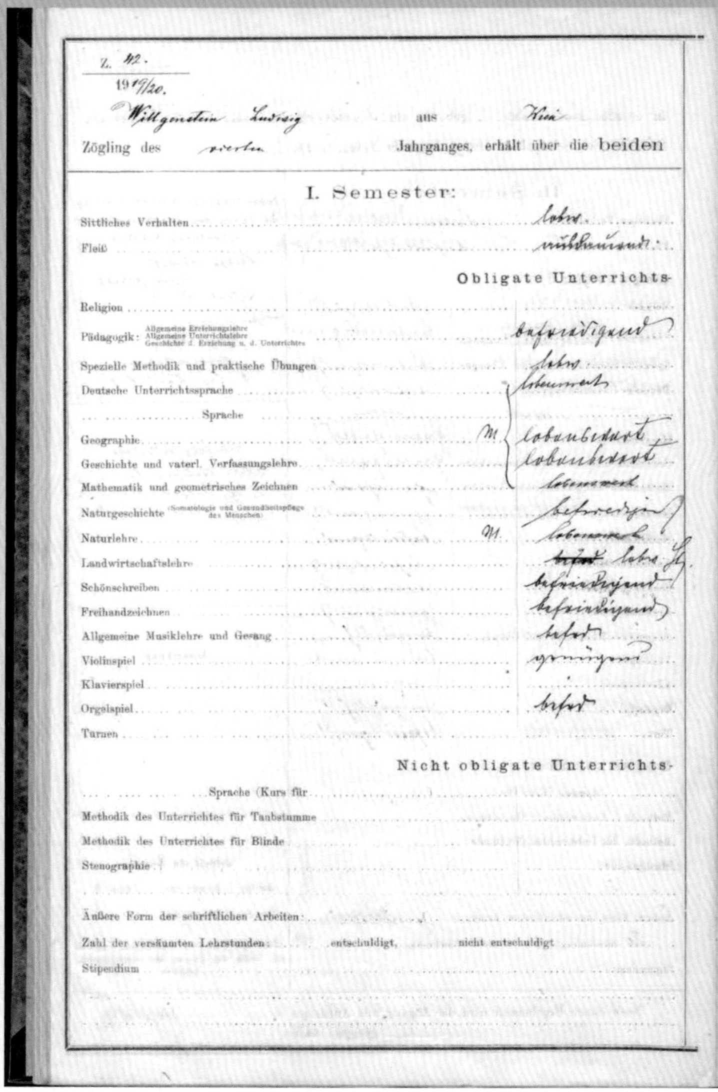
Z. 42.

1919/20.

Wittgenstein Ludwig aus Wien

Zögling des vierten Jahrganges, erhält über die beiden

I. Semester:

Sittliches Verhalten

Fleiß

Obligate Unterrichts-

Religion

Pädagogik: Allgemeine Erziehungslehre, Allgemeine Unterrichtslehre, Geschichte d. Erziehung u. d. Unterrichtes

Spezielle Methodik und praktische Übungen

Deutsche Unterrichtssprache

Sprache

Geographie

Geschichte und vaterl. Verfassungslehre

Mathematik und geometrisches Zeichnen

Naturgeschichte (Somatologie und Gesundheitspflege des Menschen)

Naturlehre

Landwirtschaftslehre

Schönschreiben

Freihandzeichnen

Allgemeine Musiklehre und Gesang

Violinspiel

Klavierspiel

Orgelspiel

Turnen

Nicht obligate Unterrichts-

Sprache (Kurs für)

Methodik des Unterrichtes für Taubstumme

Methodik des Unterrichtes für Blinde

Stenographie

Äußere Form der schriftlichen Arbeiten:

Zahl der versäumten Lehrstunden: entschuldigt, nicht entschuldigt

Stipendium

in *Nd. Österreich*, geboren am *26. April 1889, röm. kath.* Konfession,

Semester des Schuljahres 19*19/20* folgende Noten, u. zw.:

II. Semester:

Sittliches Verhalten ... *lobenswert*

Fleiß ... *ausdauernd*

Gegenstände:

Religion	—
Pädagogik: Allgemeine Erziehungslehre, Allgemeine Unterrichtslehre, Geschichte d. Erziehung u. d. Unterrichtes	*lobenswert*
Spezielle Methodik und prakt. Übungen	*lobenswert*
Deutsche Unterrichtssprache	—
... Sprache	—
Geographie	—
Geschichte und vaterl. Verfassungslehre	—
Mathematik und geometrisches Zeichnen	—
Naturgeschichte (Somatologie und Gesundheitspflege des Menschen)	*befriedigend*
Naturlehre	—
Landwirtschaftslehre	*lobenswert*
Schönschreiben	*befriedigend*
Freihandzeichnen	*befriedigend*
Allgemeine Musiklehre und Gesang	*lobenswert*
Violinspiel	*befriedigend*
Klavierspiel	—
Orgelspiel	*befriedigend*
Turnen	*Wert.* —

Gegenstände:

... Sprache (Kurs für ...)	
Methodik d. Unterrichtes f. Taubstumme	
Methodik des Unterrichtes für Blinde	
Stenographie	
...	

Äußere Form der schriftlichen Arbeiten: ... +

18 entschuldigt, — nicht entschuldigt

Stipendium ...

Name, Stand und Wohnort (Wohnung) des Vaters, resp. Vormundes oder verantwortlichen Aufsehers

Leopoldine Wittgenstein
Private
Hochreit
Post Hohenberg N. Ö.
Wohnung: Neue Gasse
III. St. Veitg. 17

Vorbildung des Zöglings

Realschulmatura Linz,
Univ. Cambridge

Anmerkung

Erhielt ein Zeugnis

über das I. Semester vom ... Februar 19..

über das II. Semester vom ... 19..

Wenn kein besonderer Behebungstag eingesetzt ist, wurde das Zeugnis am Ausstellungstage behoben.

Nach diesen Ergebnissen wird der Zögling zum Aufsteigen in den ... Jahrgang als ... geeignet erklärt.

calligraphy, free-hand drawing, music, violin playing and organ playing did Wittgenstein and the other career switchers receive the same instruction as everyone else. He completed all the pedagogical school subjects with a grade of "commendable," which is equivalent to a "B."

Like all other trainee teachers, Wittgenstein regularly shadowed the five classes of the training elementary school. Teaching tests were held in these classes a few times a year in the presence of the director, a subject teacher and the teacher of the training school class.[12]

The school building during the era of the teacher training college

Completed in 1877, the school building was divided into two parts. However, the partition walls in the corridors were located in different places on each floor. The teacher training college had more rooms on the first floor, while the preparatory school had more on the second floor. There was little contact between the two schools. However, there were students who experienced all three levels of the educational system in the school building during the course of their school careers, graduating from the model elementary school, spending the lower grades in the preparatory school, and then attending the teacher training college.

The school building was symmetrically designed and had two entrances. The teacher training college was accessed at that time through the ground floor entrance, which is used today only as an emergency exit from the basement of the preparatory school. At that time, the stairs from the entrance gate led up to the first floor. The only trace of the teacher training college in the school building today is a memorial plaque in the former entrance area. This honors three professors who retired in 1913 with the dedication *Den Lehrerbildnern, in Treue, ihre Schüler* (To the teacher trainers, from their loyal students). Whether this plaque was hanging as early as 1919 or 1920 cannot be conclusively determined. The school chronicle, which was maintained very thoroughly from 1877 to 1910, contains many lacunae afterwards.

According to the building plans, the classes of the teacher training college were taught on the second floor, in the part of the building facing Geusaugasse. Some classes also had their windows facing the garden of the former Rasumofsky Palace. Class 4 of the teacher training college had its classroom where the chemistry room of the Kundmanngasse preparatory school is located today.

The room of the teacher training college's 4th year in 1902–1903.

A subject which was not included in the curriculum of the teacher training college in 1919–20 is thus taught there today.

The classrooms were very cramped at the time, and in most cases were packed with over 40 students. They were equipped with the usual school desks of the time. The walls were paneled with wood up to a height of about one meter in order to protect the brickwork. The window niches were also decoratively paneled with wood, while the windows and doors were painted dark brown. Instead of a checkroom, there were coat hooks for jackets and hats in the classes. Some classrooms had chests for storing materials, as well as the musical instruments that were needed for the music lessons. Since the schoolhouse was not fully electrified until 1925,[13] there were gas pipes and lamps on the ceiling throughout the building, even in Wittgenstein's time. In the photos from 1902–3, however, the classrooms are only very sparsely fitted with white glass lampshades, and it can be assumed that some of them repeatedly broke. The classrooms used to be heated with coal stoves, sometimes from the hallway. The only two entries in the school chronicle for the whole of 1919 concern building-related processes. Due to fuel shortages after World War I, the school experimented with alternatives such as coal dust and fuel residues, achieving higher temperatures with these than with coal. The second entry records façade repairs as an employment measure for the unemployed[14] and to repair war

The first-grade training school 1902–3 during an observation lesson.

damage. The area of the first floor adjacent to the Geusaugasse housed the model classrooms, where the trainee teachers sat in on elementary school lessons and occasionally practiced teaching themselves. Desks and benches were placed at the back of each room for the observing trainee teachers.

At that time, the elementary school was an all-boys school with five classes of up to 45 pupils each. The class registers detail the children's home addresses, occupations of their fathers, and religious confessions. This information shows that nearly all the children lived in the immediate vicinity of the school and the vast majority were Roman Catholic, while 15–20% of the pupils were Jewish and a smaller proportion were Protestant (Augsburg and Helvetic Confessions). Most of the fathers had skilled professional jobs and counted many civil servants, lawyers, merchants, doctors, military personnel and professors among their number, as well as engineers and a few craftsmen.[15] The elementary school enjoyed a good reputation, because the teachers there were trained in the latest teaching practices and the children were taught by experienced teachers.

The shortage of essential resources in the post-war period evidently also affected the health of the children. The class records show that a number of students had many (excused) absences. Next to the records of absences, it is often noted: "Could not be classified (= moved up a grade) due to sickness-related absences." As a result, some children continued to be taught at home as so-called privatists, only to take an annual examination as external students. One boy from the third grade in 1919–20 died after a long illness.[16]

In his letters, Wittgenstein wrote twice about the children in the training elementary school. On 19 February 1920, he told Paul Engelmann:

> *The one good thing in my life just now is that I sometimes read fairy-tales to the children at school. It pleases them and relieves the strain on me.*[17]

And in September 1920, at the beginning of his teaching career in Trattenbach, he compared the children there with those from the training elementary school:

> *I also like the children here, because thank God there is no comparison between them and the disgusting devious gang in Vienna.*[18]

Were the differences between city and country schools already apparent at that time?

Wittgenstein was very eager to live a scrupulously honest life (not only as a teacher) and therefore was curious to know how others evaluated the quality of his work. According to Leopold Baumruck, a classmate of his at the teacher training college, Wittgenstein had a good relationship with the principal, Dr. Rudolf Latzke. The principal's office was on the first floor, overlooking the garden. Today, the teachers' kitchenette can be found where Wittgenstein spent the breaks talking to Latzke,[19] according to Leopold Baumruck. However, to get Latzke's professional opinion, Wittgenstein sent his friend Ludwig Hänsel to his office.

On 2 March 1920, Wittgenstein and Hänsel met briefly in the school building when he was on his way to inquire about Wittgenstein's performance with Latzke. According to his letter on the same day, Wittgenstein was in a hurry because his next teaching test was imminent. In a letter dated 5 March 1920, Hänsel informed Wittgenstein about the details of his conversation with the principal:

The property Kundmanngasse No. 19 (on the right), long before the construction of Palais Stonborough by Ludwig Wittgenstein in 1926–28.
© Archive Dr. Christoph Römer, 1030 Vienna

Wittgenstein (standing, far right) with his pupils in Otterthal, Lower Austria, 1925.
© Stonborough Family

> *The principal, Dr. Latzke "elaborated" with all due seriousness that the entire faculty had unanimously expressed its praise of you: serious... knows what he is doing... white raven among high school graduates.... great respect [for you] ... also in your model teaching. Even more confident than when asking questions in class.... wishes only that he would find in this profession the satisfaction that he seeks in it...*[20]

Wittgenstein remained in contact with Dr. Latzke later on. In 1921, he had some pipe tobacco sent to him. In 1924, with Latzke's support, he published a dictionary for elementary schools at the publishing house Hölder-Pichler-Tempsky, since at that time there was no spelling dictionary that seemed suitable to him for teaching. Apart from the *Tractatus*, this was Wittgenstein's only publication during his lifetime.

After his year at the teacher training college, Wittgenstein worked as a teacher in Lower Austria for another six years, before turning to architecture. Together with his friend Paul Engelmann, he designed a house for his sister Margaret Stonborough, located directly opposite the teacher training college. The choice of Kundmanngasse No. 19 as the location was pure coincidence and had nothing to do with the time that her brother spent there as a trainee teacher.

This article was originally written in German by two philosophy classes taught by Xenia Baumann at the Kundmanngasse Preparatory College School in Vienna's third district. The classes explored both the history of their schoolhouse and its relation to one of the most important philosophers of the 20th century.

1919–1922: "Pearls before Swine ..." The Difficult Publication History of the *Tractatus Logico-Philosophicus*

Alfred Schmidt

"As far as I am concerned, you can show the manuscript to the philosophy professor (although showing a philosophical work to a professor of philosophy is like casting pearls ...). At any rate he won't understand a word of it."

Ludwig Wittgenstein to Ludwig von Ficker,
22 November 1919.[1]

Viewed at a remove of one hundred years, the troublesome publication odyssey of Wittgenstein's *Tractatus Logico-Philosophicus* – one of the most influential philosophical works of the 20th century – can seem absurd and incomprehensible. The fact that the work's fundamental intellectual significance was not immediately recognized is not surprising, however, considering that Wittgenstein was a completely unknown name in philosophy at the time and he was not established academically either. Above all, his work broke completely new ground, both in form and content, in a way that could only cause irritation. This lack of understanding was probably no surprise to Wittgenstein himself, since even his closest philosophical kinsmen and teachers – such as Gottlob Frege – did not know what to do with the work at first.[2]

In the following article, I will attempt to trace the path from the completion of the typescripts 202 and 204 of the *Logisch-philosophische Abhandlung* (hereafter LPA) in August 1918 to the publication of the bilingual edition of the *Tractatus Logico-Philosophicus* (TLP) in London in November 1922.[3] In particular, it is Wittgenstein's correspondence that allows a fairly accurate reconstruction of the individual stages leading up to publication.

Jahoda & Siegel

We can assume that Wittgenstein dictated the LPA in the form of typescript 204 during his last extended furlough at the end of August 1918, while the later and more important Ts 202 was produced concurrently as a carbon copy. (The question of how it was possible for Wittgenstein to dictate the LPA in the version of Ts 204/202 on the basis of the manuscript 104 – the so-called

"*Prototractatus*" – has still not been fully clarified and cannot be further addressed here.)[4]

Wittgenstein's search for a publisher began immediately after the completion of the typescripts 202/204, which shows that he was very keen to have his treatise published as soon as possible, in contrast to his hesitant attitude towards publications in his later years. In September 1918, he sent the typescript (most probably Ts 204) to the publishing house Jahoda & Siegel, which, as Karl Kraus's publisher, was apparently his first choice. Whether this was also done with the ulterior motive that Kraus might put in a good word for him and thereby dispel any doubt on the part of the publisher remains an open question.[5] In his letter to Paul Engelmann of 9 October 1918, he already complains that the publisher "*has still not condescended to give me his judgment*."[6] And in his next letter to Engelmann of 22 October 1918, he repeats: "*Still no reply from the publisher! And I feel an insuperable repugnance against writing to him with a query. The devil knows what he is doing with my manuscript. Perhaps he is examining it chemically as to its fitness.*" By this time, however, the publisher's negative decision had already been made. In a letter dated 21 October 1918, Hermine Wittgenstein informed her brother that Jahoda had rejected the book, adding a few words of consolation about the exceptionally unfavorable circumstances at the time: "*I heard last year about someone who*

Annals of Natural Philosophy
No. 14 (1921), issue 374
© ANL

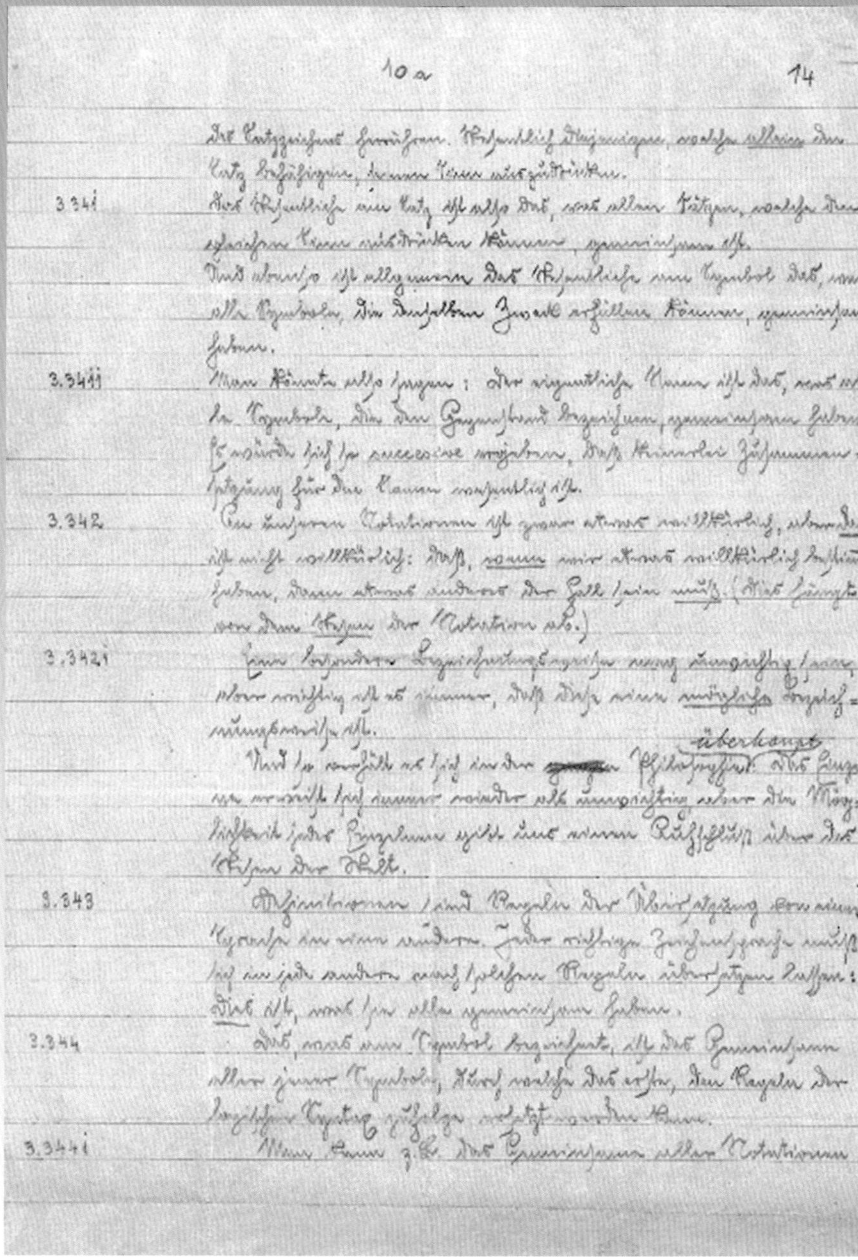

10 a 14

das Satzzeichen herrühren. Wesentlich diejenigen, welche *allein* den Satz befähigen, seinen Sinn auszudrücken.

3.341 Das Wesentliche am Satz ist also das, was allen Sätzen, welche den gleichen Sinn ausdrücken können, gemeinsam ist.
Und ebenso ist allgemein das Wesentliche am Symbol das, was alle Symbole, die denselben Zweck erfüllen können, gemeinsam haben.

3.3411 Man könnte also sagen: der eigentliche Name ist das, was alle Symbole, die den Gegenstand bezeichnen, gemeinsam haben. Es würde sich so successive ergeben, daß keinerlei Zusammensetzung für den Namen wesentlich ist.

3.342 An unseren Notationen ist zwar etwas willkürlich, aber *das* ist nicht willkürlich: Daß, *wenn* wir etwas willkürlich bestimmt haben, dann etwas anderes der Fall sein *muß*. (Dies hängt von dem *Wesen* der Notation ab.)

3.3421 Eine besondere Bezeichnungsweise mag unwichtig sein, aber wichtig ist es immer, daß diese eine *mögliche* Bezeichnungsweise ist.
Und so verhält es sich in der ~~[illegible]~~ Philosophie überhaupt: Das Einzelne erweist sich immer wieder als unwichtig, aber die Möglichkeit jedes Einzelnen gibt uns einen Aufschluß über das Wesen der Welt.

3.343 Definitionen sind Regeln der Übersetzung von einer Sprache in eine andere. Jede richtige Zeichensprache muß sich in jede andere nach solchen Regeln übersetzen lassen: *Dies* ist, was sie alle gemeinsam haben.

3.344 Das, was am Symbol bezeichnet, ist das Gemeinsame aller jener Symbole, durch welche das erste, den Regeln der logischen Syntax zufolge, ersetzt werden kann.

3.3441 Man kann z.B. das Gemeinsame aller Notationen

The handwritten page 10a copied by Hänsel, which remained in Ts 204, where it still can be found today *undertook to deliver 1000 pigs for the publication of his book, but I'm afraid you won't want to do that!"*[7]

Karl Kraus
© ANL

Technical difficulties were given as the reason for the rejection, as Wittgenstein later explained to Engelmann in a letter of 25 October 1918. This is understandable, considering that the *Treatise* is full of logical and mathematical special characters that would have made tricky demands on the printer. In the same letter to Engelmann, Wittgenstein wrote: *"I would very much like to know what Kraus said about it. If you had the opportunity to find out, I would be very pleased. Perhaps Loos knows something."*

On 3 November 1918, Wittgenstein was taken prisoner of war in Italy. Anxious weeks of uncertainty followed, during which all contact with the family was broken off. His brother Paul placed advertisements in the press inquiring about Ludwig's whereabouts, addressed to his war comrades returning home:

> *Request to returning officers and soldiers. Officers and soldiers who know more about the whereabouts and condition of Lieutenant Ludwig Wittgenstein, Mountain Artillery Regiment No. 11, Battery 8, last battery commander in Como near Gallio di Miletta, are requested to send their messages to Paul*

Wittgenstein, Vienna, 4th district, Alleegasse 16.
(Neue Freie Presse, 6 December 1918).[8]

It was not until the end of December 1918 that a telegram arrived from Ludwig in captivity.

Hermine had already sent a copy of the LPA to Frege on 24 December 1918.[9] In view of this, and by drawing on a meticulous reconstruction by Gerd Graßhoff and Timm Lampert,[10] we can clarify the mystery of the handwritten page 10a in Ts 204. In Ts 204, which had remained with Hermine in Vienna, there was evidently a missing page, namely from sentence 3.34 (2nd part) to 3.411. This page was therefore also missing in the copy for Frege, which is now lost. Hermine then asked her brother to copy the missing page from Ts 202, which he had with him in the prison camp in Italy.[11] Wittgenstein apparently did not do this himself, but asked Ludwig Hänsel, whom he had met in the prison camp, to do it for him. This is why sheet 10a in Ts 204 shows Hänsel's handwriting rather than Wittgenstein's. Hermine received the missing page and had it typed for Frege. On 3 March 1919, she wrote to Ludwig: *"The copied manuscript page is being sent to Frege today."*

Braumüller

The next stages in the publication history of the *Tractatus* only occurred after Wittgenstein's return from captivity at the end of August 1919. Immediately afterwards, in September 1919, he sent Ts 204 to Braumüller. This renowned Viennese scholarly publishing house, a family business with a rich history going back to its founding in 1783, had recently enjoyed great success with Otto Weininger's *Sex and Character* (first edition 1903; by 1925, the book was in its 26th edition) and Oswald Spengler's *The Decline of the West* (Vol. 1, 1918). Wittgenstein admired both authors,[12] which was perhaps a motive for approaching this publisher. However, Braumüller insisted on an appraisal by an expert, for which Wittgenstein approached Bertrand Russell.[13] Russell was already familiar with the LPA at this point, since he had received Ts 202 via John Maynard Keynes in June 1919, while Wittgenstein was still held captive in Monte Cassino.[14] Despite a glowing letter of recommendation from Russell, Braumüller insisted that the printing and paper costs be borne by Wittgenstein himself, which he indignantly rejected, as he wrote in a letter to Ludwig von Ficker around 7 October 1919:

> *(Of course, I told him quite frankly that he would not make any money with my book since no one will read it, even less understand it.) … Second, I could get the money, but I do not want to, for I consider it to be indecent to force a work upon the world – to which the publisher belongs – in this way. The writing was my affair; but the world must accept it in the normal manner.*

Thus, the second attempt at publication likewise ended in failure.

Frege and the Brenner

In September 1919, Wittgenstein began his training at the teacher training college in the Kundmanngasse in Vienna's third district, only a few steps away from the property on which the house for his sister Margaret was to be built a few years later. In his further efforts to have the LPA published, Wittgenstein turned first to Gottlob Frege. After a long period of silence, Frege responded to the sending of the LPA with an in-depth letter dated 28 June 1919, in which he quite openly pointed out numerous ambiguities in the text. Wittgenstein commented on this in a letter to his sister Hermine, making the remark quoted earlier, that Frege had probably understood nothing of his treatise.[15] Nevertheless, Wittgenstein asked him to support the publication of the treatise in the journal "*Contributions to the Philosophy of German Idealism,*" in which Frege's article

Bertrand Russell
© ANL

Gottlob Frege
Wikimedia Commons

"Der Gedanke" (The Thought)[16] had just appeared.[17] Frege replied on 30 September 1919 that he would recommend Wittgenstein to the editors as a *"serious thinker,"* but that he could not assess the LPA itself: *"not because I do not agree with the content, but because the content is not clear enough to me."* Furthermore, Frege pointed out the hopelessness of approaching this journal, if only because of the sheer scope of the work, which would fill an entire number. We learn about the unsuccessful outcome of this attempt from Wittgenstein's letter to Ludwig von Ficker, written around 7 October 1919:

> *Finally I turned to a professor in Germany who knows the publisher of a sort of philosophical journal. From him I received the promise to take over the work if I would mutilate it from beginning to end, and, in a word, make another work out of it.*

It is only now that Wittgenstein remembered Ludwig von Ficker, the editor of the *Brenner* journal. Shortly before the outbreak of the First World War, he had asked Ficker to distribute a generous donation to writers in need, and could therefore be assured of Ficker's goodwill. The following correspondence with Ficker contains some of the most interesting and important documents relating to the *Tractatus*. In the letter already quoted (around 7 October 1919), Wittgenstein first summarizes all the previous unsuccessful attempts at publication, before finally offering the LPA to Ficker for the *Brenner*. This is followed by a highly interesting characterization of the work: *"The work is strictly philosophical and at the same time literary, but there is no babbling in it."*

Wittgenstein's claim to have created both a philosophical *and* a literary work is noteworthy and obviously directly related to the LPA's very peculiar form of presentation.[18] Towards the end of October 1919, Ficker received the manuscript together with a letter from Wittgenstein. In this well-known letter, which is reproduced below in full, Wittgenstein refers to the unwritten second part of the LPA as being the actual important part:

> *Dear Mr. Ficker!*
>
> *I am sending the manuscript to you together with this letter. Why didn't I immediately think of you? Believe me, I did think of you right away; however, at a time when the book could not yet be published, because it was not finished yet. When it had come to that point, however, we were at war, and it wasn't possible to think of your help. Now, however, I am pinning my hopes on you. And it will probably be helpful for you if I write a few words about my book: For you won't – I really believe – get too much*

out of reading it. Because you won't understand it; the content will seem quite strange to you. In reality, it isn't strange to you, for the point of the book is ethical. I once wanted to give a few words in the foreword which now actually are not in it, which, however, I'll write to you now because they might be a key for you: I wanted to write that my work consists of two parts: of the one which is here, and of everything which I have not written. And precisely this second part is the important one. For the Ethical is delimited from within, as it were, by my book; and I am convinced that, strictly speaking, it can ONLY be delimited in this way. In brief, I think: All of that which many are babbling today, I have defined in my book by remaining silent about it. Therefore the book will, unless I'm quite wrong, have much to say which you want to say yourself, but perhaps you won't notice that it is said in it. For the time being, I'd recommend that you read the foreword and the conclusion since these express the point most directly. –

The MS which I'm sending you now isn't the corrected version, but only a hastily corrected copy, which will, however, suffice for your orientation. The corrected copy has been thoroughly revised; presently, however, it is in England with my friend Russell, to whom I sent it while in captivity. He will be sending it back to me shortly, however. And thus I wish myself a lot of luck for the time being.

Frank Plumpton Ramsey
Wikimedia Commons

Ludwig von Ficker
© ANL

Paul Engelmann
Wikimedia Commons

With kind regards,

Sincerely yours,
Ludwig Wittgenstein

My present address is:
XIII St. Veitgasse 17
with Mrs. Sjögren

Ficker was at a loss: on the one hand he did not want to disappoint his generous patron, but on the other he was obviously deeply skeptical about the idea of publishing the LPA in the *Brenner*. In his letter of 18 November 1919, he openly expressed his reservations, but at the same time offered to look for another publisher, with Rainer Maria Rilke's help. He also signaled that he would like to show the work to a professor at the "local university." Although the aforementioned professor[19] – as Ficker notes in his letter – was familiar with Russell's work, Wittgenstein reacted angrily in his reply of 22 November 1919:

> *Your letter, naturally, wasn't pleasant for me, although I wasn't really surprised by your answer. I don't know where I can get my work accepted either. If I myself were only somewhere else than in this lousy world! –*
>
> *As far as I'm concerned, you can show the manuscript to the philosophy professor (although showing a philosophical work to a professor of philosophy is like casting pearls ...) At any rate he won't understand a word of it.*

Ficker – obviously dismayed by Wittgenstein's violent reaction – relented and replied that in order not to disappoint the trust placed in him, he wanted to print the work, even at the risk of jeopardizing his own existence as a publisher. At the same time, he cautiously inquired whether Wittgenstein might be willing to dispense with the decimal numbering of his sentences. At first, Wittgenstein did indeed seem willing to accept Ficker's offer,[20] but only two days later he retracted it, explaining that he did not want to endanger Ficker's financial viability by publishing his treatise. He adopted a conciliatory tone and showed interest in Rilke's efforts to find another publisher (presumably Insel). Ficker's final refusal regarding publication in the *Brenner* came a little later in his letter of 16 January 1920:

> *With or without Russell: the printing of your treatise is, under the present circumstances, a risk that no publisher in Austria can take on today. Least of all me, for I am already at my wit's end with my journal.*

Reclam Verlag

Even before this, however, the prospects of publication had improved considerably. From 12 to 27 December 1919, Wittgenstein had met with Bertrand Russell in The Hague,[21] where he tried to explain the LPA to him in detail. While still in The Hague, Wittgenstein wrote to Paul Engelmann, apparently in good spirits, that Russell had suggested a bilingual German and English edition of the *Treatise* and was also willing to write a preface.[22] In another letter to Paul Engelmann dated 29 December 1919, Wittgenstein mentions the Reclam publishing house for the first time. Reclam seemed actually willing to print the LPA together with Russell's introduction.[23] Wittgenstein received Russell's introduction at the beginning of April 1920[24] and had it translated into German. The result of this translation, however, was so unacceptable to Wittgenstein that he informed Russell that he did not wish to have the introduction printed,[25] even at the risk that Reclam would not print the work at all – a prediction that ultimately came to pass. On 30 May 1920, he notified Engelmann that the publisher had pulled out: *"Reclam won't take my book. I don't care about it now, and that's good."*

This marked the end of the first phase in the *Tractatus's* publication history. At this point, a frustrated Wittgenstein gave up trying to find a publisher himself. In a letter of 7 July 1920, he put the practicalities of publication into Russell's hands, authorizing him to proceed entirely as he saw fit.

7 July 1920

Dear Russell!

Very many thanks for your kind letter! Reclam has, naturally, not accepted my book and for the moment I won't take any further steps to have it published. But if you feel like getting it printed, it is entirely at your disposal and you can do what you like with it. (Only, if you change anything in the text, indicate that the change was made by you.)[26]

The "pirate print" in the *Annalen der Naturphilosophie* and Ogden's bilingual edition, London 1922

As Russell was travelling to China for an extended stay in the fall of 1920, he entrusted the matter to Dorothy Wrinch, a young scholarly protégé of his. At first, she too had little success: Cambridge University Press refused to print the LPA.[27] Wrinch then turned to several German journal editors, including Wilhelm Ostwald, who had published his *Annalen der Naturphilosophie* (*Annals of Natural Philosophy)* in Leipzig since 1901. Ostwald, a successful chemist and Nobel Prize winner, was primarily interested in interweaving philosophy and science from a monistic perspective. Ostwald immediately agreed to print Wittgenstein's LPA solely on the basis of his esteem for Bertrand Russell, emphasizing that Russell's introduction to it would be particularly welcome. In March 1921, he received Ts 202 and Russell's introduction from Dorothy Wrinch, and both appeared in Issue 3/4 of the 14th and last volume of the Annalen der Naturphilosophie, which was probably not available in print until April 1922.[28] Wittgenstein himself initially knew nothing of this. Since the fall of 1920, he had been teaching at the elementary school in Trattenbach, a small village in southern Lower Austria, and had apparently abandoned the idea of publishing his LPA.

He did not receive a copy of the *Annalen* from Charles K. Ogden until April 1922, and in a postcard to Paul Engelmann dated 5 August 1922[29] he expressed his disappointment:

The treatise has already been printed once – in Ostwald's Annals of Natural Philosophy (No. 14). However, I consider this a pirated edition, it is full of errors! But in the next weeks the thing will come out in London, in both German and English.[30]

The term "pirated edition" is probably exaggerated in this context, since Wittgenstein had expressly given Russell free rein to

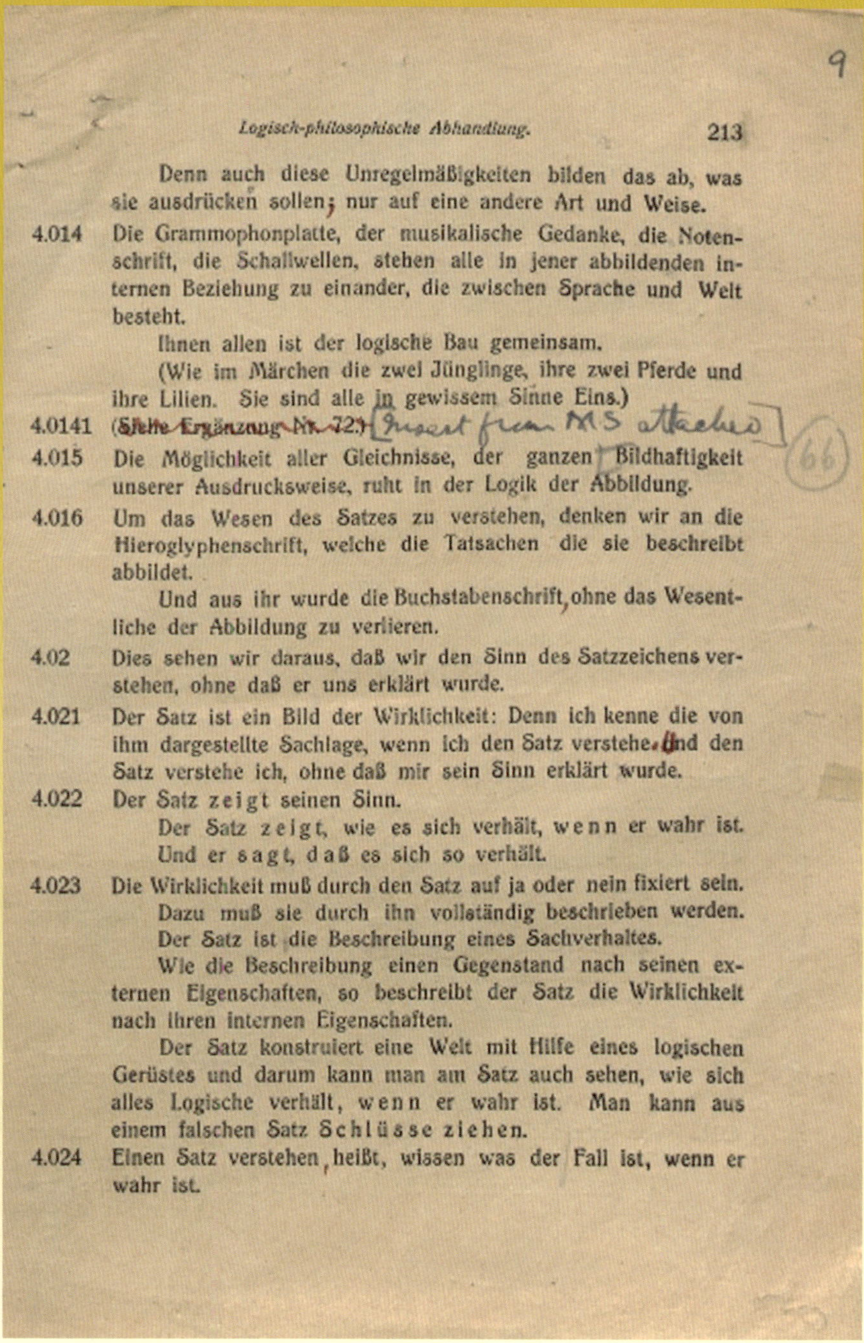

9

Logisch-philosophische Abhandlung. 213

Denn auch diese Unregelmäßigkeiten bilden das ab, was sie ausdrücken sollen; nur auf eine andere Art und Weise.

4.014 Die Grammophonplatte, der musikalische Gedanke, die Notenschrift, die Schallwellen, stehen alle in jener abbildenden internen Beziehung zu einander, die zwischen Sprache und Welt besteht.

Ihnen allen ist der logische Bau gemeinsam.

(Wie im Märchen die zwei Jünglinge, ihre zwei Pferde und ihre Lilien. Sie sind alle in gewissem Sinne Eins.)

4.0141 ~~(Siehe Ergänzung Nr. 72.)~~ [Insert from MS attached] (66)

4.015 Die Möglichkeit aller Gleichnisse, der ganzen Bildhaftigkeit unserer Ausdrucksweise, ruht in der Logik der Abbildung.

4.016 Um das Wesen des Satzes zu verstehen, denken wir an die Hieroglyphenschrift, welche die Tatsachen die sie beschreibt abbildet.

Und aus ihr wurde die Buchstabenschrift, ohne das Wesentliche der Abbildung zu verlieren.

4.02 Dies sehen wir daraus, daß wir den Sinn des Satzzeichens verstehen, ohne daß er uns erklärt wurde.

4.021 Der Satz ist ein Bild der Wirklichkeit: Denn ich kenne die von ihm dargestellte Sachlage, wenn ich den Satz verstehe. Und den Satz verstehe ich, ohne daß mir sein Sinn erklärt wurde.

4.022 Der Satz zeigt seinen Sinn.

Der Satz zeigt, wie es sich verhält, wenn er wahr ist. Und er sagt, daß es sich so verhält.

4.023 Die Wirklichkeit muß durch den Satz auf ja oder nein fixiert sein.

Dazu muß sie durch ihn vollständig beschrieben werden.

Der Satz ist die Beschreibung eines Sachverhaltes.

Wie die Beschreibung einen Gegenstand nach seinen externen Eigenschaften, so beschreibt der Satz die Wirklichkeit nach ihren internen Eigenschaften.

Der Satz konstruiert eine Welt mit Hilfe eines logischen Gerüstes und darum kann man am Satz auch sehen, wie sich alles Logische verhält, wenn er wahr ist. Man kann aus einem falschen Satz Schlüsse ziehen.

4.024 Einen Satz verstehen, heißt, wissen was der Fall ist, wenn er wahr ist.

First print of the *Logical-Philosophical Treatise* with Wittgenstein's corrections in: *Annals of Natural Philosophy* No. 14 (1921), issue 374
©ANL, Cod.Ser.n. 39.597

publish the LPA. Still, the reprint in the *Annalen* is indeed laden with errors, as can be seen from Wittgenstein's personal proof copy, which is now in the Austrian National Library (Cod. Ser.n. 39.597)[31] and which later served as the master copy for the bilingual edition in London in 1922. A great deal of the special logical characters are incorrectly represented, which makes most of the logical formulae almost incomprehensible. However, Wittgenstein was not entirely blameless in this. These special signs (such as the negation sign ~ or the logical implication (⊃) were apparently not available when dictating Ts 204/202, which led to other signs being used that were not consistently corrected by Wittgenstein later on.[32] Each of these uncorrected symbols were transferred to the Ostwald print. In addition, there are several other confusing errors (e.g., in sentence 2.0233: "*extreme Eigenschaften*" instead of "*externe Eigenschaften*"). The most curious is probably sentence 4.0141: "See supplement no. 72," a remark that was actually intended as an instruction to the printer to insert a further remark here that was on an extra sheet.

The remaining stages in the publishing history of Wittgenstein's seminal work went surprisingly smoothly and quickly. Dorothy Wrinch evidently did not consider the matter to be concluded with the print in Ostwald's *Annals*. In the fall of 1921, an approach was made to Charles K. Ogden by either Wrinch or Bertrand Russell, who had returned from China at the end of August 1921.[33] That year, Ogden had become editor of the renowned series "*International Library of Psychology, Philosophy and Scientific Method*" published by Kegan Paul in London. Taking up Russell's original idea of a bilingual edition of the LPA, Ogden had Frank Ramsey produce an English translation of the LPA at the end of 1921, based on the proofs of the Ostwald print. It was at this juncture that the Latin title *Tractatus Logico-Philosophicus (TLP)*, suggested by G.E. Moore and alluding to Spinoza's well-known treatise, first entered the picture.[34] Wittgenstein received the English translation (also housed today in the ANL)[35] with Ogden's letter of 20 March 1922 and returned it, together with corrections and detailed comments, on 23 April 1922. In the meantime, Ostwald had sent the print of the LPA in the *Annalen* as well as its source typescript (Ts 202) back to Ogden, who in turn sent these to Wittgenstein.

Wittgenstein now used Ts 202 to correct both the English translation and the Ostwald print. Together with Ogden's letter of 3 May 1922, Wittgenstein received a list of questions regarding the English translation.[36] He added annotations to this list and returned it to Ogden with his letter of 10 May 1922.

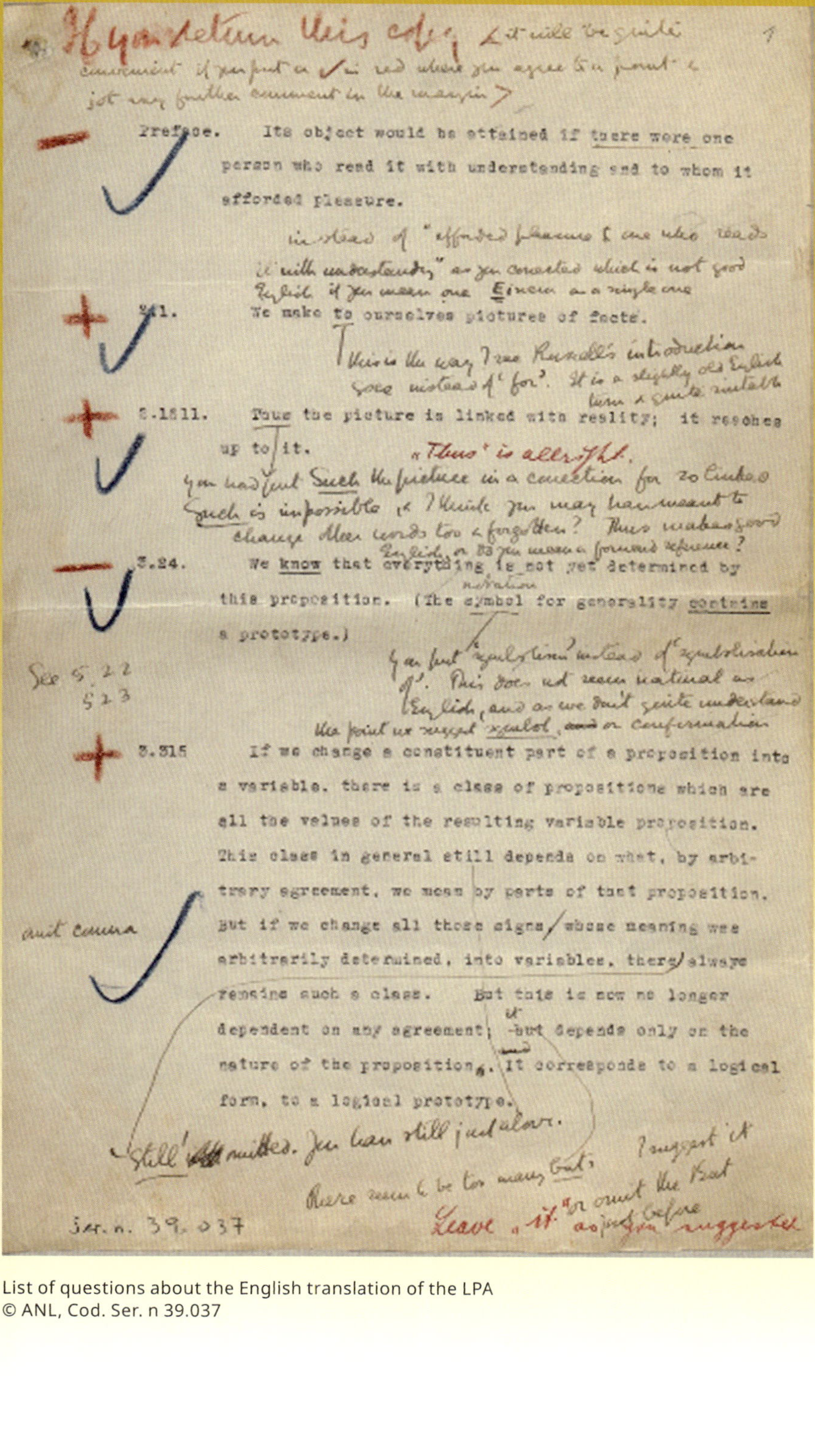

If you return this copy (it will be quite convenient if you put a ✓ in red where you agree to a point & jot any further comment in the margin)

Preface. Its object would be attained if there were one person who read it with understanding and to whom it afforded pleasure.

2.1. We make to ourselves pictures of facts.

2.1511. Thus the picture is linked with reality; it reaches up to it.

"Thus" is allright.

3.24. We know that everything is not yet determined by this proposition. (The symbol for generality contains a prototype.)

See 5.22 5.23

3.315 If we change a constituent part of a proposition into a variable, there is a class of propositions which are all the values of the resulting variable proposition. This class in general still depends on what, by arbitrary agreement, we mean by parts of that proposition. But if we change all those signs, whose meaning was arbitrarily determined, into variables, there always remains such a class. But this is now no longer dependent on any agreement; but depends only on the nature of the proposition. It corresponds to a logical form, to a logical prototype.

omit comma

Ser. n. 39.037

List of questions about the English translation of the LPA
© ANL, Cod. Ser. n 39.037

Soon after, in July 1922, Wittgenstein received the galley proofs for the bilingual edition from Ogden[37] and returned them with his corrections on 4 August 1922. The bilingual edition of the *Tractatus Logico-Philosophicus* was finally published in November 1922 by Kegan Paul in London. In a letter to Ogden of 15 November 1922, a satisfied Wittgenstein wrote:

> *Thanks so much for your letter & the books which arrived yesterday. They look very nice. I wish their contents were half as good as their external appearance.*

Thus, the publication odyssey of the *Tractatus Logico-Philosophicus* reached its happy conclusion.

Overview of the genesis of the *Tractatus Logico-Philosophicus*

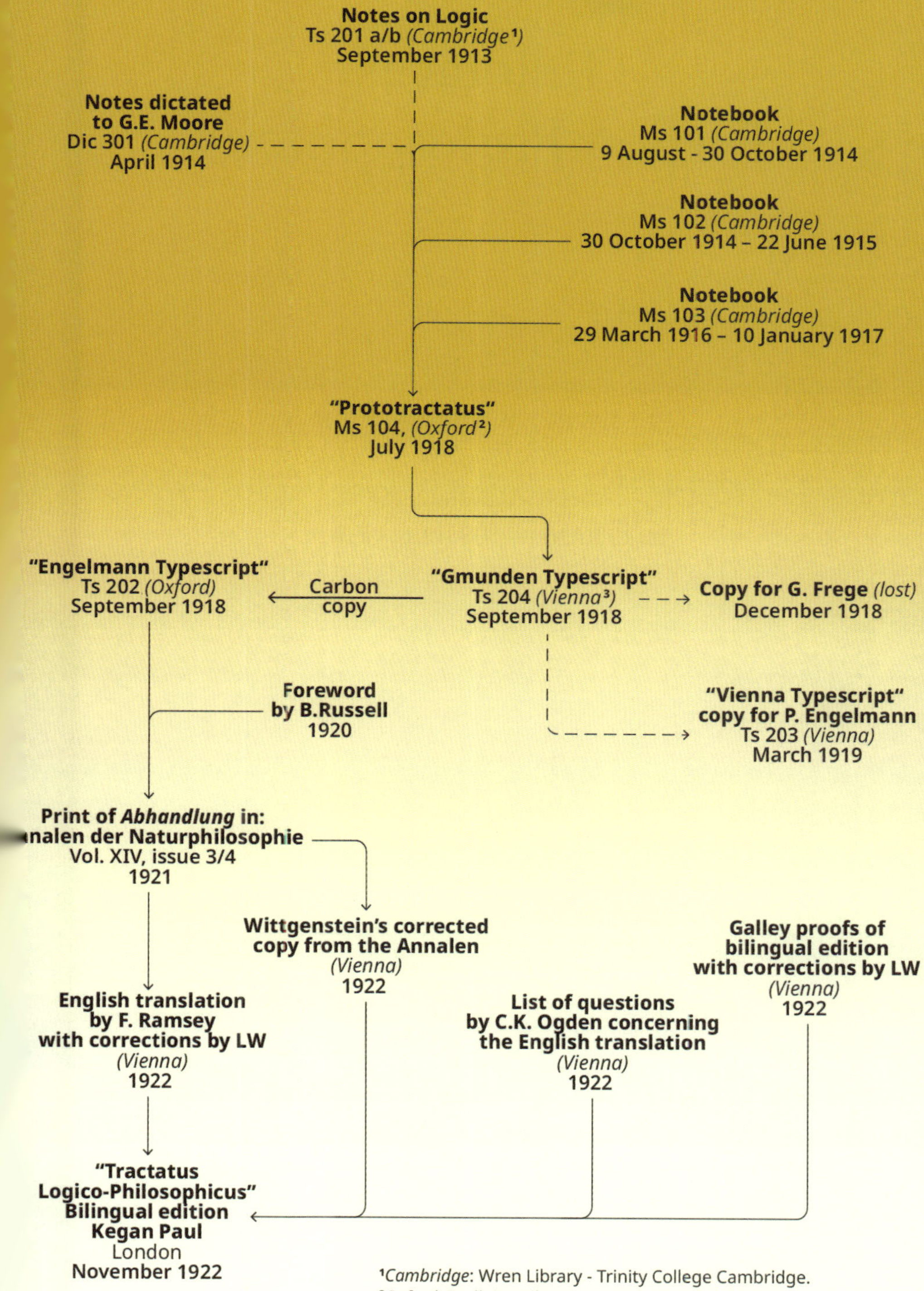

[1]*Cambridge*: Wren Library - Trinity College Cambridge.
[2]*Oxford*: Bodleian Libraries, University of Oxford.
[3]*Vienna*: Austrian National Library.

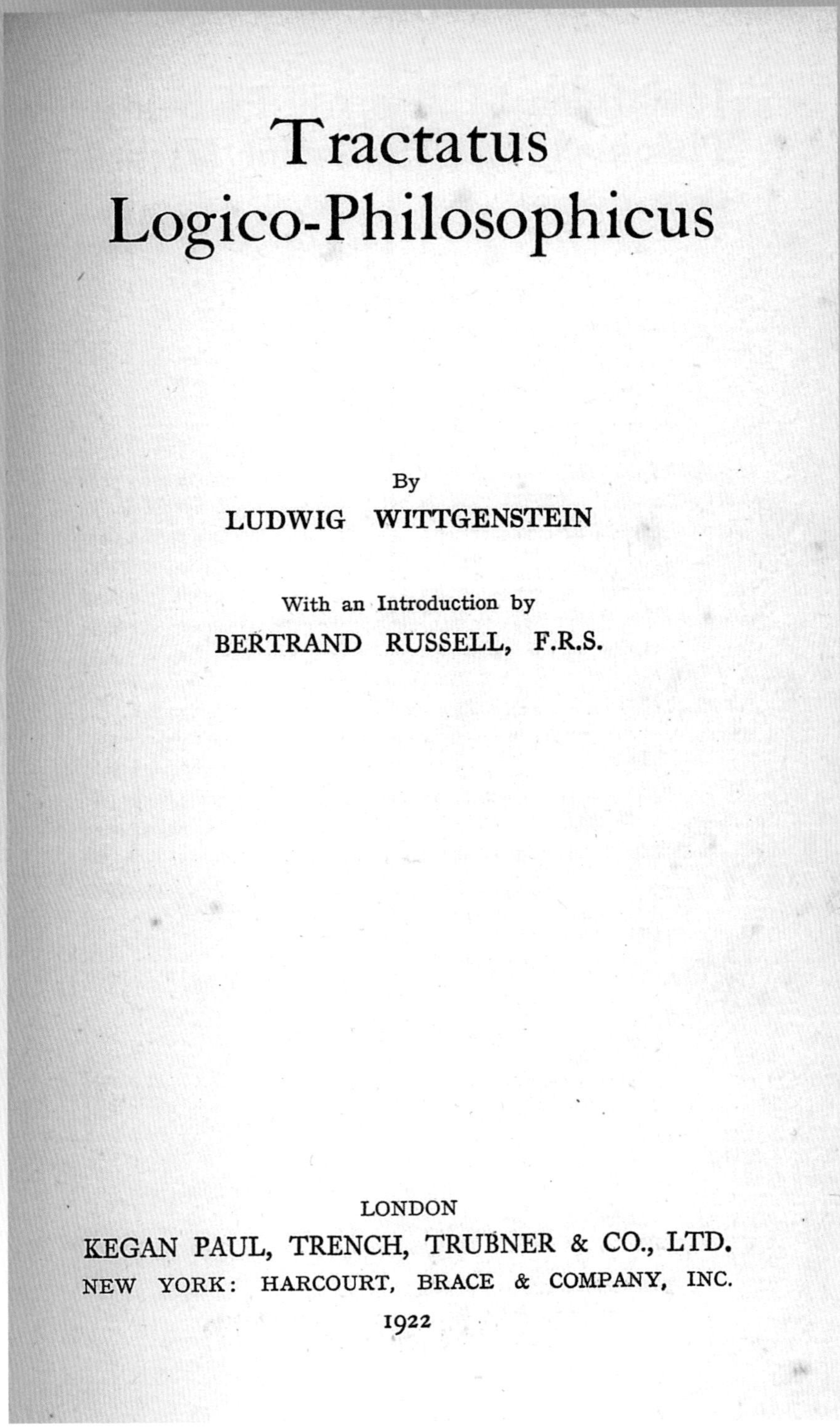
Tractatus
Logico-Philosophicus

By
LUDWIG WITTGENSTEIN

With an Introduction by
BERTRAND RUSSELL, F.R.S.

LONDON
KEGAN PAUL, TRENCH, TRUBNER & CO., LTD.
NEW YORK: HARCOURT, BRACE & COMPANY, INC.
1922

Title page of the bilingual first edition, London 1922
© ANL, Sign. 2.110.011-B-ALT-Rara

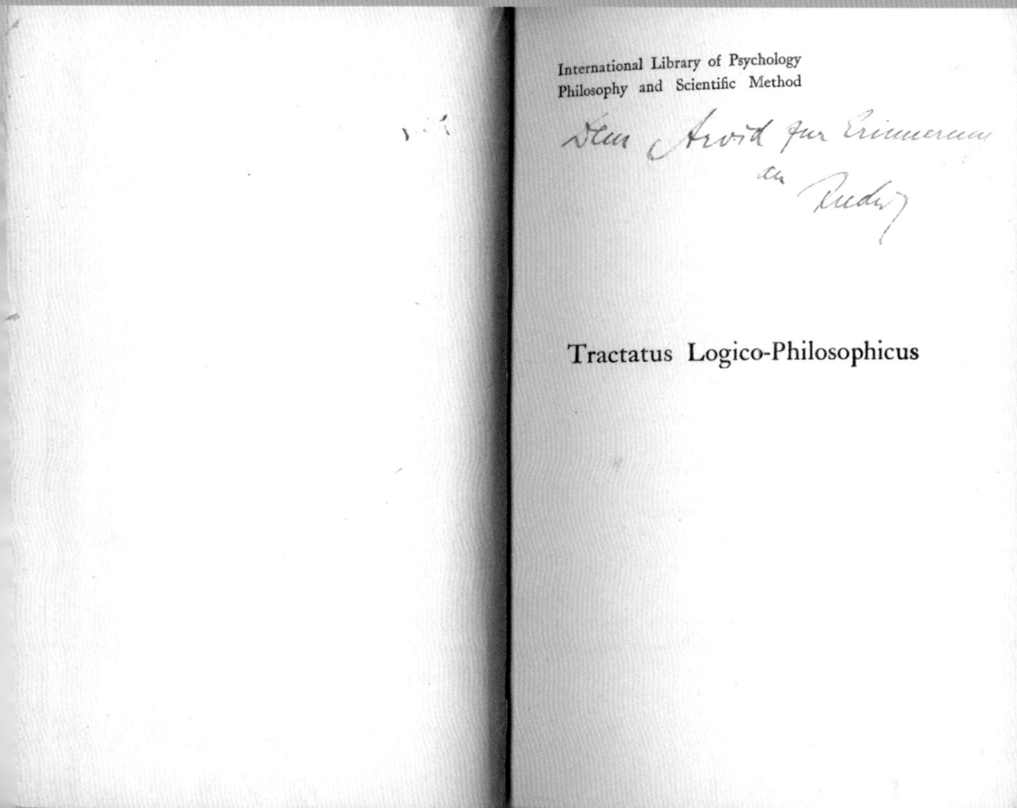
International Library of Psychology
Philosophy and Scientific Method

Tractatus Logico-Philosophicus

Ludwig Wittgenstein's dedication of the *Tractatus Logico-Philosophicus'* first edition to Arvid Sjögren

Those who know how rarely Wittgenstein passed on his Tractatus, how extremely rare his dedications are, will be pleased to get at least a dull glimpse of it. The original was donated to the Brenner Archive by Annick and Arvid Sjögren a hundred years after its publication. Facsimile No. 15 is thus also an address of thanks. Order for 10 € at sekretariat-brenner-archiv@uibk.ac.at. Please indicate whether you want the German-language or the English-language text.

Ludwig Wittgenstein Nachlass item Ms103,35v&36r as published at www.wittgensteinsource.org/BFE/Ms-103,35v_f and www.wittgensteinsource.org/BFE/Ms-103,36r_f

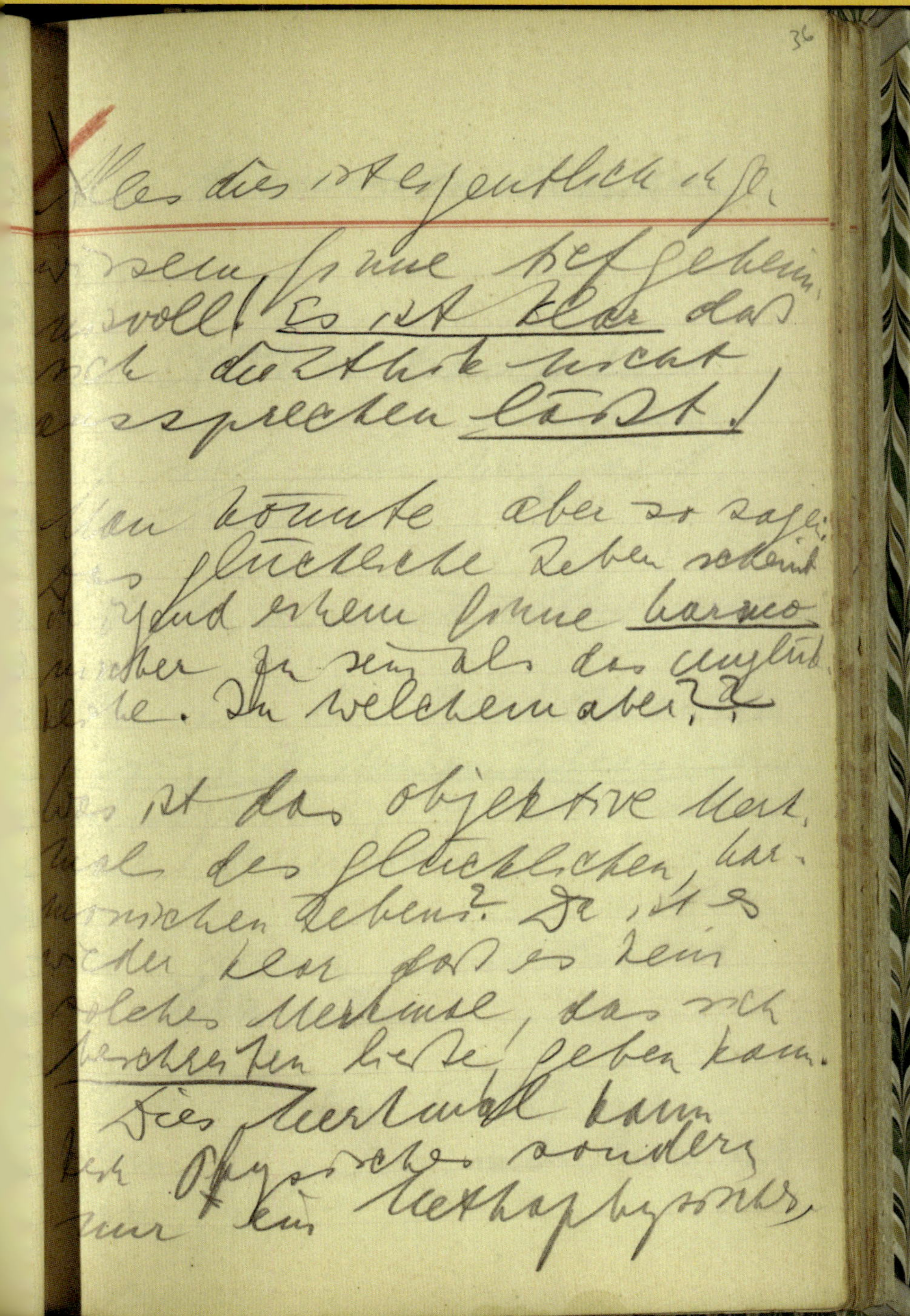

Alles dies ist ja eigentlich in gewissem Sinne tief geheimnisvoll! Es ist klar daß sich die Ethik nicht aussprechen läßt!

Man könnte aber so sagen: Das glückliche Leben scheint irgend wie harmonischer zu sein als das unglückliche. In welchem aber??

Was ist das objektive Merkmal des glücklichen, harmonischen Lebens? Da ist es wieder klar daß es kein solches Merkmal, das sich beschreiben ließe, geben kann.

Dies Merkmal kann kein physisches sondern nur ein metaphysisches

The Poetics of the *Tractatus*

Marjorie Perloff

—*The work is strictly philosophical*
but at the same time literary.[1]

For a reader new to Wittgenstein's *Tractatus*, a reader who has conscientiously read through the first five parts, which put forward, using the language of logical symbolism and mathematical equation, the picture theory of meaning as well as the distinction between *telling* and *showing* and the twin notions of tautology and contradiction, it is surely a shock to come, in 6.4, to the proposition:

> *All propositions are of equal value.*[2]

How can all propositions be of equal value? *Value:* when Wittgenstein uses that word in his cryptic and moving Preface, it refers to the putative *value* of his entire enterprise in the *Tractatus*:

> *If this work has a value it consists in doing two things. First that in it thoughts are expressed, and this value will be the greater the better the thoughts are expressed. ...*
>
> *On the other hand the truth of the thoughts communicated here seems to me unassailable and definitive. I am therefore of the opinion that the problems have in essentials been finally solved (C&V 1998, p. 28).*

The root problems of logic, it is confidently announced here, have been solved. But now comes the Preface's surprising final sentence:

> *And if I am not mistaken in this, then the value of this work secondly consists in the fact that it shows how little has been done when these problems have been solved.*

An astonishing disclaimer for a book that set out to be a treatise on logic! In his Introduction to the 1922 bilingual edition (translated by Frank Ramsey), Bertrand Russell complained that Wittgenstein's turn to "mysticism" left him "with a certain sense of intellectual discomfort." Why, for example, should "the whole subject of ethics" be "placed by Mr. Wittgenstein in the mystical, inexpressible region" where nothing can be said?[3]

To counter such charges, which continue to be made, it is important to remember that, as early as Part 4, Wittgenstein carefully delimited the power and role of logical propositions. *"Philosophy is not a theory but an activity,"* we read in 4.112. And again, *"Everything that can be said can be said clearly"* (4.116). But it is only in 5.6–5.641 that Wittgenstein turns his attention to what cannot be said, beginning with his startling proposition (5.631) *"The thinking, presenting subject; there is no such thing,"* that the "I" who speaks and perceives is only a *limit* of the world. But here, and especially in the pages from 6.41 to the end of the book, the elucidation inherent in philosophical discourse gives way to an aphoristic mode we associate less with the philosophical than the poetic. Consider the passage that follows the pronouncement that "All propositions are of equal value":

> *6.41* *The sense of the world must lie outside the world. In the world everything is as it is and happens as it does happen. In it there is no value – and if there were, it would be of no value.*
>
> *If there is a value which is of value, it must lie outside all happening and being-so. For all happening and being-so is accidental. ...*
>
> *It must lie outside the world.*
>
> *6.42* *Hence also there can be no ethical propositions.*
>
> *Propositions cannot express anything higher.*
>
> *It is clear than ethics cannot be expressed.*
>
> *6.421* *Ethics is transcendental.*
>
> *(Ethics and aesthetics are one.)*

Notice, for starters, how odd the numbering system is. 6.42, "Hence also there can be no ethical propositions," can be said to follow 6.41, but the startling pronouncement that follows – "Ethics and aesthetics are one" – produces a new idea and might logically be designated as 6.43. And what makes the numbering system – always mysterious in its arbitrariness[4] – even stranger is the passage's prominent repetition, not only of words like *Value, World, accidental, outside of, happening*, and *ethics,* but also whole clauses and sentences, with minor variations, as in "The sense of the world must lie outside the world," "it must lie outside all happenings," "It must lie outside the world."

Such differential repetition recalls no one as much as Gertrude Stein: like hers, Wittgenstein's repetitions, far from clarifying the issue, make it more obscure. In the world, we learn, there is no value, "and if there were, it would be of no value." Why not? If the philosopher can find value in the world – and most do – why would that state of affairs have no value? Conversely, if all value lies *outside the world*, how can we talk of value at all as of course we all do in everyday life? This, the *côté mystique* of Wittgenstein, made Russell throw up his hands in despair. And what is especially disconcerting is that Wittgenstein will use constructions like "It is clear" and "Hence," when nothing is clear and nothing is derived from the previous aphorism, Wittgenstein having emphatically rejected "the causal nexus" in 5.134 and following. In 6.421, for example, aesthetics, which has not been mentioned so far, is equated with ethics: *"Ethics and aesthetics are one."* Are "beauty" and "goodness" therefore equivalent? And what about the pair John Keats made famous: beauty and truth?

Here and throughout the last few pages of the *Tractatus,* Wittgenstein's terse and repetitive aphorisms recall such poetry as the opening lines of Hölderlin's "Patmos": *"Nah ist / Und schwer zu fassen, der Gott"* ("Near is / and hard to grasp, God"). *"In the world everything is as it is and happens as it does happen"*: such remarks, drawn from Wittgenstein's *Notebooks*, which were composed in the last years of the war when he was engaged in active combat on the Eastern Front,[5] are as provocative as they are suggestive. Indeed, they seem to stem, not from any sort of rational analysis, but from the depths of personal feeling. The War, as Wittgenstein himself was to declare, had changed everything.[6]

"Really, philosophy should only be written as a form of poetry" ("Philosophie dürfte man eigentlich nur *dichten"),* Wittgenstein famously declared in a notebook entry of 1933–34.[7] This sentence has been extensively parsed, especially since the German verb *dichten* has no adequate counterpart in English.[8] Certainly, Peter Winch's translation, "really one should write philosophy only as one *writes a poem*" (C & V, 28e) is unsatisfactory, given that *dichten* by no means refers to the writing of an individual poem – or even to poetry rather than fiction – but rather to what Roman Jakobson and the Russian Formalists referred to as *poeticity* as a feature of language. To shift from philosophy to what is normally considered the poetic, is to

shift from *clarity of presentation* ("Everything that can be said can be said clearly," 4.116) to the intentional unclarity, indeterminacy, and fragmentation we associate with the non-linear discourse of poetry. In the collection of Wittgenstein fragments called *Zettel*, we read:

> *The way music speaks. Do not forget that a poem, even though it is composed in the language of information, is not used in the language-game of giving information. (#160).*[9]

It is the language-game, that controls discourse, and the language game of poetry is close to that of music. *Philosophie dürfte man eigentlich nur dichten:* it is not, for Wittgenstein, a question of purporting to write a *poem*: he has no illusions on that score. But in shifting from the philosophical, in the accepted term, to the poetic – a shift that will characterize his later writings even more fully although less dramatically than here – Wittgenstein is emphasizing the impossibility of making valid ethical and aesthetic propositions (6.42) of defining "the sense of the world" (6.41).

Wittgenstein's mentor Gottlob Frege understood this right away. In a letter of 16 September 1919, responding to the *Tractatus* manuscript Wittgenstein had sent him, Frege observes:

> *The pleasure of reading your book does not derive from its already well-known content, but rather from its form, in which the uniqueness of its author reveals itself. Accordingly, the book is an artistic rather than a scientific accomplishment; for what is said in it takes second place to how it is said.*[10]

Not what but *how*: this is the hallmark of poeticity, of literariness. And the *how* in Wittgenstein can be understood in the context of two important propositions: the first, earlier in the *Tractatus* in the discussion of the limits of logic: "*The limits of my language* mean the limits of my world," and the second from the Cambridge Lectures 1930–32: "Language is not *contiguous* to anything else."[11]

If language is not contiguous to anything else, if, that is to say, there are no thoughts outside of language, then it follows that "Whereof one cannot speak, thereof one must be silent" (#7). But – and this has not always been understood – it is a basic human tendency to want to speak of the central issues of life even if and when one knows that speech cannot be adequate. Hence the repetitiousness of Wittgensteinian discourse. Consider the treatment of the adjective *glücklich* (*happy*). In the *Notebook* version on which the *Tractatus* draws, the word *happy* first appears in an entry of 6 July 1916:

> *And in this sense Dostojevsky is right when he says that the man who is happy is fulfilling the purpose of existence.*

What produces or defines happiness? On 8 July 1916, Wittgenstein writes, *"I am either happy or unhappy, that is all. It can be said: good or evil do not exist."* But no sooner has Wittgenstein unlinked the definition of happiness from value judgment, then he seems dissatisfied and adds, *"A man who is happy must have no fear. Not even in the face of death. / Only a man who lives not in time but in the present is happy."* And a few lines later, *"In order to live happily I must feel at home in the world. And that is what 'being happy' means."* And the question of ethics keeps recurring: *"For example: it makes me unhappy to think that I have offended such and such a man. Is that my conscience?" / Can one say: "Act according to your conscience whatever it may be?"* But is this always possible or desirable? Wittgenstein quickly gives it up and sets down the simple imperative *"Live happily!"*

Happiness, it seems, cannot be connected to a particular mode of being or ethical action. When Wittgenstein comes back to the happiness calculus on 29 July 1916, we read "And it is also clear that the world of the happy is a *different* world from the world of the unhappy." And finally,

> *The world of the happy is a happy world.*

Tautology, it seems, is the only permissible assertion. On 30 July 1916, Wittgenstein remarks, *"What is the objective mark of the happy, harmonious life? Here it is again clear that there cannot be any such mark that can be described."* And yet it is human to keep trying to define the elusive word. Three months later (21 October 1916), Wittgenstein, contemplating another large concept, *beauty*, writes, *"And the beautiful is what makes us happy."* The desire to draw meaningful conclusions, to make connections, dies hard.

Philosophy, let's remember, is not a theory but an activity (4.112). By taking a ordinary word like *happy* – surely one of the most frequently used adjectives in the language – and placing it in such a great variety of possible contexts, Wittgenstein creates a kind of conceptual poetry, allowing the reader to participate in the strenuous thinking involved in trying to determine what is good or true or beautiful. But in the *Tractatus,* Wittgenstein has, so to speak, already thrown away the ladder. Here he selects from the many notebook entries on the meaning of *happy*, the single aphoristic statement, "The world of the happy is quite another from that of the unhappy" (6.43).

Nothing more, it seems, can be said. But although the *Tractatus* rejects the various suppositions as to what makes one *happy*, the childlike assurance of 6.43 quickly gives way to two much more questionable propositions:

> *6.4311* *Death is not an event of life. Death is not lived through.*
>
> *If by eternity is understood not endless temporal duration but timelessness, then he lives eternally who lives in the present.*

As in a poem by Rilke or Celan where B often doesn't seem to follow A, these axioms are enigmatic. Of course, the living have never experienced death, but one could argue that to experience the death of another is certainly an event in life, indeed one of its most significant events. As for the conception of eternity as the continuous present rather than, in its accepted sense, as timelessness, duration without beginning or end, or specifically, in its religious application, as the afterlife, such displacement is surely imaginative, indeed poetic. Wittgenstein goes on to compare "our life" to the visual field: *"Our life is endless in the way that our visual field is without limit."* The analogy only works if we take our visual field to be without limits, but again, such limitlessness is hardly a matter of fact or even common belief.

Wittgenstein knows this well enough, but he speaks of the "eternity" of the present so as to emphasize that ordinary life, when understood correctly, is as mysterious and intriguing as is the very notion of eternity.[12] He is preparing the reader for the important 6.44:

> *Not <u>how</u> the world is, is the mystical, but <u>that</u> it is.*

Not how the world is but that it exists at all: this is the greatest mystery – one no scientific theory can satisfactorily explain. *"We feel*

Ludwig Wittgenstein Nachlass item Ms103,36v&37r as published at www.wittgensteinsource.org/BFE/Ms-103,36v_fand www.wittgensteinsource.org/BFE/Ms-103,37r_f

...ch transcendentes

...ist.

Die Ethik ist transcendent.

1. 8. 16.

Wie sich alles verhält, ist Gott.

Gott ist, wie sich alles verhält.

Nur aus dem Bewußtsein der Einzigkeit meines Lebens entspringt Religion – Wissenschaft – und Kunst.

2. 8. 16.

Und dieses Bewußtsein ist das Leben selber.

Kann es eine Ethik geben, wenn es außer mir kein Lebewesen gibt?

that even if all possible scientific questions be answered, the problems of life have still not been touched at all. Of course there is then no question left, and just this is the answer" (6.52).

Here is Wittgenstein as poet, refusing the language game of giving information. No theory can explain why there is life in the first place and why death: we can only take their *what* as a given: they show themselves. Fellow philosophers like Russell made much of the fact that 6.44 uses the noun *das Mystische*, but note that Wittgenstein is not referring to religious doctrine: an atheist could say, "Not *how* the world is, is the mystical," as easily as can a Christian. Indeed, the *mystical* – the unknown, mysterious other – the sense of the world that lies outside the world – can only be referred to negatively. Its domain is the language of the imagination. In the *Tractatus,* as subsequently in the *Philosophical Investigations* and the later writings, philosophy, the showing of what *cannot* be said, thus takes on poetic overtones. The favored poetic device is repetition with variation, unveiling for the reader a field of possibilities. It takes many considerations of the word *Welt* (World) to determine what cannot be said, just as the aphorism *"The world of the happy is a happy world"* challenges the reader to unpack the tautology. Such statements are the rungs of the ladder Wittgenstein's reader must climb if he is to "see the world rightly." And when all the faulty suppositions have been exposed, then there is nothing left to say and so we come to the seventh and final part of the *Tractatus* with its single proposition.

Whereof one cannot speak, thereof one must be silent.

Note that if we came to this aphorism cold, it would sound merely pretentious like "Silence is golden," and rather hypocritical, given that Wittgenstein is here making a statement that he takes to be valid. It does not allow for argument or contradiction. Yet, coming as it does, after the strenuous mental exercise that has preceded it throughout the *Tractatus*, #7 is deeply moving.

In October 1919, when Wittgenstein wrote to Ficker, urging him to take on the manuscript of the *Tractatus,* he pointed to a major publication problem: the "pamphlet," as it stood, contained only 60-odd pages. "Who writes 60-page type brochures about philosophical matters?" he commonsensically asks. But, as he suggests to Ficker, the *Tractatus* – *his* "Lifework" – could not be longer: it says what needs saying and no more, and so he can't pad it out. Not surprisingly, Ficker hesitated and made excuses, and so when, a month later, Bertrand Russell offered to have the manuscript published and translated into English, Wittgenstein accepted.

In refusing to expand the book, Wittgenstein oddly resembles another poet who felt his book, although too short for "normal" publication, could not be made longer. I am thinking of T. S. Eliot: *The Waste Land* (434 lines) was considered to be too short by a number of potential publishers. It was published first in periodicals – *The Criterion* in the UK and *The Dial* in the U.S. – and only then in book form by Boni and Liveright with the infamous appended notes, designed to flesh things out.

By a nice coincidence, both *The Waste Land* and the *Tractatus* were published in 1922: another book that appeared in that *annus mirabilis* was James Joyce's *Ulysses*. Wittgenstein, one would think, would have been pleased to have the *Tractatus* in such "poetic" company. The irony is that he had read neither Eliot's poem nor Joyce's novel. Still, Wittgenstein left open the possibility that others might undertake a comparison between the three very different "poetic" texts. Then again, such comparison would demand a different language game.

Ludwig Wittgenstein: After the *Tractatus*

1923		Puchberg in Lower Austria, elementary school teacher
1924	September	Meeting with Adolf Loos in Vienna
		Otterthal in Lower Austria, elementary school teacher
1925	August	In England as guest of John Maynard Keynes in Lewes
1926		*Dictionary for Elementary Schools* is published
	April	Leaves the teaching profession
	26 April	Works as a gardener at the Barmherzigen Brüder cloister in Hütteldorf, in the outskirts of Vienna
	03 June	Death of his mother Leopoldine Wittgenstein
	August	Work on Palais Stonborough in the Kundmanngasse
1927	February	First meeting with Moritz Schlick from the Vienna Circle
1928	March	Visits a lecture on the foundations of mathematics given by the Dutch mathematician L. E. J. Brouwer
	Autumn	Completion of the work on Palais Stonborough in the Kundmanngasse
1929		Cambridge
	06 June	Oral examination by Bertrand Russell and G. E. Moore, submitting the *Tractatus* as his dissertation
	18 June	Conferment of the degree of PhD
	19 June	Scholarship from Trinity College
		Friendship with Piero Sraffa
1930		Lectures in Cambridge
	16 May	Probationary Faculty Lectureship granted
	June	Research Fellow, resides in Whewell's Court
1931		Lectures in Cambridge
	July	Skjolden in Norway, with Marguerite Respinger
1932		Lectures in Cambridge
1933		Lectures in Cambridge
1934		Lectures in Cambridge
1935	Jan–May	Lectures in Cambridge
	7 September	Departure for Russia
	12–24 September	Leningrad, Moscow
	29 September	back in London
1936	Jan–May	Lectures in Cambridge
	June	End of Research Fellowship in Cambridge
	Aug–Dec	Skjolden, Norway
1937		Skjolden
	Summer	Vienna
1938		Lectures in Cambridge, lives with Francis Skinner in the East Road

1939	11 February	Successor to G. E. Moore to the Chair of Philosophy at Cambridge
	14 April	Conferment of British Citizenship
	01 October	Takes over the Chair of Philosophy at Cambridge
1940	November	First Aid training
1941	11 October	Death of Francis Skinner
	Nov–Dec	London, Laboratory Assistant at Guy's Hospital
1942		London, Guy's Hospital
	27 April	Gallbladder operation
1943		London, Guy's Hospital
1944	February	Newcastle, Swansea
	October	Cambridge
1945	January	Cambridge
	Oct–Dec	Lectures in Cambridge
1946		Lectures in Cambridge
1947		Lectures in Cambridge
	31 December	Resigns from the Chair of Philosophy at Cambridge
1948		Dublin, Oxford, Vienna
1949		Dublin, Vienna
	20 May	Diagnosed with an atypical form of anemia
	October	New York, Ithaca, as guest to Norman Malcolm
	25 November	Diagnosed with prostate cancer by Dr. Bevan
	24 December	Flight to Vienna
1950	Jan–March	Vienna
	11 February	Death of his sister Hermine Wittgenstein
		Cambridge, London
	Oct–Nov	Skjolden, with Ben Richards
	Christmas	Cambridge, guest of Dr. Bevan
1951		Oxford
	19 February	Cambridge, stays in Storeys End, Dr. Bevan's house
	29 April	Dies in Dr. Bevan's house. Elizabeth Anscombe, Yorick Smythies, Ben Richards and Maurice O'Drury are with him.

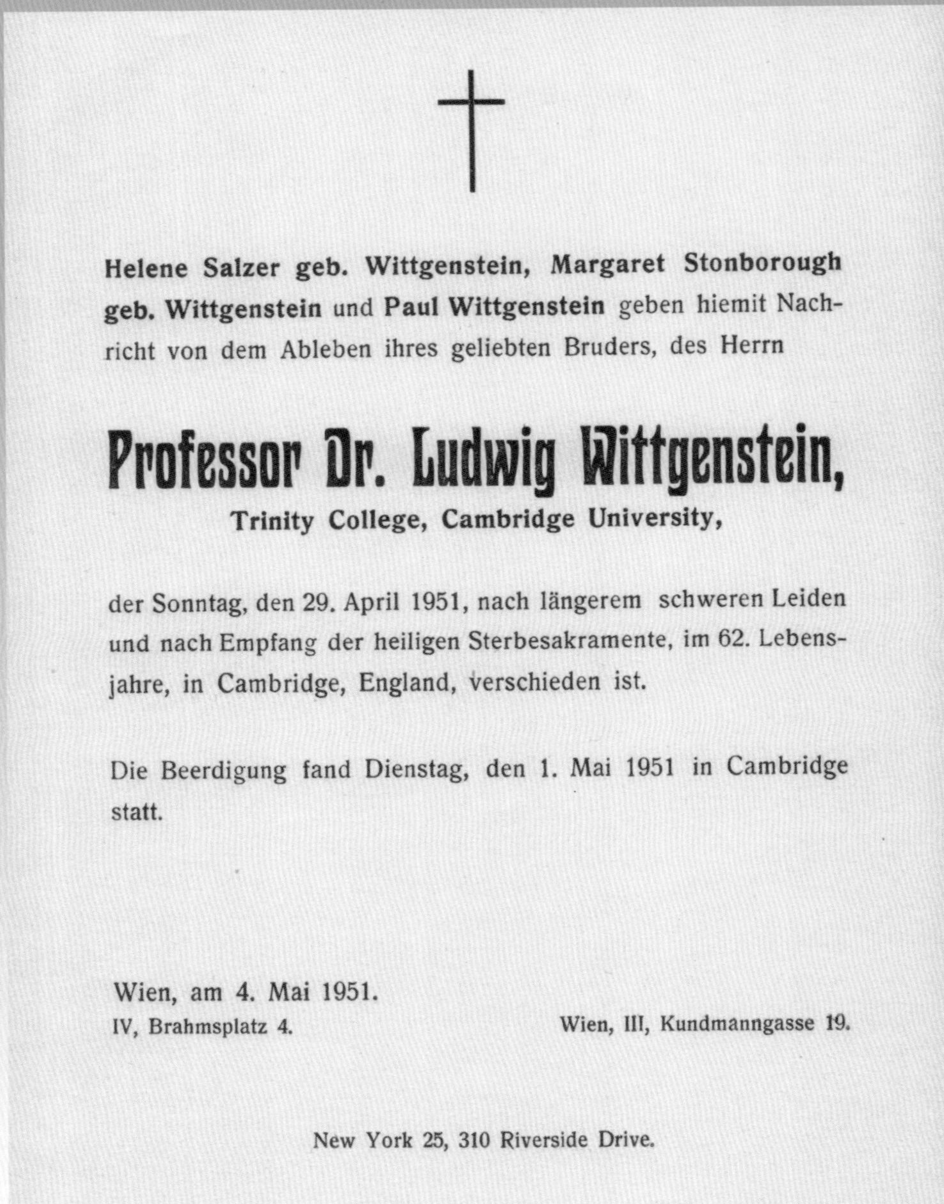

Helene Salzer geb. Wittgenstein, Margaret Stonborough geb. Wittgenstein und Paul Wittgenstein geben hiemit Nachricht von dem Ableben ihres geliebten Bruders, des Herrn

Professor Dr. Ludwig Wittgenstein,

Trinity College, Cambridge University,

der Sonntag, den 29. April 1951, nach längerem schweren Leiden und nach Empfang der heiligen Sterbesakramente, im 62. Lebensjahre, in Cambridge, England, verschieden ist.

Die Beerdigung fand Dienstag, den 1. Mai 1951 in Cambridge statt.

Wien, am 4. Mai 1951.

IV, Brahmsplatz 4. Wien, III, Kundmanngasse 19.

New York 25, 310 Riverside Drive.

Death notice issued by Wittgenstein's siblings
© Wittgenstein Initiative

ENDNOTES

1911–1913: Wittgenstein in Cambridge

1. Russell was then not yet 40 and would live another 58 years.

1914–1916: Wittgenstein in Polish Galicia

1. McGuinness 1988.
2. B. Russell. "Obituary. Ludwig Wittgenstein," *Mind* 60: 239 (July 1951). 297–298.
3. Molnár 2011: 63.
4. Group of Landwehr under the command of General Heinrich Krummer von Falkenfeld.
5. Schrott, K. "Flotylla Wis'lana monarchii austro-węgierskiej w latach 1914–1918," in: *Okręty Wojenne* 13: 61 (May 2003). 7–13.
6. McGuinness 1988: 57.
7. McGuinness 1988: 56.
8. Molnár 2011: 216.
9. McGuinness 2012: 132.
10. Ludwig Uhland "Count Eberhard's Hawthorn" transl. A. Platt (1848), in McGuinness 1967: 83–84.
11. As far as I know the only author who did justice to Keller's importance for Wittgenstein was Jacques Bouveresse in *Le Danseur et sacorde. Wittgenstein, Tolstoï, Nietzsche, Gottfried Keller et les difficultés de la foi* (Paris Agone, 2014).
12. C&V 1998: 6e.
13. C&V 1998: 6e-7e.
14. *Wittgenstein, Movements of Thought: Diaries 1930–1932, 1936–1937*, ed. I. Somavilla, in: *Ludwig Wittgenstein. Public and Private Occasions*, eds. James. C. Klagge and A. Nordmann. Lanham / Boulder / New York / Oxford: Rowman & Littlefield, 2003.
15. For the story of how the *Geheime Tagebücher* were brought to light (Spanish edition in: "Saber" 1985, German edition Turia & Kant 1990) see: I. Somavilla, "Verschlüsselung in Wittgensteins Nachlass" in: *Sprache und Welt. Proceedings des 32. Internationalen Wittgenstein Symposiums in Kichberg am Wechsel,* (Ontos Verlag, 2010), 327.

16. "Thought about Russell often these last days. I wonder if he still thinks of me? It was really odd, how we came to meet! In times of external well- being, we don't think about the weakness of the flesh; but if the time is one of need, we become conscious of it. And one turns to the spirit. — ." MS 101, 33v/34v, p. 27.
17. Wittgenstein 1914–1916: 9e.
18. On 12 September 1914 the Russians captured Sandomierz (originally their town) and destroyed the Austrian river harbor of Nadbrzezie, where important supplies of food and ammunition were stored. The inhabitants of the surrounding villages Trześń, Ostrówka, and Zarzekowice recalled the acute brutality of the Cossacks. See B. Budziło, *Gorzyce i Wrzawy. Zarys dziejów* (Kraków, 2000), 14.
19. On the fights around Tarnobrzeg, see J. Słomka, *Pamiętnik włościanina. Od pańszczyzny do dni dzisiejszych* (Tarnobrzeg, 1994), 130.
20. Phrase repeated a number of times in journal entries MS 101 under the dates 6, 9, 11, 12, 20 October 1914 etc.
21. C&V 1998: 28e.
22. The title of the entire work of which *The Gospel in Brief* is just a section is "Collection, translation and commentary (analysis) of the four Gospels" (published in 1894).
23. Regarding the similarities in the structure of the *Prototractatus*, *Tractatus* and *Gospel in Brief* we have to mention several articles: P. K. Westergaard, "A Note on Wittgenstein's *Tractatus* and Tolstoy's *Gospel in Brief*" 2009, in: Wittgenstein Repository http://wab.uib.no/agora/tools/alws/collection-9-issue-1-article-107.annotate#index.xml-back.1_div.1 accessed 14 May 2018); C. Thompson, "Wittgenstein, Tolstoy, and the Meaning of Life" in: *Philosophical Investigations* 20 (1997); T. E. Vaughan "Wittgenstein and Tolstoy: The Authentic Orientation" in: *Religious Studies* 33 (1997).
24. For example, 28 October 1914 (MS 101, 50v). For a typology of the different forms of address to God, see Martin Pilch, *Wittgensteins "Gebetsstriche" in den Kriegstagebüchern* (MSS 101–103), in: Beitrage des 39. Wittgenstein Symposiums, eds. Stefan Majetschak and Anja Weiberg, Kirchberg am Wechsel 2016, 192–195.
25. M. O'C. Drury in *Ludwig Wittgenstein: Personal Recollections*, ed. R. Rhees (Blackwell, Oxford 1981), 109.
26. See M. Pilch, Wittgensteins "Gebetsstriche" in den Kriegstagebüchern (MSS 101–103).
27. *Gospel according to Saint Matthew*, chapter 19, transl. English Standard Version.
28. See A. Waugh, *The House of Wittgenstein: A Family at War*, chapter 19, "Money Matters"; Monk 1990: 196–199; McGuinness 1988: 205–210.
29. Molnár 2011: 100.

1914–1918: The Genesis of the *Tractatus* in the First World War – Addenda to Previous Biographies

1. About the Goplana and the searchlight, see Urszula Idziak-Smoczyńska's article in this volume.
2. The three wartime notebooks (or "diaries") Mss 101, 102 and 103 range from August 1914 to January 1917, with a gap from June 1915 to March 1916, and are now kept in the Wren Library at Trinity College, Cambridge. All quotations in this article are identified only by their date and can be found on wittgensteinsource.org as follows: Ms 101 9 August–30 October 1914; Ms 102 30 October 1914–22 June 1915; Ms 103 28(?) March 1916–1 January 1917.
3. Ray Monk's biography (Monk 1992: 121) reinforces this notion when he writes that Wittgenstein "was facing death manning a searchlight amid heavy fighting." In fact, the Goplana was not involved in any such heavy skirmishes, indeed in any battles at all, and Wittgenstein's impression of grave danger was exaggerated.
4. Ms 104 in Wittgenstein's *Nachlass*, also called *Prototractatus*, is now kept at the Bodleian Library, Oxford. For a facsimile edition see www.wittgensteinsource.org.
5. Ms 101.
6. *Notes on Logic* B2 (in: Potter 2009: App. B 276).
7. "Galleys" were a long chain of towed barges, which were also used for transporting wounded combatants on the Vistula.
8. See also Susan Sterrett's contribution in this volume.
9. Cf. Wright 1982: 20 f.
10. Ms 101, cf. Pilch 2016.
11. ÖULK I: 367.
12. Ms 102.
13. See Ms 102: 3 November 1914.
14. Ms 102: 25 November 1915.
15. The information on Gürth is taken from a number of preserved files in the Vienna War Archives.
16. He also mentions this in a military postcard to Ludwig von Ficker ("am now a technical official at the *Artillerie Autodetachement*" CC 2011: From Ludwig Wittgenstein to Ludwig von Ficker [mid-Dec. 1914]; author's note: if the appointment took place on 24 December, the letter is more likely to be dated late December).
17. Files of the Vienna War Archives: *Kriegsministerium* (KM) 7. Abt. 90-1/2 (901/1915).
18. Ray Monk's *Ludwig Wittgenstein. The Duty of Genius* (Monk 1990) also did not use this material.
19. EOK 21.917 Op./1915, Enclosure 12 of Decree KM 7. Abt. 1138/1915.
20. EOK 25.422 Op./1915.

21. KM 7. Abt. 90-1/6-2 (14.621/1915), approved by Minister of War Alexander von Krobatin (1849–1933) on 30/04/1915.
22. KM 7. Abt. 27-33 (42.965/1915) fol. 3v.
23. Although Gürth himself graduated from the Technical Military Academy in 1909 and subsequently completed an "Automobile Course" in 1910 and an "Alternator Course" in 1911, his technical and mathematical knowledge was certainly inferior to that of Wittgenstein's many years of mechanical engineering studies at the Technical College in Berlin and in Manchester (McGuinness 1988: 54–72).
24. Thus McGuinness' (1988: 232) assessment: "Wittgenstein must clearly have been the best-qualified person in the workshop."
25. KM 7. Abt. 27-33 (42.965/1915) fol. 3v.
26. KM 7. Abt. 27-33 (42.965/1915) fol. 2r.
27. Gürth takes this measure already at the end of January or beginning of February and not, as McGuinness (1988: 237) and Monk (1992: 146) concur, in April 1915.
28. See CC 2011.
29. It is noteworthy that the information about Gürth's transfer was inserted later by Wittgenstein at this place.
30. KM 7. Abt. 90-1/6 (14.295/1915).
31. "*Feldzeugmeister* [General of Artillery] Leopold *Freiherr* Schleyer von Pontemalghera (1858–1920), military technician and military writer, appointed section chief in 1913 to head the technical section of the War Ministry, from the beginning of the war in 1914 he also headed the War Surveillance Office, set up within the War Ministry to counter anti-state activities." (*Österreichisches Biographisches Lexikon* 10, p. 202).
32. "Field Marshal Lieutenant Franz Kanik (1863–1931), chief of the stage system from 1913, relieved of this post in 1916, general inspector of the gendarmerie from 1917." (*Österreichisches Biographisches Lexikon* 3, p. 214).
33. KM 7. Abt. 90-1/6-2 (14.621/1915).
34. "*Oberleutnant* Randa" (not identified) KM 7. Abt. 90-1/6-5 (27.324/1915).
35. KM 7. Abt. 68-34 (16.872/1915); cf. Ms 102: 22/04/1915.
36. Cf. Ms 102: 05/05 and 08/06/1915.
37. KM 7. Abt. 68-34 (16.872/1915).
38. KM 7. Abt. 20.584/1915, co-signed with KM 7. Abt. 61-7-65-2 (21.789/1915); the Inspector of Technical Artillery, Field Marshal Lieutenant Wilhelm Pucherna, played a significant role in Wittgenstein's further military employment in WWI.
39. KM 7. Abt. 90-1/6-5 (27.324/1915).
40. Wittgenstein later exchanged letters with Wahle when the latter, transferred to the Air Force after his time with the artillery workshop

train, tried to recruit Wittgenstein as an engineer for aircraft development in the summer of 1917 (CC 2011; for the backgrounds, see Seekircher 2002).
41. KM 7. Abt. 61-7-65-2 (21.789/1915).
42. Russell 1914a.
43. McGuinness 2012: 74.
44. What should be noted about this remark is that "Scientific Method in Philosophy" here apparently refers to a work title and not to Russell's method as such (the text is written in quotation marks and capital letters); either Wittgenstein is referring here to the cover title of the 1915 American edition or to the subtitle "SCIENTIFIC METHOD IN PHILOSOPHY" of the 1914 edition, visible on all even-numbered pages in the header.
45. Cf. Ms 102: 23 April 1915 and before that already on 29 March 1915.
46. "Sensibile" (pl. "sensibilia") is the term Russell introduces in Russell 1914a for sense-data that are not perceived by a subject but could be perceived. Sensibilia are attributed to physics. Wittgenstein uses the term "minima sensibilia" on 7 May 1915 in Ms 102.
47. Russell 1914: 87–97.
48. Russell 1914a.
49. Potter 2020: 261–264.
50. Russell 1914a: 7.
51. Russell 1914a: 15.
52. Russell 1914a: 11; 1914: 107; cf. "Occam's motto" in Ms 102: 23 April 1915.
53. "Private Spaces" in a comparable sense are already addressed in Russell's *Problems of Philosophy* (Russell 1912: 29–31).
54. von Wright 1938: 18; Anscombe 1963: 11; cf. Hacker 1986: 87–104.
55. Closing Lecture at the event "Wittgenstein and the Vienna Circle – after 100 Years" in Vienna 10–12 June 2021.
56. Hacker 1986: 81–104; Birk 2006: 17–56; Potter 2020: 360–363.
57. B2, in: Potter 2009: App. B 276.
58. Note, however, that in the use of these remarks in the final context of TLP 5.6. ff. the term 'limit' at least includes the meaning of 'outer boundary'.
59. In the textual interpretation proposed here, the remark of 23 May is both a precursor of the principle of 'completeness of logical space' as expressed later at the beginning of the *Prototractatus*, and an essential mental step towards the famous remark 1 of the *Tractatus* "The world is everything that is the case."
60. The source of inspiration for this thought is also in OKEW, on page 202 f. The more far-reaching thesis that this passage forms the starting point for Wittgenstein's discussion of the "second kind of

generalization" in the *Prototractatus* (PT 5.005341; Ms 104: 21) in the context of the important distinction of three ways of determining the propositional variable in TLP 5.501 cannot be discussed here for reasons of space.

61. The belief in the existence of anything "outside my private world" and in particular "the existence of other minds" is also treated by Russell (1914: 93) and also the possible role of solipsism as a philosophical position (1914a: 12 f).
62. The choice of this unpretentious title might also have been influenced by Schopenhauer, whose dissertation *On the Fourfold Root of the Principle of Sufficient Reason* bears the subtitle *Eine philosophische Abhandlung* [A Philosophical Treatise].
63. Ms 104: 3.
64. The "class-theory of propositions" is a system element of this phase, which did not enter the *Abhandlung* as it was designed in Ms 102. The function assigned to it in the system is taken over there by the theory of truth-functions (see PT 4.1–4.4).
65. It is unlikely that Luciano Bazzocchi's (2008: 21) assumption is correct that this letter indicates that Wittgenstein had already started writing Ms 104 in April or May 1915. The positions formulated in May and June are still exploratory and full of doubts, which does not quite fit in the resolutely formulated solutions to the same logical problems of language at the beginning of Ms 104. See McGuinness 2012: 83.
66. It remains somewhat puzzling how Wittgenstein was able to write such extensive philosophical remarks as at the end of Ms 102 in view of the increased workload in the artillery workshop in June. "From 16 June onwards, five 30.5 cm and two 24 cm mortar batteries arrived for urgent reestablishment, as a result of which the artillery workshop was fully occupied." (KM 7. Abt. 90-1/6-5 27.324/1915).
67. However, this must remain a conjecture, because a notebook that is widely assumed by researchers to directly follow 22 June 1915 has not survived and the existence of such a notebook is also not indirectly proven.
68. CC 2011: From Ludwig Wittgenstein to Ludwig von Ficker (24 July 1915) also from Stanislaus Jolles to Ludwig Wittgenstein (12 August 1915).
69. KM 7. Abt. 90-1/6-7 (33.046/1915). In fact, the completion work continued until "14 August in the evening," as can be seen from a telegram to the *Etappenoberkommando* [Army Rear Area High Command] (EOK 74.116 Op./1915).
70. Major General (from 14 November 1915 onwards Field Marshal Lieutenant) Árpád Kiss de Nagy-Sitke. Head of the 7th Department in the Ministry of War (organization and administration of the artillery

weapons and artillery equipment, as well as weaponry and ammunition in the army), later section chief in the Ministry of War.

71. KM 7. Abt. 68-86 (32.602/1915).
72. Cf. CC 2011: "We hope with all our hearts that the accident that happened to you will remain without any serious consequences. 3 weeks' leave, after more than a year's service and after a wound and illness, is really a bit short." From Adele Jolles to Ludwig Wittgenstein, 12 August 1915.
73. Ray Monk (1992: 131) assumes that Wittgenstein was not individually transferred, but the whole artillery workshop was moved from Kraków to Sokal. In his account, Monk was not aware of the development and role of the trains.
74. Files in the Vienna War Archives indicate that Artillery Workshop Train No. 1 "Gürth" was moved from Sokal to Stojanow, 35 km southeast, sometime between 15 November 1915 and 21 February 1916; KM 7. Abt. 90-1/3-50 (48.296/1915) or AOK Qu. Abt. 33.039/1916.
75. KM 7. Abt. 90-1/6-8 (32.816/1915).
76. KM 7. Abt. 90-1/6-2 (14.621/1915) and EOK 44.617/1915 respectively, Supplement 3 "Staff List": the staff of each of the two trains consisted of three officers, 20 non-commissioned officers, and 66 persons with crew ranks.
77. Besides the detailed photographs of the Artillery Workshop Train No. 1 "Gürth" (in: *Im Etappenraum der I. Armee*) there is another series of 17 photographs (interior shots of all wagons as well as an overall shot of the train) of the twin train No. 2 "Allitsch," made by the Austrian *Kriegspressedienst* [war press service] on 12 July 1916 in Kowel on the occasion of the inspection by the German Colonel General Alexander von Linsingen.
78. KM 7. Abt. 27-33 (42.965/1915) fol. 19r.
79. Unfortunately, the original was burned together with the whole Frege estate during World War II. However, there is a summary note on the correspondence by Heinrich Scholz: "W. to Fr. about his treatise. New address." (Floyd 2011: 9)
80. Bieler's report is reprinted in McGuinness 1988: 234–236.
81. See Potter 2013: 27.
82. See CC 2011: From Gottlob Frege to Ludwig Wittgenstein, 16 September 1919.
83. Cf. CC 2011: From Ludwig Wittgenstein to George Edward Moore, 18 February 1914, [10? March 1914], 7 May 1914; cf. Pinsent 1994: 156.
84. Ms 104.
85. See Pilch 2015.
86. Contrary to Ray Monk's opinion (Monk 1992: 133), who claims that "the first version of the *Tractatus*," i.e. the *Abhandlung* in the form

of autumn 1915, "has unfortunately not survived" we now have evidence that the manuscript Ms 104 meticulously records the course of development of this original version in the remarks up to page 28 with all insertions, corrections, and corrections and can be regarded as the place where the philosophical thoughts were systematically formulated.

87. One can still discern traces of the transition to the numbering system on pages 4 and 5 of Ms 104 (see Pilch 2015).
88. Besides the invention of decimal-numbering as a tool Wittgenstein also seems to have developed another compositional device, namely the idea of keeping a parallel-version of the successively expanding *Abhandlung* written on "loose sheets," a form that would easily allow the insertion of new remark-numbers between already existing ones. The existence of such an early text related to the *Tractatus* (the "loose-sheet-collection") is evidenced in the same letter of 22 October to Russell, but its function either as a precursor document or as a parallel working tool is disputed (cf. Pilch 2015: 86–91; Pilch 2018: 111–116).
89. McGuinness 2012: 84.
90. These first formulations of the remarks were subsequently subjected to a large number of corrections and changes, both with regard to the propositional numbering and in the text, until the completion of the *Prototractatus* in March 1918.
91. KM 7. Abt. 27-33 (42.965/1915) fol. 2.
92. In his description, Bieler explicitly emphasizes Wittgenstein's lack of rank when he first noticed him in the mess of the train as a "slender man of about 25 years and without military rank" who, unlike the officers present, ate little, drank little, did not smoke, and, he was told, was assigned to the train as an engineer.
93. An "*Akzessist*" was the lowest officer-valued rank of military officials, recognizable by a rosette instead of a star in the rank insignia. Georg Trakl, for example, as a trained pharmacist, served as a *Medikamentenakzessist*, responsible for the production and distribution of medicines in the armed forces.
94. KM 7. Abt. 27-33 (42.965/1915) fol. 6v.
95. KM 7. Abt. 27-33 (42.965/1915) fol. 8.
96. Gürth's report on Wittgenstein, enclosed with the request, states that Wittgenstein had also rendered outstanding services in the "train work" "which Excellency *Feldzeugmeister* von SCHLEyER and *Herr Generalmayor* von KISS honorably described as pioneering in this field." KM 7. Abt. 27-33 (42.965/1915) fol. 3v).
97. KM 7. Abt. 27-33 (42.965/1915) fol. 16.
98. KM 7. Abt. 27-33 (42.965/1915) fol. 19.

99. See Pilch 2014. All time data on the progress of writing in Ms 104 are based on the assumption that Wittgenstein began writing the *Abhandlung* either while still in Vienna in August 1915 or only in Sokal and had just reached the conspicuous caesura on page 28 when he was transferred to the front in March 1916. This corresponds to about one page per week. Moreover, it is assumed that the text is evenly distributed over this time.
100. McGuinness 1988: 234 f.
101. See Ms 104.
102. It would undoubtedly have been within Pucherna's discretion to decide pragmatically in favor of promotion and to grant Wittgenstein the titular rank. His irreconcilable attitude may have had many reasons, among them the consolidation of his own position as a specialist authority outside the ministerial hierarchy, a certain competitive relationship with the section chief Schleyer, but possibly also a dislike of Gürth, whom he knew only too well personally. In his role as project supervising inspector for the planning work at the arsenal in Vienna from mid-May to early July 1915, Pucherna was Gürth's direct superior and was confronted more than once with the idiosyncratic and energetic approach of the latter.
103. It is not clear why the announcement of the order to Wittgenstein was delayed for so long. The Army High Command Quartermaster's Department (AOK Qu. Abt., formerly EOK) had already received the rejection of the request on 28 February 1916. Perhaps Gürth was still trying to prevent the loss of his most important engineer in some way. In February, his train was in serious personnel straits. Gürth's deputy, Walter Wahle, left the train on 20 February to return to his regiment, and on 21 February Gürth wrote to the AOK Qu. Abt. "requesting the assignment of a *Landsturm*-engineer or an engineer-lieutenant in place of the *Landsturm*-engineer Ing. Karl Haarhofer, against whom a military trial was initiated for embezzlement of military funds and unauthorized disposal" (AOK Qu. Abt 33039/1916). Thus, with Wittgenstein, the train loses three of its leading officers and engineers within a short period of time.
104. See also Geschkowski (2001: 77), but not McGuinness (2002: 266) who assumes that in March 1916 Wittgenstein had already reached page 70 in Ms 104.
105. McGuinness 1988: 235.
106. Czernowitz was from 1775–1918 part of the Habsburg Monarchy and capital of its most eastern *Kronland* [crown province] 'Bukovina'; today in the western Ukraine.
107. See also Potter 2013: 28.

108. Reward Request 500/1482 states, "He observed the firing of the mine launchers regardless of the heavy artillery fire on the *Koffer*[*stellung*] [a special form of infantry post] and the exploding mines and spotted them. The battery also succeeded in destroying two of the heavy-caliber mine launchers by direct hits, as the captured men later also testified."
109. This second-lowest military rank which Wittgenstein had received just a few days before on 1 June, corresponds approximatively to a non-permanent Lance-Bombardier (McGuinness 1988: 242), but combined with the prospect of being accepted into the officer's training program upon excellent probation.
110. CC 2011: Heinrich Bertl to Ludwig Wittgenstein, 12 February 1920.
111. McGuinness 1988: 243.
112. Cf. McGuinness 1988: 245.
113. ÖULK IV: 619.
114. ÖULK IV: 644.
115. Geschowski 2001: 31.
116. McGuinness 2019: 29.
117. This is also what he did with the Norwegian notebook at the beginning of the war ("Gave my large notebook to Trenkler for safekeeping." Ms 101: 9 August 1914).
118. See Potter 2009 for a reconstruction.
119. On page 35 there is also a fine, previously overlooked, horizontal demarcation line.
120. D 301 in the *Nachlass*.
121. See Pilch 2018.
122. Somavilla 2006: 85 ff.
123. Apparently, this hope was not unfounded, as can be seen from the somewhat cryptic postscript of *Oberleutnant* Schallmayer in his letter to Wittgenstein of 6 November 1916 about the ceremony: "Today the beautiful decoration has finally arrived, for which I thank you from the bottom of my heart. Probably the decoration ceremony here would be more beautiful than in the hinterland. For you this decoration will be accompanied with important consequences and then I hope to address it to the *Fähnrich* [ensign] instead of the *Einjährigfreiwilligen*." [special Austrian form of military volunteer with higher education background] (CC 2011).
124. CC 2011: 6 December 1916.
125. The personal entries stop already with his arrival in Vienna in September; it is possible that Wittgenstein kept a separate diary for this.
126. Potter 2013: 29.
127. On 23 November 1916, in Ms 103, Wittgenstein still pursues the idea that the elementary propositions could be constructed from

each other by means of a separate operation (cf. also the remarks on 15 and 16 April, 13 July and 21 November). Accordingly, he is thus looking for the formulation of a 'general form of the elementary proposition', which should form a counterpart to the 'general form of the truth-function' in the *Prototractatus*. On page 56 of Ms 104, however, this approach is obviously rejected, and PT 5.4 makes it clear that there can be no such thing as a general form of elementary propositions: "The elementary proposition consists of names. Since we cannot give the number of names with different meanings, we cannot give the composition of the elementary proposition."

128. McGuinness 2002: 265.
129. This remark was later erased by Wittgenstein.
130. Number 6.3 later changed to 6.4.
131. Using the same comparison, McGuinness (2002: 268) comes to the opposite conclusion and says that page 71 was reached as early as January 1917.
132. This reconstruction shows the original numbering of the remarks.
133. Nonetheless, around this time, he explicitly asked the War Ministry for a transfer to the infantry. It remains puzzling how he could think that the army leadership, already very averse to requests to change of service-branch [*Waffengattung*], should comply with such a request from a soldier who had just completed an elaborate special training.
134. The precise interpretation of the single pieces on the list is controversial (see e.g. Geschkowski 2001: 27 ff., there also a facsimile of the handwritten item; McGuinness 2002: 259 ff.; Potter 2013: 18 f.). What is more interesting is what is not enlisted in it: the 'loose-sheet collection' and – at least according to my interpretation – also Ms 103 is not noted. The reason for the former is that this special compositional aid and working copy was simply no longer needed after completion and it did not contain any additional information that was not already contained in the other pieces. (The 'loose-sheet collection' could therefore be lent to Heinrich Groag in Olomouc; see McGuinness 2002: 267). The reason for the absence of Ms 103 is that the many remarks it contained that went beyond logic were not intended to be part of the *Abhandlung* at that time. Thus, Ms 103 would not be necessary for the publication.
135. As Frege comments on the recent change, "I admire your capacity for change: in the Kraków fortress, on the Vistula with searchlights, with the field cannons, with the field howitzers and now with the Hussars." (From Gottlob Frege to Ludwig Wittgenstein, 26 April 1917, trans. by Burton Dreben and Juliet Floyd, in: *Interactive Wittgenstein*, Springer 2011, p. 35)
136. "I am working reasonably hard [...]" (McGuinness 1967: 5).

137. McGuinness 1967: 7.
138. "*Worüber*" [Whereof] instead of "*Wovon*" [about which] and "*reden*" [talk] instead of "*sprechen*" [speak].
139. This letter is the only reason why we have any knowledge of the "disposal" at all. In: McGuinness 2019: 28.
140. Venturinha 2011: 74.
141. I thank Josef Rothhaupt for this reference to Moore's diaries.
142. Ms 102: 8 December 1914; on this Venturinha 2011: 59 f.
143. Ludwig Sagt, *Die Aufzeichnungen der Hermine Wittgenstein*, ed. Mathias Iven (HE Verlag, 2015).
144. Following a conjecture of Nuno Venturinha (private e-mail), it is not implausible that the remark on scepticism (TLP 6.51 taken from Ms 101: 1 May 1915) at this stage had received the number 6.4 and thus was inserted between 6.3 and 7.
145. CC 2011: Gottlob Frege to Ludwig Wittgenstein, 30 June 1917
146. See Somavilla 2006: 97
147. Kurt Wittgenstein completed a cavalry officer training course in June and July 1917.
148. It is also possible that Ms 103 itself was placed in Groag's custody in Olomouc in mid-January (which would explain the plural "manuscripts" in Wittgenstein's reclamation request). The last entries date from 7–10 January 1917, when Wittgenstein had already left Vienna for Olomouc. There is a lot to be said for a safekeeping in Olomouc as opposed to the danger of being taken to the front in the Bukovina.
149. Originally, the section was numbered 6.2, and was renumbered 6.3 only in the very last phase of the *Prototractatus* (on p. 101), because 6.2 was assigned to an inserted section on mathematics.
150. "04/08–29/11: *Stellungskrieg* [positional warfare] near Czernowitz until the armistice on 29/11/1917"; files of the Vienna War Archive.
151. KM 7. Abt. 61-7/108-2 (15.303/1916).
152. On pp. 80, 87, 90–91, 94–96 of Ms 104.
153. Ms 104: 71–74; 81–88; 98–101.
154. The way the new section 6.2 is developed suggests that Wittgenstein did not have Ms 103 (and TB IIa) readily on hand. Otherwise, he would have used the material from Ms 103 used later in Ms 104: 81[8]-82[3] already at 74[2] = PT 6.26.
155. Geschkowski 2001: 78.
156. This chronological insertion of remarks taken out of Ms 103 includes with 81[8], 82[1–3] (supplemented by 87[8], 88[1] and the isolated 94[6]) also the *second* textual layer of subsection 6.3 (in the final numbering) on natural sciences.
157. See also Potter 2013: 31.

158. On this, Pilch 2018.
159. The entire frame narrative with the remark TLP 6.54, which is so central for the so-called resolute reading of the *Tractatus*, thus appears rather late in the *Abhandlung* and is – from a genetic point of view – by no means the intellectual starting point of Wittgenstein's textual composition.
160. Potter 2009: 82–85.
161. CC 2011: Letter to Ludwig von Ficker, 20 October 1919.
162. "In the terminology of Hertz we might say: Only law-like connections are thinkable." 98[6] = PT 6.363; cf. Hyder 2002.
163. Altogether nine completely new formulated remarks (Ms 104: 117[2], 117[4–7], 118[1–4]) in the *Korrektur*-section of Ms 104 are devoted exclusively to the expansion and clarification of subsection 6.2.
164. von Wright 1988: 18; Anscombe 1963: 11f.
165. McGuinness 2002: 263 FN 11.
166. In a letter to Engelmann of 31 March 1918, Wittgenstein refers to a seemingly recent meeting with Engelmann (CC 2011).
167. Reward application 41/152, 23 June 1918 (files of the Vienna War Archives).
168. From the Report of Fml. [Field Marshall Lieutenant] Fernengel on the activities of the 16th Infantry Division from 9 May–25 September 1918 dated 24 September 1922 (War Archives Vienna).
169. He must have received the news while he was still busy reworking the *Abhandlung* in Ms 104. The dedication to Pinsent is not only contained in Ts 204, but also handwritten in Ms 104 itself; this dedication erroneously led Georg Henrik von Wright to his late dating of the *Prototractatus* to 1918 ("There seems no reason to think that it had been added to the MS later." Wright 1982: 74).
170. In Section 2, four remarks are added that are also noted in Ms 104 (2.014, 2.0141, 2.033, and 2.151); the four remarks belong together systematically and make a weighty terminological change with 2.033 ("The form is the possibility of the structure."). "Form" and "structure" are no longer, as before, of one level, but in a relation of modal superordination and subordination. Form is now a potential structure. This brief remark has far-reaching implications for any use of "form" and "structure" throughout the text.
171. In Pilch 2013.
172. Potter 2013: 31.
173. CC 2011: 13 March 1919.
174. See Alfred Schmidt's article, p. 168.

Finding Our Way Home: The Philosophy of the *Tractatus*

1. Pere Borrell del Caso (1835–1910) a Spanish painter, illustrator and engraver, known for his trompe-l'œil paintings; especially Escaping Criticism (1874).

1919–1920: "To a Teachers' College to Become a Teacher"

1. McGuinness 1967: 17.
2. Hermine W 2016: 120.
3. McGuinness 1967. See also Wittgenstein's letters of 16 November 1919, 19 February 1920 and 30 May 1920.
4. In the archives of the former teacher training college there is a cutting from a 1945 edition of the school chronicle, which states that the school has the right to use the garden. In the National Socialist period, the school had been deprived of this right.
5. Information courtesy of Dr. Christoph Römer.
6. CC 2011.
7. Sienell 2004: 140–146.
8. Archive of the Austrian Academy of Sciences, No. 471a, 42.
9. McGuinness 1967: 19.
10. McGuinness 2012: 103.
11. CC 2011, translation by Radmila Schweitzer.
12. Wünsche 1985: 48.
13. GRG3 1994,45 and 66; electric lighting was permitted in the school gym as early as 1907 for safety reasons (school chronicle).
14. Archive of the Austrian Academy of Sciences, St. Anna, U1.
15. Archives of the Austrian Academy of Sciences, St. Anna, No. H 111–115.
16. Archives of the Austrian Academy of Sciences, St. Anna, No. H 113.
17. McGuinness 1967: 29.
18. Letter of 14 September 1920 to Dr. Rudolf Latzke, the principal of the teacher training college. CC 2011, trans. Radmila Schweitzer.
19. Wünsche 1985: 52.
20. CC 2011, trans. Radmila Schweitzer.

1919–1922: "Pearls before Swine ..." – the Difficult Publication History of the *Tractatus Logico-Philosophicus*

1. All English translations of the Wittgenstein-Ficker correspondence are by Allan Janik, in *Wittgenstein. Sources and Perspectives*, ed. C.G. Luckhardt (Cornell University Press, 1979).
2. Cf. Wittgenstein's letter to his sister Hermine of August 1919: "You sent me Frege's letter the day before yesterday. However, I

had always thought that he would not understand my work at all. Nevertheless, I was somewhat depressed by his letter...."

3. The most detailed study of this is Graßhoff/Lampert 2004.
4. It must be assumed that intermediate stages no longer exist today – such as a loose-leaf collection based on MS 104, cf. Pilch 2013 and the "Prototractatus Tools" published by the same author on Wittgensteinsource.
5. Cf. McGuinness 1992, 411. Wittgenstein knew Kraus personally at this time through the mediation of Adolf Loos.
6. McGuinness 1967.
7. CC 2011, trans. Radmila Schweitzer.
8. Quoted in Alfred Schmidt, "Wittgenstein and World War I: some additional online sources," in: *Nordic Wittgenstein Review* 3:2 (2014), 183.
9. Graßhoff/Lampert 2004, 13.
10. Graßhoff/Lampert 2004, 13 f.
11. Letter from Hermine to Ludwig, dated 10 January 1919.
12. Whether at that time he was already familiar with Spengler's work is rather unlikely; in his letter to Ficker (around 7 October 1919) he only mentions Weininger.
13. Letter dated 30 August 1919.
14. Cf. Wittgenstein's letter to Russell of 12 June 1919 and the letter from John Maynard Keynes to Ludwig Wittgenstein, 25 June 1919: "Your book has safely reached me and I am forwarding it immediately to Russell."
15. He wrote to Russell on 19 August 1919: "I also sent my M.S. to Frege. He wrote to me a week ago & I gather that he doesn't understand a word of it all."
16. Contributions to the *Philosophy of German Idealism* 2 (1918–1919), 58–77.
17. Letter of 16 September 1919.
18. He had already argued along similar lines with Russell, cf. the latter's letter to Lady Ottoline of 28 May 1912: "I told him he ought not simply to state what he thinks true, but give arguments for it, but he said arguments spoil its beauty, and that he would feel as if he was dirtying a flower with muddy hands." Quoted from McGuinness 1988: 104.
19. This was presumably Alfred Kastil.
20. Letter of 4 December 1919.
21. Cf. McGuinness 1992, 447 f.
22. Letter to Paul Engelmann, 15 December 1919.
23. Letter to Russell, 19 January 1920.
24. Letter to Russell, 9 April 1920.
25. Letter to Russell, 6 May 1920.
26. McGuiness 2012: 121.

27. Letter of 7 January 1921, cf. McGuinness 1992: 445.
28. Cf. the letter of Ogden to Wittgenstein of 4 April 1922.
29. Engelmann, who had already received a copy of the LPA from Wittgenstein's sister Hermine in 1919, namely Ts 203, apologized in his letter to Wittgenstein on 23 June 1922 for not yet having returned the manuscript. Wittgenstein responded to this in his letter of 5 August.
30. McGuiness 1967: 49.
31. Also available as a full digital copy: http://data.onb.ac.at/dtl/5559796
32. Cf. von Wright 1990, 106.
33. Whether the initiative for this came more from Dorothy Wrinch, who was supposedly good friends with C.K. Ogden, as McGuinness writes (McGuinness 1992: 458) or by Russell himself, as von Wright suggests (von Wright 1990: 103) remains unresolved.
34. In his letter to Bertrand Russell of 5 November 1921, Ogden already mentions the Latin title, but also thinks that Russell's title *Philosophical Logic* would be commercially more advantageous (cf. von Wright 1990: 103–104).

    Wittgenstein wrote in his letter to Ogden of 4 April 1922 that the title proposed by Moore would not be ideal, but would at least be much better than Russell's proposal, which he rejects as completely inappropriate: "There is no such thing as philosophical logic. (Unless one says that as the whole book is nonsense the title might as well be nonsense too)."
35. Cod.Ser.n. 39.598, full digitization at: http://data.onb.ac.at/dtl/5558923
36. ANL, Cod. Ser. n. 39.037. Both the proof copy of the Ostwald print and the English translation with Wittgenstein's corrections were first published in Graßhoff/Lampert 2004.
37. ANL, Cod. Ser. n. 39.039. Full digital copy available at: http://data.onb.ac.at/dtl/6017908

The Poetics of the *Tractatus*

1. Wittgenstein, Letter to Ludwig Ficker, mid-October 1919, CC 2011.
2. Wittgenstein 1922: 22.
3. Bertrand Russell, Introduction to the *Tractatus,* in Wittgenstein 1922: 28.
4. On the arbitrariness of the number system in the *Tractatus*, see Marjorie Perloff, *Wittgenstein's Ladder: Poetic Language and the Strangeness of the Ordinary* (University of Chicago Press, 1996), 41–43.
5. *Notebooks 1914–1916,* Second Edition, ed. G. H. von Wright and G. E. M. Anscombe (University of Chicago Press, 1979). The

translation is so awkward that I have occasionally amended it for clarity's sake.

6. See Perloff, "The Making of the *Tractatus*: Russell, Wittgenstein, and the 'Logic' of War," *Wittgenstein's Ladder*, 25–48.
7. MS14625v: see C&V 1998: 28.
8. For an important recent discussion of the proposition, see Allan Janik, "The Dichtung of Analytic Philosophy: Wittgenstein's Legacy from Frege and Its Consequences," in *New Essays on Frege Between Science and Literature*, ed. Gisela Bengtsson, Simo Säätelä, Alois Pichler (Springer, 2018). Janik argues that the "poetic" aspect of Wittgenstein's philosophy has been greatly overstated by critics, myself included, preferring to regard *dichten* as referring less to lyric poetry than to fiction: "Philosophy should only really be conceived as fiction," 142–44. I discuss the English translations by Peter Winch et. al. in "But isn't *the same* at least the same?": Wittgenstein and the Question of Poetic Translatability," *The Literary Wittgenstein*, ed. John Gibson and Wolfgang Huemer (London and New York: Routledge), 38–45.
9. *Zettel*, Bilingual Edition, ed. G. E. M. Anscombe and G. H. von Wright (University of California Press, 1967), 28.
10. Frege. *Briefe an Ludwig Wittgenstein*, ed. Allan Janik (Graz, 1989). My italics.
11. *Wittgenstein's Lectures, Cambridge 1930–32*. From the Notes of John King and Desmond Lee, ed. Desmond Lee (Chicago: University of Chicago Press, 1989), 75.
12. An important passage in MS 109 28: 22.8.1930, which is reproduced in Wittgenstein's so-called *Kringel-Buch* and again in *Culture and Value* (6–7) takes up this issue.

ABBREVIATIONS

C&V 1998: Wittgenstein, Ludwig. *Culture and Value*, eds. G. H. von Wright and H. Nyman, rev. ed. A. Pichler, transl. P. Winch. Oxford: Blackwell, 1998.

CC 2011: *Ludwig Wittgenstein: Complete Correspondence*, Innsbruck Electronic Edition, ed. Monika Seekircher. Charlottesville, Virginia, USA: InteLex Corporation, 2011.

Fleck 2012: Fleck, Stefanie. *Die Wiener Lehrerbildungsanstalten in der Zeit des Nationalsozialismus*, PhD thesis, University of Vienna, 2012. Saarbrücken: AV Akademikerverlag, 2013.

Graßhoff/Lampert 2004: Gerd Graßhoff and Timm Lampert: *Ludwig Wittgenstein's Logical-Philosophical Treatise: History of Its Creation and Publication of the Typescripts and Correction Copies*. Vienna [et al.]: Springer, 2004.

GRG3 1994: *Festschrift on the occasion of the 125th anniversary of the Landstraßer Gymnasium*, ed. Wolf Peschl. GRG, 1994/95.

Hacker 1986: Hacker, Peter. *Insight and Illusion. Themes in the Philosophy of Wittgenstein*, 2nd edition. Oxford: Oxford University Press, 1986.

Hermine W 2016: Wittgenstein, Hermine. "My Brother Ludwig," in: *Portraits of Wittgenstein*, vol. 1, eds. F.A. Flowers III and Ian Ground. London: Bloomsbury Academic, 2015. 120–129.

McGuinness 1967: Engelmann, Paul and Ludwig Wittgenstein. *Letters from Ludwig Wittgenstein, with a Memoir*, ed. B. F. McGuinness, transl. L. Furtmuller. Oxford: Basil Blackwell, 1967.

McGuinness 1988: McGuinness, Brian. *Wittgenstein: A Life. Young Ludwig 1889–1921*. Berkeley/Los Angeles/London: University of California Press, 1988.

McGuinness 2002: McGuinness, Brian. "Some pre-*Tractatus* manuscripts," in: *Approaches to Wittgenstein. Collected Papers*. London and New York: Routledge, 2002. 259–269.

McGuinness 2012: McGuinness, Brian. *Wittgenstein in Cambridge. Letters and Documents 1911–1951*. Malden: Wiley-Blackwell, 2012.

McGuinness 2019: *Corresponding with Ludwig. Wittgenstein's Family Letters*, ed. Brian McGuinness. London: Bloomsbury Academic, 2019.

Molnár 2011: Molnár, Ferenc. *Galicja 1914–1915. Zapiski korespondenta wojennego*, transl. to Polish A. Engelmajer. Warszawa: Most, 2011.

Monk 1990: Monk, Ray. *Ludwig Wittgenstein. The Duty of Genius*. London: J. Cape, 1990.

OKEW: Russell, Bertrand. *Our Knowledge of the External World. As a Field for Scientific Method in Philosophy*. London: The Open Court Publishing Company, 1914.

ÖULK: *Österreich-Ungarns letzter Krieg 1914–1918*, ed. E. Glaise von Horstenau, Bde. I u. IV (Vienna, 1931–1938).

Pilch 2013: Pilch, Martin. "From Prototractatus to *Tractatus*," in: *Mind, Language and Action*, eds. Danièle Moyal-Sharrock; Volker A. Munz; Annalisa Coliva. Proceedings of the 36th International Ludwig Wittgenstein Symposium. Kirchberg am Wechsel, 2013. 319–321.

Pilch 2014: Pilch, Martin. "Der Ur-*Tractatus*," in: Proceedings of the 37th International Ludwig Wittgenstein Symposium, eds. Sonja Rinofner-Kreidl and Harald A. Wiltsche. Kirchberg am Wechsel, 2014. 210–213.

Pilch 2015: Pilch, Martin. "A Missing Folio at the Beginning of Wittgenstein's MS 104," in: *Nordic Wittgenstein Review* 4: 2 (2015) 65–97.

Pilch 2016: Pilch, Martin. "Wittgensteins 'Gebetsstriche' in den Kriegstagebüchern (MSS 101–103)," in: Proceedings of the 39th International Ludwig Wittgenstein Symposium, eds. Stefan Majetschak, Anja Weiberg. Kirchberg am Wechsel, 2016. 192–195.

Potter 2009: Potter, Michael D. *Wittgenstein's Notes on Logic*. Oxford: Oxford University Press, 2009.

Potter 2013: Potter, Michael D. "Wittgenstein's Pre-*Tractatus* Manuscripts. A New Appraisal," in: *Wittgenstein's* Tractatus: *History and Interpretation*, eds. Peter Sullivan and Michael Potter. Oxford, Oxford University Press, 2013. 13–39.

Potter 2020: Potter, Michael D. *The Rise of Analytic Philosophy, 1879–1930: From Frege to Ramsey*. New York and London: Routledge, 2020.

Schmidt 2016: Schmidt, Alfred. "Facsimile Edition of *Tractatus* Publication Materials (LPA)," in: Wittgenstein Source, edited by the Wittgenstein Archives at the University of Bergen under the direction of Alois Pichler. http://www.wittgensteinsource.org

Sienell 2004: Sienell, Stefan. "Das Archiv der Wiener Normalschule und späteren Lehrerbildungsanstalt St. Anna (1775–1963/67)," in: *Wiener Geschichtsblatter* (Viennese Historical Gazette) 59: 2 (2004). 140–146.

Somavilla 2006: Wittgenstein, Ludwig and Paul Engelmann. *Wittgenstein – Engelmann. Briefe, Begegnungen, Erinnerungen*, ed. Ilse Somavilla. Innsbruck & Wien: Haymon, 2006.

Venturinha 2011: Venturinha, Nuno. "Wittgenstein Reads Nietzsche: The Roots of Tractarian Solipsism," in: *Unsocial Sociabilities: Wittgenstein's Sources*, ed. E. Ramharter. Leeds: Academia, 2011. 59–74.

Wittgenstein 1914–1916: Wittgenstein, Ludwig. *Notebooks 1914–1916*, eds. G.H. von Wright and G.E.M. Anscombe, transl. G.E.M. Anscombe. Oxford: Basil Blackwell, 1961.

Wittgenstein 1921: Wittgenstein, Ludwig. "Logisch-Philosophische Abhandlung," in: *Annalen der Naturphilosophie* 14: 3/4 (1921) 185–262.

Wittgenstein 1922: Wittgenstein, Ludwig. *Tractatus Logico-Philosophicus*. London: Kegan Paul, 1922.

Wittgenstein 1990: Wittgenstein, Ludwig. *Geheime Tagebücher: 1914–1916*, ed. W. Baum. Vienna: Turia and Kant, 1990.

Wittgenstein 2000: Wittgenstein, Ludwig. *Wittgenstein's Nachlass*. The Bergen Electronic Edition (BEE). Oxford: Oxford University Press, Wittgenstein Archives at the University of Bergen, The Wittgenstein Trustees, 2000.

Wright 1982: Von Wright, Georg Henrik. *Wittgenstein*. Oxford: Blackwell, 1982.

Wright 1983: Letters to C. K. Ogden, with comments on the English translation of the *Tractatus Logico-Philosophicus*; and an appendix of letters. Oxford: Blackwell [et al.], 1983.

Wünsche 1985: Wünsche, Konrad. *Der Volksschullehrer Ludwig Wittgenstein*. Frankfurt am Main: Suhrkamp, 1985.

SELECTED BIBLIOGRAPHY

Anscombe, G.E.M. *An Introduction to Wittgenstein's Tractatus,* 2nd edition. New York: Harper and Row, 1963.

Bazzocchi, Luciano. "The Date of *Tractatus* Beginning," in: Proceedings of the 31st International Ludwig Wittgenstein Symposium, eds. Alexander Hieke & Hannes Leitgeb. Kirchberg am Wechsel, 2008. 20–22.

Birk, Andrea. *Vom Verschwinden des Subjekts. Eine historisch-systematische Untersuchung zur Solipsismusproblematik bei Wittgenstein*. Paderborn: Universität Paderborn, 2006.

Bouveresse, Jacques. *Le Danseur et sa corde. Wittgenstein, Tolstoï, Nietzsche, Gottfried Keller et les difficultés de la foi.* Paris: Agone, 2014.

Dobrzeniecki, Marek. *The Conflicts of Modernity in Ludwig Wittgenstein's Tractatus Logico-Philosophicus*. Frankfurt am Main: Peter Lang, 2016.

Frege, Gottlob. "Briefe an Ludwig Wittgenstein," ed. Allan Janik and Christian Berger. *Grazer Philosophische Studien* 33 (1989). 5–33.

Hyder, David. *The Mechanics of Meaning. Propositional Content and the Logical Space of Wittgenstein's Tractatus*. Berlin; New York: De Gruyter, 2002.

Janik, Allan. "The Dichtung of Analytic Philosophy: Wittgenstein's Legacy from Frege and Its Consequences," in: *New Essays on Frege Between Science and Literature*, eds. Gisela Bengtsson, Simo Säätelà and Alois Pichler. Cham, Switzerland: Springer Nature, 2018.

Janik, Allan. Translation of the Wittgenstein-Frege Correspondence, in: *Wittgenstein. Sources and Perspectives*, ed. C. Grant Luckhardt. Ithaca, NY: Cornell University Press, 1979.

Keller, Gottfried: *Der Grüne Heinrich*. Verlag Goschen, 1880.

Olejko Andrzej: *Karpacka Wojna Trzech Cesarzy. Z działańwojennych I wojnyświatowej na lądziei w powietrzu*. Wydawca: Carpathia Rzeszow, 2013.

Perloff, Marjorie. *Wittgenstein's Ladder: Poetic Language and the Strangeness of the Ordinary*. Chicago: University of Chicago Press, 1996. 41–43.

Pilch, Martin. "Frontverläufe in Wittgensteins *Prototractatus*. Zur gedanklichen Entwicklung von Krakau bis Sokal (1914/1915)," in: *Wittgenstein-Studien* 9 (2018). 101–154.

Pilch, Martin. "The Structure of Wittgenstein's Logical Space," in: *Wittgenstein-Studien* 8 (2017). 15–60.

Pinsent, David Hume. *A Portrait of Wittgenstein as a Young Man: From the Diary of David Hume Pinsent 1912–1914*, ed. G.H. von Wright. Oxford: Blackwell, 1990.

Prokop, Ursula. *Margaret Stonborough-Wittgenstein*, transl. to French by F. Stonborough. Lausanne: Noir sur Blanc, 2010.

Russell, Bertrand (1914a). "The Relation of Sense-Data to Physics," in: *The Collected Papers of Bertrand Russell Vol. 8*, ed. J.G. Slater. London: G. Allen & Unwin, 1986. 3–26.

Russell, Bertrand. *The Problems of Philosophy.* London: Oxford University Press, 1912.

Rzymowska, Luiza. "*Tractatus Logico-Philosophicus* Ludwiga Wittgensteina w s'wietlemenory. Nowe odczytanie kompozycji," in: *Forum Ars Rhetoricae* 4: 43 (2015).

Schrott, Karl. "Flotylla Wis'lana monarchii austro-węgierskiej w latach 1914–1918," in: *Okręty Wojenne* 13: 61 (May 2003).

Schulte, Joachim. "Der Glückliche und seine Welt," in: *Klassiker Auslegen. Ludwig Wittgenstein. Tractatus logico-philosophicus*, ed. W. Vossenkuhl. Berlin: Akademie Verlag, 2001. 305–326.

Seekircher, Monika. "Wittgenstein und die Flugtechnik," in: *Personen. Ein Interdisziplinärer Dialog.* Proceedings of the 25th International Ludwig Wittgenstein Symposium, eds. E. Runggaldier, C. Kanzian and J. Quitterer. Kirchberg am Wechsel, 2002. 225–227.

Shunichi, Takagi. *Wittgenstein and the 'Kantian Solution of the Problem of Philosophy' (10 February 1931).* PhD Thesis, Department of Philosophy, University College London, 2021.

Somavilla, Ilse. "Verschlüsselung in Wittgensteins Nachlass," in: *Sprache und Welt. Proceedings des 32. Internationalen Wittgenstein Symposiums in Kichberg am Wechsel.* Heusenstamm, Germany: Ontos Verlag, 2010.

Waugh, Alexander. *The House of Wittgenstein: A Family at War.* London: Bloomsbury, 2008.

Wittgenstein, Ludwig. "Wittgenstein Source Bergen Nachlass Edition," in: Wittgenstein Source, edited by the Wittgenstein Archives at the University of Bergen under the direction of Alois Pichler. http://www.wittgensteinsource.org

Wittgenstein, Ludwig. *Zettel,* Bilingual Edition, eds. G. E. M. Anscombe and G. H. von Wright. Berkeley: University of California Press, 1967.

"Wittgenstein, Ludwig," in: *1914–2014: 100 Jahre erster Weltkrieg, Akten zum 1. Weltkrieg im Wiener Kriegsarchiv* (100 Year Anniversary of World War, Files on the First World War in the Vienna Archives). Accessed 26 July 2017. http://wk1.staatsarchiv.at/kriegseuphorie/ludwig-wittgenstein/

Wittgenstein's Lectures, Cambridge 1930–32: From the Notes of John King and Desmond Lee, ed. Desmond Lee. Chicago: University of Chicago Press, 1989.

ABOUT THE AUTHORS

Prof. Dr. Allan Janik was born in Chicopee, Massachusetts in 1941. He studied philosophy and classics at Saint Anselm College, received his MA in philosophy from Villanova University, where he began his studies in Wittgenstein's philosophy with a thesis on Schopenhauer and the early Wittgenstein, and was awarded a PhD in History of Ideas from Brandeis University in 1971. He retired from teaching philosophy at Innsbruck University in 2006 but remained research fellow of the Brenner Archives there until 2013. Janik is adjunct professor of philosophy at the University of Vienna. His wide-ranging interests are mirrored in the numerous visiting professorships he has held over the years in fields such the "Skill and Technology" PhD program at Stockholm's Royal Institute of Technology, mathematics (UNAM, Mexico City), ion physics, comparative literature, German studies (Innsbruck), Jewish studies (Northwestern), leadership studies (Stockholm School of Economics), the epistemology of work (Swedish Center for Working Life), philosophy and history of science (Centre Georges Canguilhem, University of Paris 7) as well as philosophy (Graz, Bergen). His books include *Augenblicke: Berufswissen eines Schauspielers* (with Artak Grigorjan and Karin Gasser); *Assembling Reminders: Studies in the Genesis of Wittgenstein's Conception of Philosophy*; *Theater and Knowledge*; *The Use and Abuse of Metaphor*; *The Concept of Knowledge in Practical Philosophy* (in Swedish); *Style, Politics and the Future of Philosophy*; *Wittgenstein's Vienna* (with Stephen Toulmin); *Wittgenstein's Vienna Revisited* and several others, including a guide to the Austrian capital: *Wittgenstein in Vienna* (with Hans Veigl).

Prof. Ray Monk is a British philosopher and Professor Emeritus of Philosophy at the University of Southampton, where he taught from 1992 to 2018. He won the John Llewellyn Rhys Prize and the 1991 Duff Cooper Prize for *Ludwig Wittgenstein: The Duty of Genius*. Monk is also author of *Bertrand Russell: The Spirit of Solitude & The Ghost of Madness*. His interests lie in the philosophy of mathematics, the history of analytic philosophy, and philosophical aspects of biographical writing. His biography of J. Robert Oppenheimer was published in 2012.

Dr. Knut Olav Åmås born 1968, is the executive director of the Norwegian Fritt Ord Foundation. He has served as deputy minister in the Norwegian Ministry for Culture, and as 'Culture-Opinions-Science' editor at the daily newspaper Aftenposten. He holds a cand. philol. degree in philosophy and a dr. philos. degree in media studies. He has edited, translated or authored 20 books, e.g. on Wittgenstein´s thinking and a guide to Vienna, and has received several prizes for his journalism and publishing. He has served as chairman of the Norwegian government ´s media commission, presently he is the chairman of the board of the Norwegian National Encyclopaedia, chairman of the Norwegian Soloists Choir, and a board member at the international Holberg Prize.

Dr. Urszula Idziak-Smoczyńska born 1980, currently assistant professor in the Institute for the Study of Religions at the Philosophical Department of Jagiellonian University in Kraków, Poland. Her main area of interest embraces the dialogue between religion and 20th century and contemporary philosophy (Wittgenstein, Derrida, Nancy, Agamben, Marion, etc.). She is author of *Pojęcie Daru. Spór Derridy z Marionem* (2008), *The Philosophy of The Parable* (in press) and is currently finishing a book about Wittgenstein's wartime experiences, *Wittgenstein in Polish Galicia. Life and Thought Behind the Tractatus*.

Prof. Dr. Susan G. Sterrett is the Curtis D. Gridley Distinguished Professor of the History and Philosophy of Science in the Department of Philosophy at Wichita State University in Wichita, Kansas. She earned an undergraduate degree in engineering at Cornell University in 1977, after which she worked as an engineer for several years. She completed degrees in Mathematics (M.A.) and Philosophy (M.A., Ph.D.) at the University of Pittsburgh, completing her doctorate in December 1999, with a dissertation entitled *How Beliefs Make A Difference*. During graduate school, she also wrote and published *Sounds Like Light: Einstein's Theory of Special Relativity* *and Mach's Work in Acoustics and Aerodynamics*. She then taught at Duke University. She was awarded a Woodrow Wilson National Foundation fellowship for work on *Wittgenstein Flies a Kite: A Story of Models of Wings and Models of the World*, published by Penguin in 2005. Other publications include articles on Darwin's use of analogy, on Wittgenstein and gramophone records, on Alan Turing and the philosophy of artificial intelligence, and on the use of models in science.

She spent a term at the Center for Philosophy of Science at the University of Pittsburgh in Spring 2010, then taught at Carnegie Mellon University while finishing *Three Views of Logic: Mathematics, Philosophy, Computer Science*, co-authored with the computer scientist Donald W. Loveland and the mathematician Richard E. Hodel.

Dr. Martin Pilch born in 1963, studied theoretical physics and philosophy in Graz and Vienna. PhD (1989) with a thesis on quantum field theory (lattice gauge theory). He was postdoc at the University of Graz (physics), then research associate at the University of Vienna (philosophy); later working on the natural philosophy of Schelling and Hegel. From 1990, he pursued additional studies in jurisprudence and history of law; a doctorate (2003) followed with a thesis on normativity (legal customs) in the early Middle Ages. Since 2003, he has been Deputy Head of the Department for Technical-Economic Research at the Austrian Federal Ministry for Science, Research and Economy, responsible for the Christian Doppler Research Laboratories. His two book publications are *System des transcendentalen Etatismus. Staat und Verfassung bei Carl Schmitt* (1994) and *Der Rahmen der Rechtsgewohnheiten* (2009). Since 2010, he has conducted research on Ludwig Wittgenstein's early work; most recently, editing a diplomatic transcription of Ms 104 and Ts 202. Prototractatus Tools (PTT) at www.wittgensteinsource.org, 2016.

Dr. Ian Ground has taught philosophy in a range of roles, including senior lecturer in philosophy, at the universities of Newcastle, Sunderland, Durham and Edinburgh. A specialist in making philosophical ideas accessible to the wider public, and in enabling people to think critically about current ideas and trends, he has been an innovator in the sectors of adult education and lifelong learning. Ground has won awards for Teaching Innovation and the UK's National Award in Lifelong Learning. He has published in the philosophy of mind, especially our understanding of animal minds, in the philosophy of art, and on the thought and life of the philosopher Ludwig Wittgenstein. His books include *Art or Bunk?, Can We*

Understand Animal Minds?, and *Portraits of Wittgenstein*, a comprehensive collection of memoirs. He is currently Visiting Research Fellow in Philosophy at the University of Hertfordshire and Vice-President of the British Wittgenstein Society.

Dr. Alfred Schmidt born in 1959 in Linz on the Danube, completed high school in Vienna in 1977, then studied philosophy, psychology and art history in Vienna and in Freiburg/Breisgau, and earned his doctorate with a thesis on Edmund Husserl. Alfred Schmidt works as a research assistant to the Director General at the Austrian National Library. He has been working for many years on the philosophy of Ludwig Wittgenstein, in particular on the part of his *Nachlaß* held at the Austrian National Library. He is a regular guest and lecturer at the Wittgenstein Symposium in Kirchberg am Wechsel. He worked on the 2016 Edition of the *Tractatus* Publication Materials on the Wittgenstein Source online portal supervised by Alois Pichler (http://wittgensteinsource.org); and in 2018, designed the Wittgenstein part of the exhibition *Berg, Wittgenstein, Zuckerkandl. Central Figures of Viennese Modernism* at the Literature Museum of the Austrian National Library.

Currently Alfred Schmidt is preparing the first publication of the correspondence between Ludwig Wittgenstein and Ben Richards.

Prof. Dr. Marjorie Perloff is the Sadie D. Patek Professor of Humanities Emerita at Stanford University. and Florence Scott Professor Emerita of English at the University of Southern California. She is the author of many books (and hundreds of articles) on 20th and 21st century Poetry and Poetics, including, *Frank O'Hara: Poet among Painters* (1977), *The Poetics of Indeterminacy: Rimbaud to Cage* (1981), *The Futurist Moment: Avant-Garde, Avant-Guerre, and the Language of Rupture* (1986, new edition, 1994), *Wittgenstein's Ladder: Poetic Language and the Strangeness of the Ordinary* (1996), *21st Century Modernism* (2002), *Unoriginal Genius: Writing by Other Means in the New Century* (2011), and *Poetics in a New Key* (2014), a collection of interviews and essays. Her most recent books are *Edge of Irony: Modernism in the Shadow of the Habsburg Empire* (2016), which enlarges on the theme of her 2004 memoir *The Vienna Paradox*, and *Infrathin: An Experiment in Micropoetics* (2022). A two-volume collection of her book reviews from 1969 to the present is forthcoming under the title *Circling the Canon*. Her books have been translated into many languages, including Chinese, Portuguese, and Serbian. She was 2006 President of the MLA, is currently co-president of CAAP, the Chinese-American Poetry Foundation, and is a member of the American Academy of Arts and Sciences and the Philosophical Society of America. Perloff has held many visiting Chairs and fellowships: in 2016 she was the first Wittgenstein Guest Professor at Innsbruck University in Austria, where she also received an honorary degree.

In 2022, Perloff translated and edited for the first time in English Ludwig Wittgenstein's coded remarks from the verso pages of his wartime notebooks (*Wittgenstein's Private Diaries*, Norton Liveright 2022).

Radmila Schweitzer, Editor, studied musicology and philosophy at the universities of Prague and Copenhagen, receiving her Master's Degree with Summa cum Laude in 1994. After years in classical music management in Vienna and Munich, in 2014 she founded the Wittgenstein Initiative in Vienna, together with descendants of the Wittgenstein family and some of the foremost Wittgenstein scholars worldwide. The Initiative is an international forum and aims to "bring back" Wittgenstein to his native city and to open his legacy to a wide audience, beyond philosophy — in literature, arts, and music. In 2018, she edited, together with Brian McGuinness, Wittgenstein's correspondence with his siblings (Haymon Innsbruck 2018, Bloomsbury UK 2019, and Flammarion Paris 2021). The exhibition *The Tractatus Odyssey* and its catalog (Vienna 2018) are traveling to Warsaw, Rome, Moscow, Paris, Oslo, and others, and are the basis of the present volume.